NABOKOV TRANSLATED

*A Comparison of Nabokov's
Russian and English Prose*

BY

JANE GRAYSON

OXFORD UNIVERSITY PRESS

1977

Oxford University Press, Walton Street, Oxford OX2 6DP

OXFORD LONDON GLASGOW NEW YORK
TORONTO MELBOURNE WELLINGTON CAPE TOWN
IBADAN NAIROBI DAR ES SALAAM LUSAKA ADDIS ABABA
KUALA LUMPUR SINGAPORE JAKARTA HONG KONG TOKYO
DELHI BOMBAY CALCUTTA MADRAS KARACHI

ISBN 0 19 815527 1

© *Oxford University Press, 1977*

*Printed in Great Britain
at the University Press, Oxford
by Vivian Ridler
Printer to the University*

ACKNOWLEDGEMENTS

I OWE thanks to a great many people for their help in the preparation of this book—to friends, colleagues, tutors, librarians, and in the latter stages to the staff of the O.U.P. I would like to express my especial thanks to Ronald Hingley and Anne Pennington for their ready criticism, their timely guidance, and their unfailing encouragement. I am indebted to Michael Scammell and Michael Glenny for the use of their manuscript material.

CONTENTS

CONVENTIONS   ix

INTRODUCTION   1

1. THE TRANSLATIONS   5

2. NABOKOV'S THEORY OF TRANSLATION   13

3. MAJOR REWORKINGS: *LAUGHTER IN THE
   DARK*   23

4. MAJOR REWORKINGS: *DESPAIR* AND *THE
   EYE*   59

5. MAJOR REWORKINGS: *KING, QUEEN,
   KNAVE*   90

6. MINOR REWORKINGS   119

7. THE AUTOBIOGRAPHY   139

8. TECHNIQUE OF TRANSLATION   167

9. STYLE   182

CONCLUSION   213

APPENDICES
   A. Translations of Nabokov's Works into English and Russian   220
   B. Added and Rewritten Passages in *King, Queen, Knave*   222
   C. Versions of the Autobiography   224
   D. Nabokov's Use of Autobiographical Material in Fiction   227
   E. Nabokov in Russian Criticism   232

BIBLIOGRAPHY   238

INDEX   253

CONVENTIONS

NOTE ON TRANSLATION

Citations from Nabokov's Russian works have been left in Russian. To have translated them might perhaps have made them more intelligible to the non-specialist reader, but would have undermined the purpose of this book. Nevertheless, every effort has been made to describe the points illustrated by the quotations.

TRANSLITERATION

The system of transliteration is that followed in *The Oxford Slavonic Papers*, New Series, i.e. a modified version of British Standard 2979, 1958, omitting diacritics, and using -y to express -й, -ий, -ий, and -ый at the end of proper names.

ABBREVIATIONS

CE	*Conclusive Evidence: a Memoir*
CO	*Camera Obscura* (Russian and English versions)
DB	*Drugie berega*
E1, E2, E3	First, second and third English version
EO	*Eugene Onegin*, translated from the Russian by Vladimir Nabokov
IB	*Invitation to a Beheading*
KDV	*Korol', dama, valet*
KQKn	*King, Queen, Knave*
LD	*Laughter in the Dark*
Lolita E	English edition of *Lolita*
Lolita R	Russian translation of *Lolita*
MG	Michael Glenny
MO	*Mademoiselle O* (French version)
MS	Michael Scammell
NRF	*La Nouvelle Revue française* (Paris)
PF	*Pale Fire*
PMLA	*Publications of the Modern Language Association of America* (New York)
PN	*Poslednie novosti* (Paris)
R	Russian version
RB	*A Russian Beauty and Other Stories*
SEEJ	*The Slavic and East European Journal* (Madison)

SEER	*The Slavonic and East European Review* (London)
SM	*Speak, Memory: an Autobiography Revisited*
SZ	*Sovremennye zapiski* (Paris)
VF	*Vesna v Fial'te i drugie rasskazy*
VN	Vladimir Nabokov
Voz Ch	*Vozvrashchenie Chorba: rasskazy i stikhi*
ZL	*Zashchita Luzhina*

NOTE ON REFERENCES

In lists of examples and in passages where a text is cited frequently the page references are given in parentheses following the quotations. Elsewhere they are given in footnotes.

Square brackets are used in some quotations to denote passages which are new in a second version or translation. For example: ' "A beggar", he repeated again and again [, now leaning with both hands on his stick and swaying a little].' In this example taken from *Despair* the brackets indicate an addition made in the second English translation.

Full details of works and articles referred to in the text are given in the Bibliography and not in the footnotes, except in cases where confusion might otherwise result.

Quotations are from the following editions of Nabokov's works:

In Russian

Camera Obscura, serialized in 4 parts in *Sovremennye zapiski* (Paris), Nos. 49–52, 1932–3.

Dar, Chekhov Publishing House, New York, 1952.

Drugie berega, Chekhov Publishing House, New York, 1954.

Korol', dama, valet, Slovo, Berlin, 1928.

Lolita, Phaedra, New York, 1967.

Mashen'ka, Slovo, Berlin, 1926.

Oblako, ozero, bashnya, Russkie zapiski (Paris), No. 2, 1937.

Otchayanie, serialized in 3 parts in *Sovremennye zapiski* (Paris), Nos. 54–6, 1934.

Podvig, serialized in 4 parts in *Sovremennye zapiski* (Paris), Nos. 45–8, 1931–2.

Priglashenie na kazn', Dom knigi, Paris, 1938.

Soglyadatai, Sovremennye zapiski (Paris), No. 44, 1930.

Solus Rex, Sovremennye zapiski (Paris), No. 70, 1940.

Vesna v Fial'te i drugie rasskazy, Chekhov Publishing House, New York, 1956.

Vozvrashchenie Chorba: rasskazy i stikhi, Slovo, Berlin, 1930.

Zashchita Luzhina, Éditions de la Seine, Paris, 1967.

In English

Ada or Ardor: a Family Chronicle, Weidenfeld and Nicolson, London, 1969.

Camera Obscura, translated from the Russian by Winifred Roy, John Long, London, 1936.

Conclusive Evidence: a Memoir, Harper and Bros., New York, 1951.

The Defence, Weidenfeld and Nicolson, London, 1969.

Despair, translated from the Russian by the author, John Long, London, 1937.

Despair, revised translation, Weidenfeld and Nicolson, London, 1966.

Eugene Onegin, translated from the Russian by Vladimir Nabokov, Bollingen Series, Pantheon Books, New York, 1964, 4 vols.

The Eye, Weidenfeld and Nicolson, London, 1966.

The Gift, Weidenfeld and Nicolson, London, 1963.

Glory, Weidenfeld and Nicolson, London, 1972.

Invitation to a Beheading, Weidenfeld and Nicolson, London, 1960.

King, Queen, Knave, Weidenfeld and Nicolson, London, 1968.

Laughter in the Dark, Weidenfeld and Nicolson, London, 1969.

Lolita, Weidenfeld and Nicolson, London, 1965.

Mary, Weidenfeld and Nicolson, London, 1971.

Nabokov's Dozen, Heinemann, London, 1959.

Nabokov's Quartet, Weidenfeld and Nicolson, London, 1967.

Nikolay Gogol, Weidenfeld and Nicolson, London, 1973.

Pale Fire, Weidenfeld and Nicolson, London, 1962.

Pnin, Heinemann, London, 1957.

Poems, Weidenfeld and Nicolson, London, 1962.

The Real Life of Sebastian Knight, Weidenfeld and Nicolson, London, 1960.

A Russian Beauty and Other Stories, Weidenfeld and Nicolson, London, 1973.

The Song of Igor's Campaign, translated from the Russian by Vladimir Nabokov, Weidenfeld and Nicolson, London, 1961.

Speak, Memory: an Autobiography Revisited, Weidenfeld and Nicolson, London, 1967.

Strong Opinions, McGraw-Hill, New York, 1973.

Transparent Things, McGraw-Hill, New York, 1972.

INTRODUCTION

BEFORE and after the Revolution hundreds of Russian writers and artists left Russia to settle in western Europe. The older established writers—writers such as Bunin and Remizov—could continue to draw upon their memories of Russia and the resources of the Russian literary tradition. The situation was rather different for the younger generation, for writers like Nina Berberova, Fel'zen, and Gazdanov, who began their literary careers in emigration. Their experience of Russia and Russian life was more short-lived; they were less insulated against the influence of western European literature and culture. The Russian *émigré* Press frequently expressed its concern for the difficult conditions affecting these younger writers and voiced its fears that they might lose their links with the Russian literary tradition and that they might even give up writing in their native language.

Nabokov belonged to this younger generation. Born in St. Petersburg in 1899, he had published nothing prior to his emigration apart from a verse brochure and a collection of poems, both privately printed. His Russian period dates roughly from 1920 to 1940 when he was resident in Europe and where, writing under the pen-name Vladimir Sirin, he became acknowledged as the foremost writer of his generation. But in 1940, shortly after the outbreak of war, he emigrated to the United States and there began writing in English.[1] Certainly conditions were not favourable to a continuing production in Russian. Towards the end of the 1930s Russian *émigré* writers were beset by increasing difficulties, both financial and political. The two main centres of *émigré* literature in the 1920s and 1930s had been Berlin and Paris, but with the growth of Nazism and the threat of war more and more publishing houses were forced to close down. *Sovremennye zapiski*, the most eminent *émigré* journal, and *Poslednie novosti*, the chief Paris newspaper, both ceased publication in 1940. Nevertheless, the

---

[1] Nabokov's first English novel, *The Real Life of Sebastian Knight*, was in fact written in France in 1939. It was published in the United States two years later.

significant fact remains that Nabokov is the *only* outstanding *émigré* writer to have done what the jealous guardians of the Russian literary tradition so much feared: 'turned his coat', and adopted another language. As Nikolay Andreyev puts it, 'he is the exception that proves the rule'.[1]

The corpus of Nabokov's work in English is, to date at least, not as great as in Russian. It is none the less considerable, comprising some fourteen poems, nine stories, and eight novels. It is this production which has earned him recognition as one of the major American writers. To be successful in not one, but two languages is indeed a rare achievement. Many bilingual writers, Conrad being a notable example, have written exclusively in their adopted language. Others have written only occasional pieces in one or the other language. To earn a high standing in two literatures is a distinction which Nabokov shares with only one other living writer, the novelist and dramatist Samuel Beckett.[2]

An achievement of this order invites curiosity. How was Nabokov equipped to make the difficult change from Russian to English, and be successful? A major factor, obviously, was his upbringing. Nabokov grew up speaking three languages: Russian, English, and French, and before he was twenty had read quite extensively in English and French as well as Russian literature. But more important is Nabokov's attitude to his art. He has never identified himself closely with any one national literary tradition. As he has himself said in interview: 'I have always maintained, even as a schoolboy in Russia, that the nationality of a worthwhile writer is of secondary importance. . . . The writer's art is his real passport.'[3] A revealing commentary on Nabokov's attitude is provided by *émigré* criticism of his work. Already, before he began writing in English, before he 'betrayed' his native language, he was accused of being 'un-Russian' and 'foreign'. Mikhail Osorgin, for example, suggested that *Korol'*,

[1] 'Ob osobennostyakh i osnovnykh etapakh razvitiya russkoi literatury za rubezhom', p. 20. This article contains some valuable references to the history of the period. There are few surveys of *émigré* literature, Gleb Struve's book, *Russkaya literatura v izgnanii*, being one of the most complete. The *émigré* newspapers and journals provide a rich but diffuse source of information on the literary developments of the time.

[2] For a general discussion of bilingualism see Leonard Forster, *The Poet's Tongues*. See also an article by Robert Auty on Prešeren: 'Prešeren's German Poems'.

[3] 'An Interview with Vladimir Nabokov', conducted by Appel, 1967.

dama, valet might meet with equal success in translation;[1] Georgy Adamovich said of *Zashchita Luzhina* that it could well have appeared in the pages of *La Nouvelle Revue française*.[2] The same sentiment was reiterated by Georgy Ivanov in a hostile review article which appeared in *Chisla* in 1930:

> В «Короле, даме, валете», старательно скопирован средний немецкий образец. В «Защите Лужина» — французский.

In the light of Nabokov's later development statements such as these have the piquancy of prophecy. They give perspective and point to a comparison of his writing in the two languages.

In turning to English Nabokov has not divorced himself entirely from his Russian past. On the contrary, he has brought out a substantial proportion of his Russian production in English translation and even translated two of his English works back into Russian.[3] These 'auto-translations' occupy a key position in Nabokov's œuvre. They constitute a living link between his writing in Russian and his writing in English. They provide some answers to the questions which arise in a study of any bilingual writer. What are the distinctive features of Nabokov's work in the two languages, what imprint does he make upon his adopted English medium, and what traces of 'foreignness' can be detected in his attitudes and his style?

This, however, is not the only interest of these translations. Not all of them are faithful reproductions of the originals. Nabokov is a compulsive reviser and when translating his own work he frequently takes the opportunity to incorporate substantial modifications and reworkings. If Nabokov's translation practice has interest for a comparative linguist, his revisions are of primary

---

[1] Review of *Korol', dama, valet*, 1928:

> ...талантливый роман, который мог появиться на любом языке, естественнее всего — на немецком, и который в переводах будет, вероятно, иметь успех не меньший, чем в подлиннике.

[2] Review of *SZ*, No. 40, 1929:

> «Защита Лужина» вещь западная, европейская, скорее всего французская. Если бы напечатать ее в «Нувель Ревю Франсэз», например, она пришлась бы там вполне ко двору.

[3] Beckett has also translated a number of his own works, many of which incorporate revisions. For discussions of his translations see Cohn, 'Samuel Beckett Self-Translator'. See also Janvier, *Pour Samuel Beckett*, and Fletcher, *The Novels of Samuel Beckett*.

importance to a student of his creative development. The changes which Nabokov introduces are many and varied, but the most striking development is towards increasing stylization, increasing deployment of artifice. The controlling hand of the author is more openly revealed, the reader is continually reminded that the action and the characters are but products of the artistic imagination. These same features were not absent from Nabokov's early work. Indeed, the poet Khodasevich, who reviewed much of Nabokov's Russian production, saw at an early stage that for Nabokov 'human interest', conventional notions of character and plot, were of only secondary importance, and that his primary concern was with the theme of artistic creation and the creative personality.[1] Julia Bader in a study of six of Nabokov's English novels has sought to demonstrate that artifice is the central preoccupation in Nabokov's English writing.[2] A comparison of Nabokov's translations with their originals makes it possible to assess the growth of this preoccupation with art and artifice. To date this area has not attracted the amount of critical attention it deserves. While isolated studies have appeared of three novels,[3] no attempt has hitherto been made to consider all the auto-translations in relation to the general development of Nabokov's writing.

The purpose of this book is to examine this broad issue in Russian and English versions of Nabokov's prose. In the first part (Chapters 3–5) the emphasis is on the alterations Nabokov makes when translating and reworking his fiction and his autobiography. Successive versions are analysed for development in narrative technique, structure, characterization, and style. In the second part (Chapters 6–7) the translations are examined for the light they shed on Nabokov's method of translation and method of composition, and distinctive features of his style in English. Chapters 1 and 2 are introductory; they describe Nabokov's part in the translation of his own work and outline his theory of translation.

[1] See, for example, 'O Sirine', 1937.
[2] *Crystal Land*, 1972.
[3] Proffer, 'From *Otchaianie* to *Despair*' and 'A New Deck for Nabokov's Knaves'; Hughes, 'Notes on the Translation of *Invitation to a Beheading*'.

1

THE TRANSLATIONS

TRANSLATION INTO ENGLISH

THE first English translations of Nabokov's work came out in the 1930s while Nabokov was still writing in Russian. It seems evident that the control which Nabokov exercised over his translations was a good deal less rigorous at the outset than it was later to become. The first two works to appear in English were translated completely independently of the author. These were two stories translated by Gleb Struve: *The Return of Tchorb* (*Vozvrashchenie Chorba*) and *The Passenger* (*Passazhir*). The first translation appeared in 1932 in Paris, and the second in 1934 in London. Struve has said that while Nabokov gave the translations his approval, he had no part in their preparation.[1] Another English translation of a story, also made independently of the author, appeared in 1939. This was a translation of *Kartofel'nyi El'f* by Serge Bertensson and Irene Kosinska which was published in *Esquire* under the title *The Potato-Elf*.[2]

The first of Nabokov's novels to appear in translation was *Camera Obscura* which was published by John Long in London in 1936 in a translation by Winifred Roy. It seems clear that Nabokov was not satisfied with this translation for he later referred to it in interview as 'insufficiently revised by me'.[3] Nabokov himself prepared the translation of the next novel which appeared. This was *Despair* (*Otchayanie*), which was published in London in 1937, also by John Long. The following year Nabokov brought out a new English version of *Camera Obscura*—this time his own. It was published in New York, under a different title: *Laughter in the Dark*. These translations were Nabokov's first publications in

[1] Letter to this author, 18 October 1970. Speaking of his translation of *Vozvrashchenie Chorba* Struve adds: 'It appeared with a number of editorial cuts and changes about which neither I nor the author was consulted, and should, in all honesty, be described as an "adaptation" of Nabokov's original.'

[2] In 1973 Nabokov published a new translation of the story, made in collaboration with his son.

[3] 'An Interview with Vladimir Nabokov', conducted by Appel, 1967.

English. Before then he had done a number of translations from English into Russian, of poetry as well as prose, but this was his first *active* use of the English language. Shortly afterwards, in 1940, Nabokov left Europe for America and there he abandoned translating for a time and concentrated on creative writing in English. Apart from three Russian stories which came out in English soon after his arrival in America, Nabokov left his Russian production untouched until the late 1950s. It was only then, after he had made his reputation as a writer of English—after *The Real Life of Sebastian Knight*, *Bend Sinister*, *Conclusive Evidence*, *Pnin* and, of course, *Lolita*—that he set about revising his Russian works in translation.

In thirteen years, from 1959 to 1972, Nabokov brought out English versions of all his Russian novels. A list of these translations, with their dates of publication, is given in Appendix A. It will be observed that the sequence of publication does not correspond to that of the originals. The order appears to be random: *Mashen'ka* and *Korol', dama, valet*, for instance, Nabokov's first novels, are among the last to be translated. It seems unlikely that there is any conscious intention behind this sequence—Nabokov's personal preference, estimations of what was most likely to appeal to American readers, and presumably other factors all come into play. The effect of this random order of publication has, however, been to present the English reading public with a distorted image of Nabokov's development as a novelist. This distortion has been accentuated by popular editions of his works. The front cover, for example, of the Panther Books edition of *The Gift* has: '*The Gift*, by the author of *Lolita*'. The same publisher advertises '*The Defence*, by the author of *Lolita*', and the dust cover even of the Weidenfeld and Nicolson edition of *Glory* has: 'A novel by the author of *Lolita* and *Ada*'.

Though the corpus of Nabokov's Russian novels is dismembered in English translation, at least all the parts are there, which is more than can be said of other areas of Nabokov's Russian production. His drama, his verse, and his short stories are, as yet, by no means as adequately represented in English. In all, Nabokov wrote seven plays or fragments of plays in Russian out of which only his last, *Izobretenie Val'sa* (*The Waltz Invention*), has appeared in English. As for his poetry—and he has written a good deal—until 1970 only a small proportion had been translated. In that year, however,

Nabokov brought out a collection entitled *Poems and Problems*, which includes translations of thirty-nine Russian poems. More recently Nabokov has been engaged in the translation of his short stories. A collection, *A Russian Beauty and Other Stories*, appeared in 1973 and *Tyrants Destroyed and Other Stories* in 1975. Out of a total of fifty Russian stories recorded thirty-one had appeared in English by the end of 1975. This figure includes the two translations by Struve which were done independently of Nabokov.

This is the sum total of Nabokov's Russian production which exists up to this date in English. By no means all the translations are the author's own work. It is true that all the versions of poetry are his, including all the verses contained within the novels and stories.[1] But among the prose works Nabokov is solely responsible for the translation of only two novels. These are the second revised version of *Camera Obscura* (*Laughter in the Dark*, 1938) and two different versions of *Otchayanie*: *Despair*, 1937, and *Despair*, 1966. (For convenience these two versions will be referred to as *Despair 1* and *Despair 2*.) The rest of the prose translations have been written in collaboration with other translators. Nabokov's supervision of the later translations, published after he moved to America, is considerably more careful than it appears to have been in the 1930s. Here it is Nabokov who takes the initiative every time; he it is who decides upon which work he wants translated; he it is who engages a translator and who prepares the final text which is submitted to the publishers.

Nabokov's first partnership was with Peter Pertzov, a partnership which yielded three stories: *Cloud, Castle, Lake* (1941), *The Aurelian* (1941), and *Spring in Fialta* (1947).[2] In 1973, Simon Karlinsky translated the story *Krasavitsa* (*A Russian Beauty*). Nabokov's most fruitful collaboration, however, has been with his son Dmitri, who has translated twenty-five stories (1963–75), one play: *The Waltz Invention* (1966), and four novels: *Invitation to a Beheading* (1959), *The Eye* (1965), *King, Queen, Knave* (1968), and *Glory* (1971). Dmitri also started work on a translation of *Dar*, but completed only the first chapter. The remaining four chapters

---

[1] See Nabokov's Foreword to *The Gift*: 'I am responsible for the versions of the various poems and bits of poems scattered throughout the book.' In his revision of Glenny's translation of *Mashen'ka*, Nabokov rewrites all the jingles and fragments of poetry.

[2] All three stories have been reprinted in the collections *Nine Stories* (1947) and *Nabokov's Dozen* (1958).

were translated by Michael Scammell (*The Gift*, 1963). Scammell went on to translate *Zashchita Luzhina* (*The Defence*, 1964). A few years later Michael Glenny translated *Mashen'ka* (*Mary*, 1970). In all these partnerships Nabokov has made it clear that he requires from his translator an accurate literal rendering, reserving to himself alone, as author, the right to make changes. Of the stories translated in collaboration with Pertzov, he writes: '[I] am alone responsible for any discrepancies between them and the original texts.'[1] In his Foreword to *King, Queen, Knave* he refers to a 'literal translation' prepared by his son which he then revised by collation with the Russian original.[2] He has admitted on occasion that he finds it difficult to resist the temptation to emend his early work when translating, and Scammell recalls a discussion in which Nabokov explained that this was one reason why he commissioned others to do the work. Nabokov's professional dealings with Scammell and Glenny give some insight into his recent methods of collaboration. In both cases the collaboration was conducted by post (Glenny never once met Nabokov). Nabokov asked for the translations to be submitted to him several chapters at a time. He checked the manuscript very carefully, pointing out inaccuracies and mistranslations. (He, in fact, enclosed lists of these mistranslations in two letters to Glenny.) Discussion of the translation was confined to correction. Nabokov did not discuss points of style or idiom, nor did he more than hint at some additional changes which he was making. These appear only in the final printed version.

Scammell and Glenny have both very kindly made available their manuscript versions of *The Gift*, *The Defence*, and *Mary*, which has made it possible to see exactly what changes Nabokov introduced before sending the translation to his publishers. For the translations made by Pertzov and Dmitri Nabokov no manuscripts are available, and Nabokov's part cannot be determined with the same degree of accuracy. This means that these texts cannot be used as reliable source material for an examination of Nabokov's translation technique. While certain features of vocabulary and style may be recognized as typically 'Nabokovian', they

---

[1] Bibliographical note to *Nabokov's Dozen*, p. 222.

[2] *KQKn*, pp. vi–vii: 'By the end of 1966, my son had prepared a literal translation of the book in English, and this I placed on my lectern beside a copy of the Russian edition.'

cannot be vouched for as his. It is another matter with the more substantial modifications of plot, structure, and characterization, together with the major additions and deletions. As already noted, Nabokov himself assumes all responsibility for changes in the original. It is therefore possible to use these translations to illustrate certain aspects of his creative development.

The English translations vary considerably in their closeness to the original. Some adhere closely; the changes are on a small scale, affecting vocabulary, idiom, and points of detail. Such are all the short stories, *The Waltz Invention*, and the following novels: *Camera Obscura*, *Despair 1*, *The Gift*, *The Defence*, *Invitation to a Beheading*, *Mary*, and *Glory*. The other novels have been substantially revised in translation, and in some cases whole passages have been rewritten. Reworkings tend to be more considerable when Nabokov himself makes the translation, as in *Laughter in the Dark* and *Despair 2*. However, this is not invariably the case: Nabokov's first version of *Despair*, his own translation, is very close to the Russian, whereas *King, Queen, Knave*, prepared in collaboration with his son, is considerably altered. Nor does there appear to be any correlation between the degree to which the translation has been altered and the distance in time between the translation and the original. There are examples of both free and close renderings in early, as well as in much later versions. These findings do not correspond with a statement made by Nabokov in his Foreword to *Invitation to a Beheading*:

> If some day I make a dictionary of definitions wanting single words to head them, a cherished entry will be 'To abridge, expand, or otherwise alter or cause to be altered, for the sake of belated improvement, one's own writings in translation.' Generally speaking the urge to do this grows in proportion to the length of time separating the model from the mimic ... (p. 6)

However, since *Invitation to a Beheading* was only the first of the series of translations which Nabokov made after the publication of *Lolita*, his statement cannot be taken to apply to his general practice as an auto-translator.

It is characteristic of Nabokov's writing in English that he often reworks an earlier version in successive editions. He makes minor modifications to the translations of several short stories when he reissues them in collections, and in the 1966 edition of *Despair* he subjected a thirty-year-old translation of a novel to a complete overhaul. And it is not only the translations which Nabokov retouches in this way. There is some evidence of reworking in later editions of his original English production. This, however, is not a feature of his Russian writing, in the original or in translation. None of the re-editions of Nabokov's Russian prose contains any reworking.

TRANSLATION INTO RUSSIAN

When Nabokov began writing creatively in English his use of Russian became more passive. Not that he gave up writing in Russian altogether: the story, *Ultima Thule* (1942), is his last prose work in Russian,[1] but he continued to write poetry in Russian for ten years after that date. His last collection, *Stikhotvoreniya: 1929–1951*, was published in 1952. (This was followed by a collection in English, in 1959). Nabokov has also contributed articles in Russian to American *émigré* journals, and has written a critical introduction to a Russian edition of Gogol's stories.[2] Of greater interest are his translations from Russian literature and his translations of his own English works. In 1954 he brought out a Russian version of his autobiography under the title *Drugie berega*. In 1967, he published a Russian translation of his best-selling novel *Lolita*.

The extent of alterations which Nabokov makes in these translations again varies. *Lolita* may be termed a fairly close translation, and as such classed alongside such English translations as *The Gift* and *The Defence*. *Drugie berega*, on the other hand, is very substantially rewritten, the amount of alteration being greater even than is found, for instance, in *The Eye* or *Despair 2*. These Russian translations were both made by Nabokov himself, without help from collaborators. This contrasts with his usual practice when translating into English.

TRANSLATION INTO ENGLISH AND INTO RUSSIAN

There remains Nabokov's most audacious venture into the field of auto-translation—his Autobiography. This has undergone two

---

[1] This and *Solus Rex* were in fact chapters from an unfinished novel.
[2] *Povesti: N. V. Gogol'* (New York, 1952).

language changes: the first from English into Russian, the second from Russian back again into English. The original English version, entitled *Conclusive Evidence: a Memoir*, came out in book form in 1951. In 1954, Nabokov brought out the Russian version, *Drugie berega*, which has been mentioned above. Then, twelve years later, in 1966, he published a second revised English edition, entitled *Speak, Memory: an Autobiography Revisited*. The Autobiography casts light on one of the main interests of this study, namely the part played by language in the development of Nabokov's art. In one and the same work it is possible to observe Nabokov the translator at work in two directions—from English to Russian and from Russian to English. The different editions also illustrate clearly how Nabokov's elaboration and embellishments carry *across* a change of language, for *Speak, Memory* is not just a straight reworking of *Conclusive Evidence* alone; it is also built upon *Drugie berega* and incorporates many, though not all, of the revisions made in that translation.

TRANSLATIONS FROM AND INTO FRENCH

Nabokov has made little active use of French. In the 1920s he translated some French poetry and prose into Russian. These include a translation of Romain Rolland's novel *Colas Breugnon* (*Nikolka Persik*, 1922) and some translations of Alfred de Musset and Rimbaud and other well-known French poets. Early in 1937 he delivered a lecture in French at which he read his own French translations of some of Pushkin's poems. This lecture was later published in *La Nouvelle Revue française* in March of the same year.[1] His only piece of original writing in the language is the story *Mademoiselle O* which was published in Paris in 1936. This story was translated into English in 1943 by Hilda Ward, with the collaboration of the author, and was subsequently incorporated into the memoir *Conclusive Evidence*, Chapter 5. When Nabokov left Europe for America in 1940 he abandoned writing in French. As far as can be ascertained, his only work in French since that date has been a translation of one of his Russian stories: *Muzyka*

---

[1] 'Pouchkine ou le vrai et le vraisemblable', *NRF*, No. 282. This includes translations of three lyrics: *Tri klyucha, Ne poi, krasavitsa, pri mne . . ., Mne ne spitsya, net ognya*, and one of the *Ezersky* stanzas: *Zachem krutitsya vetr v ovrage*.

(*Musique*). This appeared in *Les Nouvelles littéraires* in 1959, the year of Nabokov's return to Europe.

It remains to summarize the main points which have emerged from this description of translations of Nabokov's Russian and English writings. Little of his work has been translated from English into Russian, but what has been translated has been translated by Nabokov himself. There is a much longer history of translation into English, and here Nabokov has worked largely with collaborators. Nabokov himself is solely responsible for the translation of his poetry, his autobiography, and two novels. He first became involved in translating his works into English while he was still writing in Russian, but his interest in translation did not really develop until after he had established himself as a writer of English. Obviously, the fame which he achieved with *Lolita* in 1955 had something to do with this. After that date there was a demand for his work which had not existed before and a ready market waiting for anything he was subsequently to produce— even translations. However, this surely is not the only factor. Nabokov made no use of translations to make his name as a writer in America. He established his reputation almost entirely by original writing. Only after he had acquired an independent English style did he become seriously interested in transferring his Russian works into English. All these later translations—including those prepared by 'hired' collaborators—bear the stamp of this mature English style. It is this imprint that prevents even the most literal translation from reading like juvenilia. In this respect, then, there is no anachronism in speaking of '*The Defence*, by the author of *Lolita*', or '*Glory*, by the author of *Lolita* and *Ada*'.

2

NABOKOV'S THEORY OF TRANSLATION

> In point of fact, any translation that does *not* sound
> like a translation is bound to be inexact upon inspec-
> tion.[1]

NABOKOV's translation practice is not limited to translation of his own work. Translation of both poetry and prose has been a constant companion to Nabokov's creative writing. In *Speak, Memory* he tells how he first began translating while he was at Cambridge in the early 1920s.[2] His first translations in the 1920s and 1930s were all into Russian. In the late 1930s he brought out some translations of Russian poetry into French, but then began translating into English. These translations are many and varied. Some were undoubtedly done as a challenge and for pleasure; others were done also for profit, and others again were designed as teaching aids and contributions to scholarship. From this long practice as a professional translator Nabokov has formulated some very definite views on the necessary conditions for a good translation. In early articles, such as his article on Pushkin in 1937, he is content simply to comment generally on the difficulties involved in translation.[3] Later, he progresses towards the formulation of his doctrine of 'literal translation' which is propounded with increasing virulence and increasing repetitiveness in Russian and English, in articles, in prefaces, and in commentaries.

In his critique of Gogol, first published in 1944, there are several passing references to the cruel fate which Gogol has suffered at the hands of incompetent translators who have flattened the style and travestied the sense. Speaking of translations of *Revizor* he comments:

> I sometimes think that these old English 'translations' are remark-
> ably similar to the so-called Thousand Pieces Execution which was

---

[1] *A Hero of our Time*, p. xii. [2] p. 268.
[3] 'Pouchkine ou le vrai et le vraisemblable', *NRF*, No. 282.

popular at one time in China. The idea was to cut out from the patient's body one tiny square bit the size of a cough lozenge, say, every five minutes or so until bit by bit . . . his whole body was delicately removed.[1]

In his Foreword to the translation of Lermontov's *Geroi nashego vremeni*, made in collaboration with his son in 1958, he is equally scornful of previous renderings of the work into English: 'The book has been paraphrased into English several times, but never translated before.'[2] There he contrasts the 'experienced hack', with his malpractices of 'judicious omission, amplification and levigation', with the 'honest translator', whose principal virtue is faithfulness and who will, like himself, 'gladly sacrifice to the requirements of exactness a number of important things—good taste, neat diction and even grammar'. He inveighs against the idea that a translation 'should read smoothly' and 'should *not* sound like a translation', and insists that the good translator should not shrink from rendering faithfully the inelegancies of Lermontov's style—its dry drabness, its redundancies, its hackneyed epithets.

But most of Nabokov's theorizing about translation has arisen in conjunction with his work on the translation of Pushkin's *Evgeny Onegin*.[3] Before completing his translation in 1964, he brought out several articles in which he commented upon the problems he had encountered.[4] There is a good deal of repetition in these articles, and most of what is said there is included in the Introduction and Commentary to the translation proper. It was in 1955, in 'Problems of Translation', that Nabokov first formulated in print a definition of 'literal translation'. There he states that the translator's sole aim should be 'to produce with absolute exactitude the whole text, and nothing but the text'. He then adds: 'The term "literal translation" is tautological, since anything but that is not truly a translation but an imitation, an adaptation or a parody.' Rather less bombastically, in his Foreword to *Eugene Onegin*, he lists three types of rendering: paraphrastic, lexical, and literal. This last he defines as 'rendering, as closely as the associative and syntactical capacities of another language allow, the

---

[1] *Nikolay Gogol*, pp. 38–9.
[2] *A Hero of our Time*, Translator's Foreword, p. xii.
[3] *Eugene Onegin*, 1964.
[4] 'Problems of Translation', 1955; 'Zametki perevodchika', 1957; 'Zametki perevodchika II', 1957; 'The Servile Path', 1959.

exact contextual meaning of the original'.[1] He expands this same idea in the Commentary:

> 'literal translation' implies adherence not only to the direct sense of a word or sentence, but to its implied sense; it is a semantically exact interpretation, and not necessarily a lexical one (pertaining to the meaning of a word out of context) or a constructional one (conforming to the grammatical order of words in the text).[2]

In the light of this definition Nabokov criticizes previous poetic translations of Pushkin as so many varieties of paraphrase. He finds the translators guilty of inaccuracy, of unjustifiable embellishment and additions (*otsebyatina*), and of a 'sheer unacquaintance with Russian life in the 'twenties of the last century'.[3] He emphasizes that a faithful rendering of the original requires the translator to be thoroughly acquainted with the stylistic and lexical resources of the source language. One of the difficulties he sees in translating Pushkin is the necessity of coping with a constant intrusion of gallicisms and borrowings from French poets. As he boldly asserts in 'Problems of Translation', 'Alexandr Sergeyevich Pushkin (1799–1837), the national poet of Russia, was as much a product of French literature as of Russian culture.'[4] In subsequent articles, in 'The Servile Path' and in 'Zametki perevodchika', Nabokov lists some of the russified French locutions which abound in Pushkin's verse and advises the translator to bear these considerations in mind in his search for appropriate equivalents. Thus, for instance, he argues that it would be a mistake to look for parallels in the English Romantics whose poetic vocabulary was a good deal richer:

> Суживая пределы, убеждаешься в том, что «Онегин», в идеальном английском воплощении, ближе к общему духу 18-ого века (к духу Попа, например, — и его эпигона Байрона) чем, скажем, к лексикону Кольриджа или Китса.[5]

The true translator, then, must combine skill and patience with scholarship:

> This is my task—a poet's patience
> And scholiastic passion blent.[6]

---

[1] *EO*, Foreword, vol. 1, p. viii.   [2] Ibid., note to viii, 17–18, vol. 3, p. 185.
[3] 'Problems of Translation', p. 506.   [4] Ibid., p. 501.
[5] 'Zametki perevodchika', p. 130.
[6] 'On Translating "Eugene Onegin"', in *Poems*, pp. 37–8.

Nabokov readily admits that his exacting stipulations of accuracy will involve sacrifices. In his translation of Pushkin it is the rhyme scheme which he feels must be sacrificed: 'can a rhymed poem like *Eugene Onegin* be truly translated with the retention of its rhymes? The answer, of course, is no. To reproduce the rhymes and yet translate the entire poem literally is mathematically impossible.'[1] He points out that rhyme has a different value in Russian verse than in English. Moreover, rich feminine rhymes in English poetry often sound contrived or burlesque: 'For if in Russian and French, the feminine rhyme is a glamorous lady friend, her English counterpart is either an old maid or a drunken hussy from Limerick'.[2] A fully rhymed version in English would not only fail to convey the subtlety of the rhythm of the original but would inevitably entail unjustifiable manipulation and padding.

A 'literal translation', then, can never be more than an imperfect replica of the original. The form and content of *Evgeny Onegin* cannot be exactly reproduced in English. Nevertheless, Nabokov maintains that it is possible to compensate for all that is lost by explanations and footnotes: 'It is possible to describe in a series of footnotes the modulations and rhymes of the text as well as all its associations and other special features.'[3] And in more lyrical vein: 'I want translations with copious footnotes, footnotes reaching up like skyscrapers to the top of this or that page so as to leave only the gleam of one textual line between commentary and eternity.'[4] The Bollingen edition of *Eugene Onegin*, with its 256 pages of text as against 1,175 pages of introduction and commentary, can be seen as the realization of this vision.[5]

The theoretical position which Nabokov adopts in his discussion of *EO* inevitably raises the question of the function which he is intending his translation to fulfil. As theorists have pointed out,

[1] *EO*, Foreword, p. ix.
[2] 'Problems of Translation', p. 500.
[3] Ibid., p. 512.
[4] Ibid., p. 512. See also 'An Interview with Vladimir Nabokov', conducted by Appel, 1967: 'The only object and justification of translation is the conveying of the most exact information possible and this can be only achieved by a literal translation, with notes.'
[5] Another edition of *EO* is in preparation which Nabokov promises 'will be even more gloriously and monstrously literal than the first'. See the interview with Duffy in *Time*, 1969. See also Nabokov's 'Reply to My Critics': 'My EO falls short of the ideal crib. It is still not close enough and not ugly enough.' (*Strong Opinions*, pp. 242–3.)

it is possible to differentiate between a translation undertaken with an artistic intent and a translation which aims at being a scholarly or a pedagogical tool. Whereas the former presupposes both the ideal presence of the original and its physical absence, the latter has no independent existence and is effective only when read in conjunction with the original. Nabokov maintains that an 'artistic translation' which traduces the author and deceives the reader thereby forfeits any claims to being a true translation.[1] It is clear, though, that in his translation of *Evgeny Onegin* Nabokov has a very specific public in view—a public with some knowledge of Russian who will use the translation in order to gain a better understanding of the original. In his Foreword he tells how the writing of the book was prompted in the first instance by 'the urgent needs of my Russian-literature class at Cornell and the non-existence of any true translation of *Eugene Onegin* into English'.[2] The complete edition comprises translation, commentary, *and* the original Russian text. Nabokov's aim in *EO* is quite other than artistic—rather is it scientific. His translation is designed as but one part of the exegesis of the poem, which is complemented by the commentary. This utilitarian aim is reflected in the images he chooses to describe his labour. In his poem 'On Translating "Eugene Onegin"' he speaks of:

> my honest roadside prose—
> All thorn, but cousin to your rose.

In the Foreword to *EO* he takes up Pushkin's comparison of translators to horses changed at the post-houses of civilization, and adds: 'The greatest reward I can think of is that students may use my work as a pony.'[3] But it is in 'Problems of Translation' that Nabokov gives the fullest statement of his intentions, with a characteristic image drawn from lepidoptery:

> To the artist whom practice within the limits of one language, his own, has convinced that matter and manner are one, it comes as a shock to discover that a work of art can present itself to the would-be translator as split into form and content, and that the question

---

[1] See, for example, Nabokov's comments on Zhukovsky's translations in *EO*, note to viii, 2, vol. 3, p. 145: 'His versions of foreign poetry are not really translations but talented adaptations remarkably melodious and engaging; and they seem especially so when the original is not known to the reader.'

[2] Vol. 1, p. xi.

[3] Vol. 1, p. x.

of rendering one but not the other may arise at all. Actually what happens is still a monist's delight: shorn of its primary verbal existence, the original text will not be able to soar and to sing; but it can be very nicely dissected and mounted, and scientifically studied in all its organic details.[1]

It is clear that it is only comparatively recently that Nabokov has adopted this rigid standpoint about translation. His early translations of poetry were all into rhymed verse. Of particular interest are his French translations from Pushkin, 1937, and his English renderings of Pushkin, Lermontov, and Tyutchev in the collection *Three Russian Poets*, 1944. Nabokov himself has little to say in defence of these earlier works. When, for example, Walter Arndt uses Nabokov's own weapon of literalism to attack a translation of three stanzas from *Evgeny Onegin*, published by Nabokov in 1945, Nabokov in his reply readily disowns this earlier attempt:

> I have often been asked to allow the reprinting of my old verse translations (such as the three stanzas in the *Russian Review* 1945, mentioned by Mr. Arndt) and have always refused since they are exactly what Mr. Arndt says—lame paraphrases of Pushkin's text. They may be a little closer to it than Mr. Arndt's effort, but still have nothing in common with the literal translation I am preparing now.[2]

Then again, in a note to his translation of *Slovo o polku Igoreve*, he refers to an earlier unpublished version which he made in 1952 as 'much too "readable"', and recommends that 'mimeographed copies of that obsolete version which are still in circulation at Cornell and Harvard should now be destroyed'.[3]

However, these recantations notwithstanding, Nabokov has not entirely abandoned his old practices in later years. His translations of his own poems are all into English verse. The Foreword to to *A Hero of our Time* contains a rhymed translation of Lermontov's poem *Son*, and Nabokov also includes a rhymed translation of Pushkin's lyric: *Pora moi drug, pora* . . . in his Foreword to *Despair 2*.

---

[1] p. 504.

[2] Nabokov's postscript to Arndt's article, 'A Reply to Vladimir Nabokov: Goading the Pony'. See also 'Zametki perevodchika 11':

> ...я сам когда-то (вспоминаю со стоном) пытался переводить Пушкина и Тютчева стихами с «раскрытием образов».

[3] *The Song of Igor's Campaign*, note 18, p. 82.

This is how he introduces the rendering: 'I give it here in full, in my own translation, with the retention of measure and rhyme, a course that is seldom advisable—, nay, admissible—except at a very special conjunction of stars in the firmament of the poem, as obtains here.'[1]

In prose as well as poetry it is clear that Nabokov's developing theoretical rigorism coincides, in practice, with a growing preference for 'functional' translation, translation which is designed as an aid to scholarship. This can be illustrated by comparing an early work, such as his translation of *Alice in Wonderland* (*Anya v strane chudes*), made in 1923, with the translation of *Geroi nashego vremeni*, made in 1958 by his son under his supervision.

Alice, which Nabokov translated while still a student at Cambridge, is a delightful, ingenious, and wholly 'readable' piece of work. But in no sense is it a scholarly undertaking. There are no notes, no commentary. In rendering the puns and word-play Nabokov does not shrink from substituting his own inventions when he can find no close equivalent in Russian. More than that, he makes some alterations in Carroll's imagery and adds some word-play of his own 'in the spirit' of the original. A typical example of his method of translating the word play occurs in Chapter 3, following the Mouse's recital of 'Fury and the Mouse'. The verbal exchange:

> Alice: '. . . you had got to the fifth bend, I think?'
> Mouse: 'I had *not*!'
> Alice: 'A knot! . . . Oh, do let me help to undo it!'

—is rendered as follows:

> Аня: «Вы, кажется, дошли до пятого погиба?»
> Мышь: «Ничего подобного, никто не погиб!..
>   Вот Вы теперь меня спутали».
> Аня: «Ах, дайте я распутаю... Где узел?»   (р. 27)

Equally characteristic is Nabokov's translation of the description of the procession of the Queen of Hearts. Carroll here gives the suit of clubs and the suit of diamonds a *real* value:

> First came ten soldiers carrying clubs . . . next the ten courtiers; these were ornamented all over with diamonds, and walked two and two, as the soldiers did.

---

[1] pp. 9–10. In 'Reply to My Critics' Nabokov states that he translated this poem thirty years ago (*Strong Opinions*, p. 255).

Nabokov has:

> Впереди шли десять солдат с пиками на плечах... За ними следовали десять придворных с клеверными листьями в петлицах и десять шутов с бубнами.   (p. 69)

(*Piki* is the plural form of *pika*, meaning 'lance' and is also used for the suit of spades (cf. Carroll's clubs); *bubny* is the plural form of *buben*, meaning 'tambourine', and as the plural of *bubna* is used to denote the suit of diamonds.) An example of Nabokov altering an image occurs in Chapter 6. Here Carroll speaks of the pig-baby 'snorting like a steam-engine'. Nabokov translates:

> Оно, бедное, напряженно сопело и словно куколка, то скрючивалось, то выпрямлялось...   (p. 54)

This is a free rendering (and recalls Nabokov's interest in lepidoptery), but at least it is in keeping with the story. In the previous chapter, 'Advice from a Caterpillar', Alice has talked to the caterpillar about turning into a chrysalis and then into a butterfly. There is, however, another change which Nabokov makes in Chapter 4 which does not seem quite so justified. Describing Alice's games with the giant puppy he changes Carroll's simile:

> . . . thinking it was very like having a game of play with a cart-horse.

to:

> Ане казалось, что это игра с бегемотом...   (p. 37)

Admittedly, in Chapter 2 Alice does momentarily mistake the mouse for a hippopotamus in the pool of tears, but the whole point of the dream-construction of *Alice* is the 'making strange' of the everyday things of Alice's waking life. The cart-horse image anticipates the final page of the story where Alice's sister identifies the near-by farmyard as the source of some of the sounds in the dream: '. . . and all the other queer noises, would change (she knew) to the confused clamour of the busy farm-yard . . .' Practically all the images in the book are presented as associations which are close to Alice's own experience.

By far the most significant change which Nabokov makes in this translation is to transpose the setting from England to Russia. He renders the verse parodies by parodies from the Russian classics— from Pushkin and Lermontov. He also transposes names of characters, measurements, as well as geographical and historical references. The Mouse's 'dry' tale about William the Conqueror in Chapter 3 is, for example, replaced by an equally tedious account of Vladimir Monomakh's successors to the Kievan throne.[1]

By contrast, *A Hero of our Time* and the passages of translation included in the study of Gogol are clearly designed for the student of Russian literature. *A Hero of our Time* is equipped with a critical introduction and some 129 notes. These include explanations of geographical and historical references in the text, as well as of modes of dress and types of food and transport. There are explanations of references to Russian folklore and of allusions to Russian and foreign authors. There are also comments on inconsistencies in Lermontov's handling of the plot and on points of vocabulary and difficulties of translation. In the book on Gogol passages of translation are included simply to illustrate points of criticism. Into these passages Nabokov inserts parentheses where he comments on the style and explains details of vocabulary and Russian customs.

It is not proposed to enter here into a discussion of the merits or demerits of Nabokov's theory and practice of translation. The intention has been simply to show how Nabokov's theories arise naturally out of his developing practice as a translator. The main points of this theory may be resumed as follows:

1. The personality and views of the translator must not impinge upon the work. *Otsebyatina* is condemned.
2. The translator should endeavour to reproduce exactly the lexical and stylistic features of the original, with all its imperfections. he should not attempt to emend, improve, up-date that original. He should not sacrifice accuracy for conventional notions of 'readability' or 'smoothness'.

With two exceptions, *Laughter in the Dark* and *Despair 1*, all of Nabokov's own translations of his prose works have come out *after* he had formulated, in print, this theory of literal translation. The question naturally arises as to what influence, if any, these theories have had on his practice in his autotranslations. Clearly here different factors come into play. For one, these translations

---

[1] Karlinsky summarizes the main changes of this kind in a short article, 'Anya in Wonderland'. For further discussion of this translation see Demurova, 'Golos i skripka', and Weaver, *Alice in Many Tongues*.

do not perform the same function as do *EO* or *A Hero of our Time*. In no sense are they intended as teaching aids. Secondly, and more important, where the author and the translator are one and the same person, the requirements of 'faithfulness to the original' no longer apply. In translating his own work, Nabokov is under no obligation to reproduce his original exactly. He is at perfect liberty to emend, to elaborate. And this Nabokov does in many of his translations. (The first part of this study—Chapters 3–5—is devoted to an analysis of these emendations and elaborations.) Nevertheless, it is equally the case that Nabokov never entirely abandons his principles of literalism; he never ceases to function as a conscientious translator. (It is this aspect which will be examined in the second part of the study—in Chapters 6 and 7.)

3

MAJOR REWORKINGS: *LAUGHTER IN THE DARK*

> An author's fondest dream is to turn the reader into
> a spectator; is this ever attained?[1]

THE novels which have been most substantially revised
by Nabokov in translation are *Camera Obscura*, *Otchayanie*,
Soglyadatai, and *Korol', dama, valet*. Of these, *Camera
Obscura* and *Otchayanie* exist in two separate English versions:
Camera Obscura was translated under the same title in 1936 and
again in 1938 under a new title, *Laughter in the Dark*; *Otchayanie*
first appeared in English in 1937 entitled *Despair*, and again in
1966 under the same title. The translation of *Soglyadatai* (*The
Eye*) was published in 1965, and that of *Korol', dama, valet* (*King,
Queen, Knave*) in 1968.

In seeking to account for the amount of revision which these
novels have undergone in translation it is clearly false to suggest,
as one critic Carl Proffer does, that a decisive factor is the distance
in time between the translation and the original. In an article on
KQKn Proffer writes:

> When we triangulate to find its position in Nabokov's world, we
> discover that it is located near *Despair*, *Laughter in the Dark*, and
> *Lolita*. Nabokov has translated all of these novels, and the number
> of changes grows in inverse proportion to the author's age at the
> time of writing. The Russian *Lolita* is marked by only a few
> adjustments in allusion, the English *Despair* is changed in relatively
> minor tonal and stylistic ways, but almost every page of *King,
> Queen, Knave* differs from its Slavic model.[2]

Furthermore, he quotes a statement by Nabokov in support of his
findings.[3] However, from Proffer's article on *Despair* it is evident

---

[1] *Despair*, p. 26.   [2] 'A New Deck for Nabokov's Knaves', pp. 293–4.
[3] Ibid., p. 293. 'Nabokov has said that the urge to emend grows in proportion
to the length of time separating the model from the mimic.' Proffer is referring
to a statement made by Nabokov in his Foreword to *IB*. See above, p. 9.

that he has considered only the second, 1966, English translation, leaving out of account the earlier version which appeared only three years after the Russian original.[1] This three-year gap can be compared with the twelve years which separate the two *Lolitas*. More seriously, Proffer ignores completely the evidence of *Laughter in the Dark*. This, the most completely reworked of the novels, was published at only six years remove from the Russian and only three years after its first English translation. Proffer gives no dates in his article, which leaves it unclear what exactly is the 'pattern' he sees in the four works he mentions. If, however, they were arranged in order of increasing variation from the original this would give: *Lolita R* (published twelve years after the original), *Despair 2* (published thirty-one years after the original), *KQKn* (published at forty years remove) and *LD* (published only six years later)!

Chronology then is of no help in determining why some novels have undergone major alterations and others minor. Any speculations on this account must centre on the works themselves. One possible consideration is whether the four novels which are most completely reworked are among Nabokov's weakest. *KQKn* has never been the most highly rated of his novels, either in its Russian or its English form. Proffer, for instance, suggests that 'it is not for nothing . . . that it was among the last to be Englished'.[2] The other three novels, however, have enjoyed quite a measure of success with the reading public. Russian *émigré* reviewers admired their formal and stylistic brilliance even when they could not sympathize with their coldness, their 'inner emptiness'.[3] Georgy

---

[1] 'From *Otchaianie* to *Despair*', note 3, p. 258: 'It should also be noted that Nabokov did a translation of *Despair* in 1937. It was published in England, but so far as Nabokov knows he owns the only surviving copy.' Admittedly, Nabokov in his Foreword to *Despair 2* is not very helpful about where copies of this first translation are to be found: 'Despite that bonus, the book sold badly, and a few years later a German bomb destroyed the entire stock. The only copy extant is, as far as I know, the one I own—but two or three may still be lurking amidst abandoned reading matter on the dark shelves of seaside boarding houses from Bournemouth to Tweedmouth' (p. 8). Two English copyright libraries, the Bodleian Library, Oxford, and the British Museum, have this 1937 edition.

[2] 'A New Deck for Nabokov's Knaves', p. 293.

[3] See Terapiano's review of *CO*, 1934:

> Это лишь волшебство, увлекательное, блестящее, но не магия. Захочешь — и пусто становится от внутренней опустошенности — нет, не героев — самого автора.

Adamovich, writing in 1934, rated *Otchayanie* the most original and the most profound of Nabokov's novels:

Два вопроса и ответа:
— Какой из романов Сирина будет иметь наименьший успех у публики?
— Вероятно, «Отчаяние».
— Какой из романов Сирина — самый законченный, оригинальный и даже глубокий?
— Несомненно, «Отчаяние».[1]

Certainly, these four novels are among the most carefully constructed of Nabokov's works; nor can they be said to have dated in the same way as have parts of *Glory*, or even *Mary*. An explanation then is not to be found in any obvious inferiority of the originals.

What is noticeable, however, is how alike the four novels are in setting and theme. All are set in Berlin: the main characters of *CO/LD* and *KQKn* are all Germans. Hermann, the hero of *Despair*, though he has a Russian wife and is himself half Russian, is completely integrated into the world of small German commerce. *The Eye* centres exclusively on a Russian *émigré* milieu, but there again the nationality of the characters is not directly relevant to the action. As Nabokov says in his Foreword to the English translation: 'Actually, of course, they might just as well have been Norwegians in Naples or Ambracians in Ambridge.' In this respect these novels differ from Nabokov's other Berlin novels, *Mary*, *The Defence*, and *The Gift*, in all of which the Russian background plays a very prominent part. There are also close similarities of plot in the four novels. In all there is a love triangle. Although in *Despair* and *The Eye* this is of secondary interest, in *LD* and *KQKn* it forms the central part of the action. It is not without significance that as the tragedy of *LD* begins to develop, the husband, Albinus, finds on his desk an invitation from the Dreyers. (The Dreyers are husband and wife in *KQKn*.)[2] All the

---

[1] Review of *SZ*, No. 56, 8 November 1934.

[2] *LD*, p. 56. Until the translation of *KDV* in 1968, this allusion would, of course, have been lost on Nabokov's English readers. Allusions to characters out of other works are quite common in Nabokov's fiction. Alfyorov and Mashen'ka, characters from *Mashen'ka*, reappear in *ZL*; Robert Horn and Dorianna Karenina, characters from *CO*, reappear in *Pnin* as Robert Karlovich Horn and Dorianna Karen. *Ada* contains many cross-references to Nabokov's earlier novels, most of which are summarized by Bader in *Crystal Land*, p. 132.

novels provide variations upon the same theme—the theme of
blindness: the blindness of egoism (Dreyer, Smurov, and Hermann), the blindness of deceived love (Hermann, Smurov, Albinus,
and Dreyer), the blindness of the inferior artist (Hermann, Albinus,
and Dreyer). They are among the most gruesome of Nabokov's
novels—their stock-in-trade being torture, murder, and madness.

Perhaps more important than similarities of theme and subject
is the fact that they are all written with a consistent cold detachment. Other novels, such as *Lolita* or *Bend Sinister*, treat equally
powerful themes, but in none is the author's detachment so marked
as here, in none is the reader required to identify so little with the
characters. Pattern and plot is all, involvement and participation
is virtually nil. As Nabokov said of *KQKn*, 'the lack of any
emotional involvement and the fairytale freedom inherent in an
unknown milieu answered my dream of pure invention. I might
have staged *KQKn* in Rumania or Holland.'[1] The comment could
equally well have been made about *Despair* or *LD*. It can be suggested that it is just this degree of detachment which allows
Nabokov to treat these novels so freely in translation. The characters
remain the author's creatures, they have no life of their own and
can be manipulated at will. The dominant imagery is the imagery
of illusion: images of conjuring, of the cinema, the theatre, and of
works of fiction. And in *KQKn* a key symbol is an invention of
some life-size mannequins which Dreyer delights in for a time
and then tires of and abandons.

It has already been said that the extent of alterations varies
even in these four novels. *The Eye* is a very slight novel and undergoes the fewest alterations of all. *Despair*, a full-length novel,
undergoes similar sorts of changes, but on a rather larger scale.
The first English version, whilst containing some very imaginative
translation, makes only minor alterations to the Russian. In the
second English version, however, there are a number of significant
additions to the original text, particularly in the second and final
chapters.[2] In *KQKn* there are no additions of such a sustained
length as the addition in Chapter 2 of *Despair* which is over two
pages long. However, the total number of added passages greatly

---

[1] *KQKn*, Foreword, p. vi.
[2] Chapter 2: 'She was plump, short, rather formless . . . Otherwise, my con-
nubial bliss was complete'; Chapter 11: '"Frenchmen! This is a rehearsal. . . .
I'm coming out now".' This second passage is quoted in full on pp. 69–70.

exceeds those in *Despair*, and a number of episodes are completely rewritten. (The principal additions and reworkings are listed in Appendix B.) Many of the changes in *KQKn* affect characterization: the principal characters are given more substance, and more secondary characters are added; they enliven the margins of the narrative rather like those 'homunculi' which Nabokov comments upon in Gogol's *Revizor*.[1]

The changes made in *CO/LD* are more complex and occur at every stage of the novel's publication. It first appeared in Russian in book form in 1932, entitled *Kamera obskura* (Berlin and Paris). It was then serialized in the journal *Sovremennye zapiski*, in four parts, 1932–3.[2] In the third and fourth of these extracts Nabokov made some cuts in the text. Two whole chapters (R: Chapters 20 and 33) and parts of two more chapters (R: 23 and 35) were not included. These deletions were presumably dictated by requirements of length stipulated by the journal, but it is interesting to note that two of the omitted passages (Chapter 33 and part of Chapter 35) are ones which were to disappear altogether from the 1938 English version.[3]

The English translation of 1936, also entitled *Camera Obscura* and prepared by Winifred Roy, is a fairly close rendering of the original. There is one structural change: the Russian Chapter 5 is divided to make two chapters (5 and 6). This change, a sensible one, is carried forward into the 1938 version. There are also a number of significant small deletions and additions, some of which, but by no means all, are preserved in the second English version. It is this second version, *Laughter in the Dark*, made by Nabokov himself, which introduces the most radical changes. Firstly, there are more chapters: where the Russian version had thirty-seven chapters and E1 thirty-eight, E2 has thirty-nine.[4]

[1] *Nikolay Gogol*, p. 42: 'Gogol has a peculiar manner of letting "secondary" dream characters pop out at every turn of the play (or novel, or story), to flaunt for a second their life-like existence . . .'

[2] Whereas the title appears in Cyrillic in the book edition, it is printed in Latin script in the *SZ* edition. Since it is the *SZ* edition which has been mostly used in this study the work will be referred to by its Latin title—*Camera Obscura*.

[3] No other novel by Nabokov serialized in *SZ* was cut in any way. (This applies to *Podvig*, *Otchayanie*, *ZL*, *Priglashenie na kazn'*, and *Soglyadatai*.) However, no other novel was already available in book form prior to the completion of the serialization.

[4] In *both* Russian editions of the novel there is a misprint in the numbering of chapters. Two chapters are headed 'Chapter XVII'. This affects the sequence of all the chapters which follow.

A large part of the first chapter is rewritten; so too are Chapters 27–9 (R, 26–7; E1, 27–8). A link chapter (R, 33; E1, 35) is cut; Chapters 37 and 38 are created from just one chapter in the Russian and E1 (R, 36; E1, 37); and Chapter 37 is substantially shortened.[1] In this 1938 version the names of all the main characters are changed and alterations are made to the secondary characters. But the process of modification does not quite stop there. Minor alterations are made in subsequent editions of *LD*. There are some changes, for example, in the London edition of 1961 and further alterations are made in the London edition of 1969. The majority of these changes are textual emendations and a few are simply adaptations of Americanisms for the English reader. Some, however, are quite clearly elaborations. One such elaboration occurs in Chapter 3 in the description of one of Margot's lovers— an old man. In earlier editions Nabokov writes that he dropped fast asleep 'the moment he had stopped wheezing'. In 1969, Nabokov replaces this by '. . . dropping fast asleep the moment he had finished his messy little job'. These changes, though, are not sufficiently numerous or significant to make it necessary to class the 1969 edition as a separate version, and it is this edition which will be used in the analysis which follows.

Although the history of these English translations is different, although the amount of alteration varies considerably, the *type* of alteration shows marked similarities in all four novels. In all of them the changes affect structure, character, and style. In all of them there is a noticeable change in the authorial voice, a shift in the author's position relative to the narrative. And in the three later, post-*Lolita* translations, i.e. *The Eye*, *Despair 2*, and *KQKn*, there is evidence of an adaptation, an up-dating of subject-matter with the modern reader in view. The analysis of these translations will follow the order of their publication: *Camera Obscura/Laughter in the Dark*, *Despair*, *The Eye*, and *KQKn*.

LAUGHTER IN THE DARK

E1: *Camera Obscura*

Camera Obscura is the story of Kretschmar, a married man, and his unfortunate infatuation with a young cinema attendant, Magda. When his wife Annalisa learns of the liaison, Kretschmar

---

[1] Chapter references in the discussion which follows will be from E2, except where otherwise stated.

leaves her and their small daughter and sets up house with his young mistress. The daughter subsequently dies. The return of Magda's former lover, Robert Horn, gives rise to a classic love triangle and Magda begins deceiving Kretschmar. Kretschmar eventually learns of Magda's treachery, but immediately afterwards has a car accident in which he loses his sight. He is removed to a villa in Switzerland where Magda looks after him. Though ostensibly reconciled to Kretschmar, she profits from his blindness to continue deceiving him with Horn, who lives invisibly in the same house. Kretschmar is ultimately rescued from this torture by his brother-in-law and taken back to Berlin to his wife. The novel ends with the blind man's final attempt at vengeance. He sets out to his old flat to shoot Magda, but she succeeds in getting possession of the gun and kills him.

It has already been said that the first English version adheres fairly closely to the Russian text. It has not been ascertained what part Nabokov took in the preparation of this translation, but it would appear that his control was not as rigorous as it was later to become. Quite a number of the changes are not incorporated into the 1938 version—Nabokov's own—and it therefore seems probable that Winifred Roy did allow herself some latitude.

Perhaps the most significant feature of E1 is the toning down of the erotic content of the novel. Some of these changes are retained in E2; others, however, occur only in E1 and are subsequently abandoned. The main examples of this attenuation of the sexual detail are summarized below.

1. Chapters 2–3. Magda, Kretschmar's young mistress, is only sixteen in the Russian version. In E1, she is two years older. E2 retains this change, but puts less emphasis on her age. E1, for example, begins Chapter 3: 'She was in fact only eighteen years of age.' In E2, this reference is omitted.

2. Chapter 2. Details of Kretschmar's previous sexual experience and erotic fantasies are modified or attenuated.

(i) E1 omits the not-so-palatable details of Kretschmar's former love affairs: the doctor's wife with the unpleasant woman's illness, and the young Russian lady in Bad-Homburg who offers to take out her false teeth for him to look at. These cuts are maintained in E2. (R, p. 43; E1, p. 11, E2, p. 10)

(ii) The dreams which Kretschmar has while his wife is pregnant are less suggestive in E1. Compare:

> а по ночам ему снились какие-то молоденькие полуголые венеры и пустынный пляж... (p. 44)

E1: but at night he dreamed of some young girl on a lonely shore, and then he was overcome with a terrible fear of being caught by his wife. (p. 13)

E2 is not a literal translation of the Russian, but it does capture the erotic quality:

> but at night he dreamed of coming across a young girl lying asprawl on a hot lonely beach and in that dream a sudden fear would seize him of being caught by his wife. (p. 11)

(iii) When Nabokov describes the recurrence of this craving through the years of married life, the style of the Russian version mimics the intensity of Kretschmar's desire:

> и во всех вещах, кроме сокровенной, бессмысленной жажды обладания какими-то молоденькими красавицами, которых все равно никогда, никогда не коснешься, Кречмар был с женой откровенен... (p. 45)

E1, however, introduces a note of censure:

> and in everything, except his secret, foolish craving for some pretty young girl, Kretschmar was frank with his wife. (p. 14)

E2 restores the induction into Kretschmar's feelings:

> and he was perfectly frank with her in everything except that secret foolish craving, that dream, that lust burning a hole in his life. (p. 12)

(iv) When describing Kretschmar's desire to take a girl home while his wife is in hospital, E1 *adds* a comment on the shame which accompanied this desire:

> He felt ashamed of these persistent thoughts yet continued to toy with them. (p. 13)

This comment is absent from the Russian *and* E2.

(v) In the Russian version Nabokov explains why Kretschmar does not like sitting in cafés: he does not like watching young lovers:

> сидеть же полтора часа в кафе, слушать громкую музыку и, мучась, исподтишка, смотреть на чужих любовниц, нимало его не прельщало. (p. 46)

This explanation is omitted from E1 which has simply:

> yet neither did he feel disposed to spend an hour and a half sitting in a café. (p. 15)

It is restored in E2:

> yet neither did he feel disposed to sit and wait: the sight of other men with girl friends always upset him. (p. 13)

3. In Chapter 3, which contains a description of Magda's early life, E1 omits some small incidents suggestive of Magda's sexual awakening. The Russian version describes how when she was eight she was pinched by an old man (p. 49), and how when she was thirteen a young man in the house opposite would lean out of the window in the evenings and smile at her (p. 50). Neither of these details is in E1, and they are not restored in E2.

4. The unusual sexual demands made by Magda's ageing lover are also deleted from E1. Compare:

> Потом он начал требовать всяких странных новшеств. (p. 58)

E1: After one brief and feeble embrace he fell asleep immediately and did not wake till morning. (pp. 33-4)

E2 repairs this with a more explicit reference to their intercourse:

E2 (1938): dropping fast asleep the moment he had stopped wheezing. (p. 39)

E2 (1969): dropping fast asleep the moment he had finished his messy little job. (p. 25)

5. In Chapter 10, E1 omits some of the details of Kretschmar instructing Magda in personal hygiene:

> Она сбрила темнорусые волоски подмышками и больно порезалась жиллетным клинком. Вид крови в ней вызывал тошноту и головокружение. Кречмар бросился в аптеку, принес желтой ваты, иоду, еще чего-то. (pp. 118-19)

E2 endorses this omission (p. 59).

6. In Chapter 23, during the film show, the Russian version describes Horn's advances to Magda in more detail:

> он зато гладил ее по юбке и как-то умудрился отстегнуть ей подвязку. (p. 121)

This detail is absent from both E1 (p. 179) and E2 (p. 120). This is the most consistent type of change made in E1, which is why it has been illustrated in such detail. Not only is the erotic content minimized, but a certain moral note intrudes in the description of Kretschmar's sexual longings. It is not as easy to generalize about other changes made in E1. There are some cuts in descriptions of the private fantasies of the characters. Just as E1 gives less rein to Kretschmar's dreams, so too it curtails Magda's fantasies of stardom. In Chapter 3, the Russian version has a short passage in which Magda imagines herself being helped out of a lacquered car by a gentleman in an elegant coat with a sealskin collar; she sees herself buying a shimmering dress from a fairy-tale shop window. Neither of these fantasies is included in E1. E2 returns to the Russian, and reproduces the first of these images, but stylized in imitation of Margot's unimaginative 'superlative' vision:

> that vision of herself as a screen beauty in *gorgeous* furs being helped out of a *gorgeous* car by a *gorgeous* hotel porter under a *giant* umbrella. (p. 19)[1]

Earlier in the same chapter E1 omits the description of Magda's mother's horrific dream about a magnificent staircase which is continually being soiled by footprints. Magda's mother, it will be remembered, is a cleaner:

> Ей часто снилась по ночам сказочновеликолепная, белая как сахар лестница и маленький силуэт человека, уже дошедшего доверху, но оставившего на каждой ступени большой черный подошвенный отпечаток, левый, правый, левый, правый... Это был мучительный сон. (p. 49)

E2 restores this dream-sequence, with slight modifications (p. 16). Again, in Chapter 18, E1 minimizes the illustrations of Horn's warped sense of humour, by deleting the anecdote of the fresco painter. This is restored in E2 (p. 92). Elsewhere, there are some deletions of incidental vivid detail. One example is the description of Madame Levandovsky's dachshund in Chapter 3. Details of the dog's appearance and walk are cut in E1, but restored in E2 (R, pp. 53–5; E1, pp. 26, 29; E2, pp. 20, 22). In one or two places E1 inserts explanatory comments on character and situation. In Chapter 18, the description of Horn's poker dream is followed by the comment:

> That will-o'-the-wisp dream had pretty well ruined him, but he was incurable. He followed his desires without thought of others or of the morrow. (E1, p. 135)

---

[1] My italics.

This, like the moral comment on Kretschmar's fantasies, does not reappear in E2. On the other hand, there are instances when both E1 and E2 *delete* explanatory comments from the Russian version.

It will be clear from these examples that not only are the changes made in E1 comparatively small but few of them follow any consistent pattern, and by no means all are retained in E2. Deletions predominate over additions. It is E2, and E2 alone, which merits serious consideration as a revision.

E2: *Laughter in the Dark*

Structure

The plot of the novel, as outlined above, is a very simple one—indeed it has an almost fable-like quality. 'Love is blind' comments a postman at the end of one chapter, and this might well serve as an epigraph to the story. It is this fable-like quality which Nabokov emphasizes in his second English version. Concrete details of dates and places are cut. This is most noticeable in the introduction, in Chapter 1. The Russian version begins:

> Приблизительно в 1925 году размножилось по всему свету милое, забавное существо... существо, носившее симпатичное имя: Cheapy.　(p. 39)

E2 opens as follows:

> Once upon a time there lived in Berlin, Germany, a man called Albinus. He was rich, respectable, happy; one day he abandoned his wife for the sake of a youthful mistress; he loved; was not loved; and his life ended in disaster.　(p. 5)

Elsewhere in the novel several place-names are deleted. The Tiergarten becomes simply 'the park'. In Chapter 12, we learn that Irma, Kretschmar's daughter, has been taken 'to the country' (E2, p. 71), whereas in R and E1 she is sent to Misdroy. The exact whereabouts of the family holiday which Annalisa remembers is no longer specified. R and E1 mention Abbazia, but E2 has just 'one summer on the Italian coast' (p. 70). Nor is any indication given of the location of the holiday resort where Kretschmar takes Magda. The Russian version and E1 mention a steamer sailing 'to Ragusa', but E2 has just 'a passing steamer' (E2, p. 74).

Of more significance are the changes made in the names of the characters. The names of the principal actors in the drama lose their specifically German character. The writer, Segelkranz, becomes Udo Conrad, Magda becomes Margot, Bruno Kretschmar becomes Albert Albinus.[1] Robert Horn is renamed Axel Rex, Annalisa changes to Elizabeth, and Max, her brother, becomes Paul. Here Nabokov is obviously adapting the names of his characters for an English-reading public, but also evident is his intention to invest them with a symbolic, a 'fable-like' significance. This is very apparent in his choice of Axel Rex and Albert Albinus. Axel Rex combines associations of 'axe' and 'king', fitting allusions to the role of cruel omnipotence which he will play in the novel. Albinus greets Rex with the words:

> 'I had formed quite a different picture of you in my mind—short, fat, with horn-rimmed glasses, though on the other hand your name always reminds me of an axe.'   (p. 83)

The name Albinus fits into a pattern of colour symbolism, already present in the Russian version, but considerably elaborated in E2. The colour white dominates Albinus's characterization in the early part of the novel. White is the colour of his former life, the colour of his marriage with Elizabeth. It is this that is to contrast with the black of his blindness and the red of his passion. In Chapter 2, E2 emphasizes the whiteness of the hospital corridors where Albinus awaits news of his wife's delivery:

> Albinus walked up and down the long, *whitewashed, white-enamelled* passage . . . he hated it, hated the *hopeless whiteness* of the place and the ruddy-cheeked rustling hospital nurses with *white-winged* heads who kept trying to drive him away.   (p. 12)[2]

> Кречмар ходил взад и вперед по длинному, белому коридору больницы... сердясь на румяных, шуршащих сестер, которые все пытались загнать его куда-то.   (pp. 44–5)

In the same chapter, colours are similarly used to describe his wife's love:

> Her love was of the *lily* variety; but now and then it burst into *flame* . . .   (p. 11)

---

[1] In *SM* Nabokov reveals that the name Kretschmar was his revenge on a German lepidopterist of that name who had previously made a discovery which Nabokov had thought was his (p. 134). Field, in his remarks on *LD* (*Nabokov*, pp. 160–1), seems under the impression that Kretschmar's name is not changed in this second translation, and that Albinus is Kretschmar's Christian name. He refers to him as Albinus Kretschmar.

[2] My italics here and in the following examples.

Compare:

изредка на нее находили припадки стыдливой, нервной
страстности... (p. 44)

And when Elizabeth is away in hospital E2 stresses that Albinus
was 'tortured by two *dark* thoughts, *each of a different kind of
darkness*' (p. 11). The Russian version has merely *shaleya ot
dvukh veshchei* (p. 44). White is prominent in the description of
the bedroom which Albinus shares with Elizabeth; lying in bed
Albinus can see 'part of the central heating apparatus (*painted
white*) reflected in the mirror' (p. 31). This detail is absent from the
Russian version. The telephone on the bedside table is white in E2,
instead of black as in the two preceding versions (E2, p. 33; R, p. 65).

The theme of darkness and blindness is already present in the
Russian version. Here already there is a parallel drawn between the
sixth and final chapters. On both occasions, Albinus is searching
for Margot in his flat. On the first occasion it is night, on the
second occasion Albinus is blind; here he is groping to love, later
he will grope to kill; and both times he will be frustrated. All
versions give as one illustration of Rex's sense of humour the
situation of a blind beggar sitting down unsuspectingly on some
wet paint (see E2, p. 92). In all versions, Albinus drives past a man
in black spectacles just before his accident (see E2, p. 151).
Following the crash Elizabeth is seen in all versions reflecting on
the contrast between her black dress and the white of the ice-
cream vendor's coat: 'it seemed strange to her that he should be
dressed all in white and she all in black' (E2, p. 153). However, it
is only in E2 that Rex comments upon the fortuitousness of his
encounter with Margot with the quip: 'I couldn't believe my eyes,
as the blind man said' (p. 87). It is E2 alone which names the direc-
tor of the film in which Margot appears—he is called Schwartz
(p. 124). It is only in E2 that Albinus's suspicion of Margot's
unfaithfulness is described as 'something dark and looming, and
yet smooth and soundless, coming towards him'. He follows the
'weird bat-like shudder' of this thought, and turns round 'almost
knocking down a little girl in a black pinafore' (p. 142). Only in
this version, when confronting Margot with his suspicions, does
Albinus comment: 'Only I was blind' (p. 147). And the road on
which he is to meet disaster is changed from white to 'shiny blue-
black' (E2, p. 150).

When Albinus loses his sight the pathos of his condition is underlined in all versions by references to the coloured quality of his memory. E2, however, intensifies the irony by adding many more references to colours. Albinus's recall of the tennis racket becomes visual:

> 'But they couldn't find the tennis rackets.'
> Tennis rackets? Sun on a tennis racket. Why was that so unpleasant? Oh, yes, that nightmare business at Rouginard. (p. 155)

Compare:

> «а ракеты так и пропали». Отчего неприятно? Да, этот ужас в Ружинаре. (p. 76)

He remembers Irma 'playing with glass marbles (a rainbow in every one)' (E2, p. 165). The Russian is:

> стеклянный шарик, которым играла дочь... (p. 86)

His recall of Rouginard is more vivid and complete:

> He visualised the sky, blue distances, light and shade, pink houses dotting a bright green slope, lovely dream-landscapes at which he had gazed so little, so little ... (p. 158)

Compare:

> вспоминая уже другое, небо, зеленые холмы, на которые он так мало, так мало смотрел... (p. 79)

The description of Rouginard on that last fateful day before the accident is more vivid in E2. It is a more stylized description, with added imagery, seen as it were through Albinus's eyes. He wakes up and smiles 'at the tender blue sky and at the soft green slopes, luminous yet hazy, as if it were all a bright frontispiece under tissue paper' (p. 136). This simile is not in the Russian version nor in E1. Albinus then approaches Conrad, 'gently pushing aside the feathery foliage of a mimosa tree, which leaned wistfully in his way' (p. 137). (This detail is also not in the Russian, nor in E1.) The cicadas are described with an image: 'the creaking of the cicadas was like the endless winding-up and whirr of some clockwork toy' (p. 139). Compare:

> на стволах сидели сплюснутые цикады и трещали, трещали, пока то у одной, то у другой не кончался завод. (p. 135)

The stream is also described more imaginatively:

> A stream was running over flat stones which seemed to quiver under the knots of water. They sat down on the dry, sweet-smelling turf. (p. 139)

Compare:

> Там, из железной трубки, била ледяная струйка воды, текла по мшистой выемке, над ней дрожали желтые и лиловые цветы. (pp. 135–6)

The tops of the pine trees appear to Albinus like seaweed floating in water:

> asked Albinus, as he gazed up at the pine-tops that looked like seaweeds swimming in blue water. (p. 139)

> said Albinus, lying on his back and dreamily following with his eye the outlines of blue gulfs and lagoons and creeks between the green branches. (pp. 139–40)

Compare the Russian:

> Кречмар лег навзничь и загляделся на синеву неба сквозь озаренные, тихо шевелящиеся верхушки сосен. (p. 136)

The death scene in the final chapter is also heightened in E2 with more references to Albinus's coloured vision. Margot's perfume we learn is called *L'heure bleue*; in the corner something trembles 'like the air above sand on a very hot day by the sea' (p. 185). In the Russian, Magda's perfume has no name, and something trembles, *kak drozhit vozdukh v znoi*. Describing Albinus's sensations as he lies dying, E2 intensifies the blueness of his vision:

> 'I must keep quiet for a little space and then walk very slowly along that bright sand of pain, towards that blue, blue wave. What bliss there is in blueness. I never knew how blue blueness could be.'
> (p. 187)

Compare:

> нужно посидеть минутку совершенно смирно, посидеть, потом потихоньку пойти по песку к синей волне, к синей, нет, к сине-красной, в золотистых прожилках волне...
> (p. 105)

And E2 also adds the final glimpse of the carpet: 'bulging up at table foot in a frozen wave' (p. 187).

But Albinus is not just an ordinary man who loses his sight—
he is an art connoisseur, and Nabokov in E2 underlines the irony
of his fate by including more allusions to painting. When Albinus
is lying in hospital trying to transform sounds into corresponding
shapes and colours, Nabokov adds: 'It was the opposite of trying
to imagine the kind of voices which Botticelli's angels had' (p. 155).
Earlier, however, with another, more bitter kind of irony, Nabokov
in E2 shows up the limitations of Albinus's artistic perception.
He is unable to distinguish an original painting from a forgery.
He has in his flat what he believes to be a seventeenth-century
Baugin which Rex had faked only eight years previously (p. 94).
With this added detail Nabokov adds another dimension to
Albinus's blindness.

If white is the colour of Albinus's marriage, and black the
colour of his blindness, red is the colour of his passion. Again, E2
reinforces a symbolism which is already present in the Russian
version. The French town where Kretschmar learns of Magda's
infidelity already in the Russian has the portentous name Rouginard. In all versions Magda/Margot is frequently seen wearing
a red dress: she wears it for her first meeting with Robert Horn/
Rex; she wears it again on her first visit to Kretschmar/Albinus's
flat. It is a red cushion behind the book-stand which deceives
Kretschmar/Albinus into thinking that Magda/Margot is hiding
in the library (R, p. 74; E2, p. 44). But E2 adds another reference
to a red cushion: in Chapter 15 Margot throws one at Albinus
(p. 80). In the Russian version and E1 Magda does not throw
anything—she merely stamps her foot. The 'raspberry' reflections
of the cinema lights in the snow and wet asphalt also become more
highly coloured in E2—they become 'scarlet' and 'blood-red' (see
E2, pp. 13, 14, and R, pp. 46, 47). Margot's first sexual experiences
become associated in E2 with the colour red. The first boy to kiss
her has red hair (see p. 17). The Russian is *odin iz gimnazistov*
(p. 50). The first boy to molest her has a red motorcycle (p. 18).
The Russian is *molodoi mototsiklist* (p. 51). The effect of this
colour symbolism is to stylize the relationships of the characters.
The added allusions to blindness also intensify the irony and
stress the inevitability of the tragic outcome.

These are not the only pointers which Nabokov adds in E2 to the
outcome of the novel. In E2 an explicit connection is made between the films which Albinus sees at the cinema and his own and

his daughter's death. The poster outside the cinema 'portrayed a man looking up at a window framing a child in a nightshirt' (p. 13). Irma, Albinus's daughter, will stand in just this position shortly before she dies (see p. 103). In the Russian version and in E1 the poster has no relevance to the subsequent action. It depicts 'a fireman carrying a yellow-haired woman' (R, p. 46). The film which Albinus sees on this first visit shows a girl 'receding among tumbled furniture before a masked man with a gun' (p. 13). This is an allusion to the final scene of the novel. In the Russian version the allusion is less explicit:

> человек — спиной к публике — слепо шел на пятившуюся женщину... (p. 47)

It is omitted altogether from E1. On his second visit to the cinema Albinus sees a car 'spinning down a smooth road with hairpin turns between cliffs and abyss' (pp. 14–15). This scene clearly anticipates the car crash in Chapter 31. In previous versions there is only an oblique reference to the future catastrophe. Kretschmar sees a film about Japan entitled 'When the Cherry Trees are in Bloom'. Cherry orchards figure in the description of Rouginard, the morning before the accident (R and E1). Another pointer which Nabokov adds to the outcome of the novel is in Chapter 7. There Margot is shown innocently miming her future action:

> Often, behind her locked door, she would make all sorts of wonderful faces for the benefit of her dressing-chest mirror or recoil before the barrel of an imaginary revolver.   (p. 45)

In earlier versions she is shown miming suicide. The Russian version already provides adequate foreshadowing of Kretschmar's urges to kill Magda. There are three references in the Russian version, all of which are preserved in E2 (pp. 9, 64, 148). However, E2 adds yet another. After his first visit to the cinema, Albinus reflects, 'Like to crush her beautiful throat. Well, she is dead anyway, since I shan't go there any more' (p. 15).

The increase in the number of internal plot indicators in E2 is part of a general tightening of the novel's structure. One of the major changes occurs in the first chapter. The Russian version and E1 open with an account of Robert Horn's career as a caricaturist, and his creation of Cheepy, the guinea-pig.[1] It is described how

---

[1] The name of this guinea-pig is spelt 'Cheepy' in the Russian book edition published in Berlin, and in E1. It is spelt 'Cheapy' in the journal edition and in the book edition published in Paris.

the idea was first suggested to him by a physiologist who was campaigning against vivisection. For three years the animal enjoyed a tremendous vogue. It was reproduced in film cartoons, as models and as stuffed toys. Kretschmar is then introduced and his connection with the caricaturist outlined. Horn had sued a cosmetics firm for using for advertising purposes a picture of the actress Dorianna Karenina holding a stuffed replica of Cheepy. Kretschmar, as an art expert, had been asked to give his opinion on whether in fact the focus of the pictures was the actress or, as Horn claimed, the guinea-pig. In *LD* this opening is abandoned. There is no mention of Cheepy, and all subsequent allusions (there are several) are deleted from the text. Instead, the novel opens with Albinus and tells of his plan to make animated cartoons of famous paintings. Axel Rex is recommended to him as a talented cartoonist, and Albinus writes to him in America to enlist his help with the project.

This second exposition improves on the Russian version in several ways. It is considerably shorter and less involved. Incidental characters, such as the physiologist and the actress, are eliminated. (Dorianna Karenina makes her appearance later in the novel.) On the other hand, Udo Conrad, who *is* to play a significant part in the novel, is introduced on the very first page. It is from one of his books that Albinus has borrowed the idea of the cartoons. Albinus, the central character in the novel, is introduced first, and not Rex. The new opening also has an important bearing on the characterization, for it is Albinus who makes the overtures to Rex and not the other way round. This is more in keeping with the character of the relations of the two men in the novel, with Rex being the dominant personality. Here, too, the reader is given a first class illustration not just of Albinus's artistic sensibility, but of the superficial quality of that sensibility. Nabokov's tone, in describing the idea of the cartoons is the tone he uses for gentle satire of *poshlost'*:

> What a tale might be told, the tale of an artist's vision, the happy journal of eye and brush, and a world in that artist's manner suffused with the tints he himself had found!   (p. 6)

Cheepy gave to the characterization of Horn a certain light, slightly whimsical superficiality which is not entirely consistent with his characterization elsewhere in the novel. Not only does Horn play a sadistic role, but his humour is unrelievedly 'black'.

It seems possible that it was for these reasons of consistency that Nabokov abandoned his first exposition.[1]

The second major alteration made in E2 concerns the part played by Udo Conrad (Segelkranz) in revealing Margot's unfaithfulness to Albinus. This episode is covered by three chapters in E2 (27–9), but only two in the previous versions. In the Russian version and E1, Kretschmar runs into Segelkranz at the buffet of a railway station outside Rouginard. Kretschmar points out his carriage to Segelkranz but pauses to finish his beer. Segelkranz, presuming that Kretschmar has missed the train, seats himself in the same compartment with Magda and Horn, and overhears their intimate conversation. Kretschmar, in fact, does not miss the train, but just manages to board the last carriage. Back at the hotel, he asks Magda and Horn whether they had met Segelkranz, but they do not remember seeing anyone of that description. Kretschmar makes inquiries as to Segelkranz's whereabouts, without success. However, a few days later, out for an early morning walk, he chances upon his friend and the two men go for a walk up the hillside. Segelkranz reads Kretschmar a long-winded extract from the novel he is writing. It is a description of a dentist's waiting room, into which he has inserted with meticulous accuracy the conversation of his railway companions, including the conversation of Magda and Horn. As Kretschmar listens to this extract he guesses at the true identity of the lovers and realizes that he has been deceived. There follows the account of the crash and Kretschmar's blindness. Six chapters later, Nabokov takes up with Segelkranz again and describes his remorse at being the unwitting instrument of another man's suffering. Segelkranz returns to the Hotel Rouginard to inquire after Kretschmar and there learns of the tragedy. He then (a chapter later) proceeds to Berlin and explains to Max, Kretschmar's brother-in-law, that Kretschmar is being deceived by Magda and Horn, begging him to intervene. Max accordingly sets off for Switzerland.[2]

In E2, Nabokov reduces Conrad's involvement in Albinus's

---

[1] Field, however, regrets this deletion, and adds that Nabokov does not remember precisely why he made it. He goes on: 'While many of the omissions do tighten and improve the novel this particular frivolous symbol seems to me to be a good counterweight to the harsh and cheerless story of Albinus Kretschmar' (*Nabokov*, p. 161).

[2] It is this intervention by Segelkranz which is cut from the edition serialized in *SZ*. It takes up one and a half chapters

affairs. He is not troubled by conscience, nor does he inquire after Albinus, and he does not go to Berlin to inform Paul of the situation. Instead, Paul's suspicions are aroused by a much simpler device: his bank manager shows him the large withdrawals Albinus has been making from his account. Worried not only by the amounts, but by the handwriting on the cheques, Paul decides to go to Switzerland and find out what is going on. This plot mechanism, as well as being more concise, is also more natural: it does not hinge upon the motivation of a subordinate character. Moreover, the account of Conrad's unwitting revelation is at once more comic, more dramatic, and more logical. In a tone of light comedy Nabokov describes how Albinus chances upon Conrad at a bar by a bus-stop. Albinus misses the bus and has to wait for the next. When he returns to the hotel and asks whether Margot or Rex noticed Conrad, Rex replies that a man of that description had sat right behind them. On this note of suspense the chapter ends. The following chapter describes Albinus's walk with Conrad up the mountains. Conrad does not read any extract from his work, but he talks of what it is like to be a German resident abroad and alludes to a 'rather fascinating experience' he had listening to Albinus's two friends talking German in the bus. Again the chapter ends with Albinus still unsuspecting. It is only when he chances upon one of the hotel boarders, who asks knowingly after the 'lovers' and talks of them kissing beneath his window, that Albinus begins to perceive the truth. Only then does he call back on Conrad and ask what exactly Conrad had overheard in the bus. And Conrad tells him.

In this rendering, the discovery is made only gradually. The reader is also spared a repetition of Magda and Horn's conversation, which is a necessary part of the Russian version. Gone too is the lengthy literary parody of a second-rate imitator of Proust. (This takes up some four pages in the Russian.) In its place, there is a discussion which touches directly on Nabokov's own problems as an *émigré* writer, and which furnishes an ironic comment on this English translation. Conrad tells Albinus: 'I'd gladly write in French, but I'm loath to part with the experience and riches amassed in the course of my handling of our language' (p. 138).

The sense of logic and sense of drama which Nabokov displays in this major change is apparent, too, in minor alterations he makes to the text. It would seem superfluous to detail all of them here.

Mention may just be made of his treatment of chapter endings. Nabokov in E2 goes to considerable lengths to round off his chapters in a more telling way: some chapters abandon the action on a note of suspense; others rest with a significant detail; others lend a twist of irony to character and events. Only some ten chapter-endings are left unaltered. The final impression left by the structural changes in E2 is one of total authorial control. Nabokov has tightened up every structural feature: the development of the plot becomes more dramatic, more logical, and more inevitable.

Characterization

The alterations made to character in *LD* primarily affect the three principals. In this later version they are more sharply drawn, but are noticeably less sympathetic than their Russian counterparts. There is more colour and more comedy, but at the same time there is more irony.

From the start the reader is left in no doubt about Albinus's artistic and intellectual limitations. In the Russian version Kretschmar is introduced as follows:

> В начале 1928 года в Берлине знатоку живописи Бруно Кречмару, человеку, очень, кажется, сведущему, но отнюдь не блестящему, пришлось быть экспертом в пустяшном, прямо даже глупом деле.   (p. 41)

In E2, this comment is accompanied by a wealth of telling illustration. When Nabokov sketches his portrait in the beginning of Chapter 2 he does not stop at mentioning his slightly protruding eyes; he adds:

> the mild blue eyes which bulged a little when he was thinking hard (and as he had a slowish mind this occurred more often than it should).   (p. 9)

There is the added detail of his cartoon project, which has already been referred to, and of the fake pictures hanging in his flat which he believes to be genuine. There is also his rather questionable literary judgement. While esteeming Conrad's talent as a writer he nevertheless reproaches him for his indifference to social problems: 'he has a contempt for social problems which, in this age of social upheavals, is disgraceful and, let me add, sinful' (p. 86; see also p. 139). To the reader acquainted with Nabokov's much publicized literary credo, this is inadmissible literary criticism.[1] These views, incidentally, find an appropriate echo in Albinus's false gesture of social sympathy, when he offers some money to Magda's brother (p. 69).

Physically Albinus is rather less attractive than Kretschmar. His gestures and mannerisms are described more critically. The Russian version already mentions his *meshkovataya razgil'dyaiskaya pokhodka* (p. 63), but when describing Albinus's attempt to smile at Margot, E2 adds: '. . . and what a desperate leer it would have been had he achieved it' (p. 15). Here is another simile:

> и запоздалой улыбкой попытался смягчить выказанное раздражение.　(p. 48)

This becomes:

> and then tried to make up for his nastiness with a belated titter. (p. 15)

(E1 has 'belated smile'.) Then there are the details of Albinus's ham-fistedness. In E2 the comment is more comic, and more damning. Nabokov adds:

> He could not tie a dress-tie nor pare his right-hand nails, nor make up a parcel; he could not uncork a bottle without picking to bits one half of the cork, and drowning the other.　(p. 149)

This is not in previous versions. Slight adjustments which are made to Margot's portrait also reflect upon Albinus's lack of discrimination and perception. In E2 the cheapness of her charms is accentuated. The voice which Paul overhears on the phone is no longer 'soft and coy' (E1), it is 'vulgar' and 'capricious' (p. 47) (R: *priveredlivo i nezhno progovoril zhenskii golos* [p. 77]). When Rex sees Margot again, he is no longer bowled over by her beauty; instead, he comments laconically: 'I'm not sure that you've grown prettier, but I like you all the same' (p. 87) (R: *'Ty, znaesh', stala takoi krasavitsei'* [p. 144]). Margot's lack of talent as an actress is consistently exposed. When she mimes in front of her mirror Nabokov comments:

> And it seemed to her that she simpered and sneered as well as any screen actress.　(p. 45)

---

[1] See, for example, Nabokov's Foreword to *Despair*: '*Despair*, in kinship with the rest of my books, has no social comment to make, no message to bring in its teeth' (p. 8).

Compare:

и ей сдавалось, что у нее это выходит вовсе не хуже, чем в Холливуде.   (p. 75)

When she pretends to faint after her encounter with Otto, E2 has:

It was an indifferent performance, but it worked.   (p. 64)

Compare:

Вышло очень удачно.   (p. 123)

And in E2 Nabokov elaborates upon what already in the Russian version is a comic and merciless exposure of her appalling film début:

1. Her first appearance on the screen:

She was reading a book; then she slapped it down and lurched to the window . . .   (p. 120)

она читала, потом бросала книгу и бежала к окну...   (p. 121)

2. She leans out of the window:

and then broke in two with her stomach on the window sill and her buttocks to the spectators.   (p. 120)

легла грудью на подоконник, задом к публике.   (p. 121)

3. She opens her mouth:

Margot opened her mouth, as in real life she never opened it, and then, with drooping head and dangling arms, came out into the street again.   (p. 122)

Невеста открыла рот, как Магда никогда не открывала.   (p. 122)

If Albinus and Margot are less sympathetic characters than their Russian counterparts, they are indisputably more vivid creations and furnish more entertainment for the reader. It has already been mentioned how Nabokov gives more insight into Albinus's inner life, his artistic aspirations, and his painful adjustment to his blindness. His idiom, particularly his words of endearment to Margot, is also more individualized in the second English translation. Similar comments may be made of Nabokov's new treatment of Rex. He is no longer introduced as the inventor of Cheepy, an amusing piece of commercial gimmickry. Instead, full weight is given to his cleverness and talent as an artist, and to his dangerous and macabre taste in humour. His superiority to Albinus is stressed. He has more artistic talent and he is the more perceptive critic. It is he who has painted the forgery Albinus has in his flat; and at the dinner-party (Chapter 16) he expresses his indifference to the depiction of social problems in literature (p. 85). (Horn takes the same view in the Russian version, but since Kretschmar does not express any opinion on the subject the remark has little significance.) Rex's sense of comedy is made more subtle. Nabokov suppresses two of the more slapstick illustrations: the idea of watching a woman in bed trustfully devouring some pâté which he had concocted out of refuse; the idea of leaving a smouldering cigarette end to eat its way through some costly Eastern silks (pp. 149–50). Nabokov comments, 'He despised practical jokes', and substitutes the example of the uncle dressed up as a masked man (p. 92). This sort of 'superhumour' in which the reader is also duped is indeed very akin to the humour favoured by Nabokov himself in some of his other novels.[1] Rex's conversation also becomes a good deal cleverer. For instance, there is his tale of the man and the fish which he tells Margot, which is not in the Russian version (p. 87). His comments on Albinus's sanctification of his wife's memory are more elaborate:

> 'he has come to look upon her as a precious saint painted on glass. He will not care to smash that particular church-window.'   (p. 169)

Compare:

> «он причислил ее к лику святых...»   (p. 90)

When enjoining the maid to secrecy, Rex warns her that Albinus 'has already seriously injured one old woman (much like you in many respects, though not so attractive) by stamping on her face' (p. 161). The Russian version does not make any reference to a resemblance between poor Emilia and Albinus's purported victim (R, p. 83). Situations involving Rex are also made much funnier, through Rex's—and Nabokov's—gift for comedy. Particularly successful examples are Paul's visit to Albinus (Chapter 20) at which Rex is present, and the incident of Rex

---

[1] See, for example, the incident of the glass bowl in *Pnin*, Chapter 6. The bowl does *not* get broken, despite a good deal of build-up by Nabokov and implicit allusions to the unfortunate oriental vase in *The Idiot*.

getting caught in the lace of Margot's dress and being surprised by Albinus (Chapter 19).

In contrast with the three principals, the characterization of Albinus's family—Paul, Elizabeth, and Irma—is muted and rather more sympathetic in *LD*. They represent the solid values of family life and love which Albinus abandons for the fantastic nightmare world of Margot and Rex, and Nabokov stylizes their characterization to reinforce the contrast. The very ordinariness of Elizabeth and Paul's new names emphasizes their normality. Paul is depicted in all versions with a certain amount of gentle humour, but E2 pares away extraneous biographical details of his bachelor life (see E1, Chapter 7). Gone too is the extreme reluctance to go and see his brother-in-law in Switzerland. In E2 he is troubled, but when he finds that Elizabeth has packed his suitcase, he sets off without demur. This elimination of incidental motivation in a minor character recalls the changes Nabokov makes in the presentation of Segelkranz/Conrad. Elizabeth herself is, if anything, more pale and ethereal in *LD*. The detail of her 'plump white fingers' (*belye pukhlye pal'tsy* [p. 65]) is changed to 'her delicate fingers' (p. 33). Her gift of second-sight (a stylized motif of her love) also receives more emphasis. Not only does she sense some crisis when Paul and Irma return from the ice-hockey match (this is in all versions), but she packs Paul's bags for Switzerland before he has even told her that he is thinking of going (p. 176).

These changes which Nabokov makes in characterization in *LD* are of the same order as the changes which he makes in the structure. In stylizing his characters he shifts his point of view—he views them from a greater distance and with greater detachment. And the accumulation of colour symbolism and thematic indicators, the tightening of both outer and inner form—all this has the same effect. It encloses the life of the novel in a controlled authorial perspective. The characters move rather like caged mice through a carefully constructed maze. But Nabokov goes further. At various points in the narrative he lifts off the top of the cage and exposes the mechanism of his creation in asides to the reader. In Chapter 7, when Paul overhears Margot telephoning Albinus, he adds, '(fate's classical method: eavesdropping)' (p. 47). In Chapter 26, as Albinus rattles the locked door of the bathroom through which Margot has disappeared to join Rex, he comments

that Albinus was 'quite unconscious of the queer part doors
played in his and her life' (p. 132). On two occasions Nabokov
describes a scene as if it were a stage set. Chapter 9 ends with the
words:

> He went out. Frieda was sobbing in the wings. Someone carried
> out the luggage. Then all was silent.   (p. 58)

> Он вышел. Фрида всхлипывала в прихожей. Кто-то
> выносил сундуки. Потом все стихло.   (p. 117)

In Chapter 39, he emphasizes a scenic parallel which is already
present in the Russian:

> Stage directions for last silent scene: door—wide open. Table—
> thrust away from it.   (p. 187)

> Тишина. Дверь широко открыта в прихожую. Стол ото-
> двинут...   (p. 106)

Devices such as these preclude the possibility of the reader
identifying completely with the sufferings of the characters.

Nabokov's abundant use of comedy and irony in E2 accentuates
this distancing of perspective. Very few situations are free from
the author's irony—only Irma's death stands out for its unrelieved
pathos. Elsewhere, the most intense moments of the characters'
feelings are constantly being punctured by the sharp point of
Nabokov's pen. When Albinus, for instance, steals down at night
to the library hoping to find Margot but finds only a red cushion,
Nabokov in E2 adds the comic irrelevancy:

> But it was only a scarlet silk cushion which he himself had brought
> there a few days ago, to crouch on while consulting Nonnen-
> macher's *History of Art*—ten volumes, folio.   (p. 44)

> Это была красная шелковая подушка с воланами, которую
> он сам же на-днях принес, чтобы на полу, у низкой полки,
> просматривать фолианты.   (p. 74)

When Margot, greatly distraught, runs from Rex and into the
house, in the Russian version she gives the door a loud bang:

> Дверь бухнула ему в лицо.   (p. 145)

In E2, Nabokov writes: 'The door would have banged, had it not
been of the reluctant, pneumatic kind' (p. 88)—a classic comic

device to be found again in Jacques Tati's *Playtime*.[1] As the tragic truth of Margot's unfaithfulness is gradually revealed to Albinus, again comedy intrudes: old men suck their pipes and argue among themselves about bus routes; a French colonel makes tactless witticisms 'with what the French call a *goguenard* look in his porcelain-blue, bloodshot eye'; and Conrad, the arch-representative of Nabokovian detachment, ponders over his unwitting blunder with the words:

> 'I wonder . . . I wonder, whether I haven't committed some blunder (. . . nasty rhyme, that! "*Was* it, I *wonder*, a—*la*, la la—blunder?" Horrible!).' (p. 143)

Even Albinus's death is not without a touch of farce—he is wearing felt slippers!

Field, in his brief remarks on the novel, sees a certain 'softening' in Nabokov's second English version.[2] Since this observation seems to run counter to much of what has been said above it deserves some consideration here. The example which Field quotes in support of his statement has already been given (example 5, p. 31), and concerns the deletion of the detail of Kretschmar teaching Magda to shave under her armpits. In fact, this particular alteration was made by Winifred Roy in E1. Nevertheless, the detail was not restored by Nabokov in E2 and it can therefore be assumed that the deletion had his sanction. It has already been seen that Nabokov's practice regarding alterations made in E1 is not consistent. Some deletions of erotic detail are sustained in E2, but in other cases Nabokov restores the original Russian. However, it is important to note that Nabokov makes hardly any *additions* of this sort of detail in E2. Moreover, he makes further deletions from the text. Some examples of these deletions made in E2 are given below.

1. In Chapter 25, E2 omits details of Margot undressing before she makes love to Rex:

---

[1] Nabokov was to use this same effect in his first English novel, *The Real Life of Sebastian Knight*:

> I turned on my heel and slammed the door after me— at least, I tried to slam it—it was one of those confounded pneumatic doors which resist. (p. 116.)

[2] *Nabokov*, p. 161: 'On the other hand, there are many little ways in which the later version is somewhat softened.'

Присутствие маленького мольберта у окна и пыльный сноп солнца через комнату напоминали ей, как она была натурщицей, и теперь, торопливо снимая платье, она с улыбкой вспоминала, как бывало ей иногда холодно выходить голой из-за ширмы.

Одевалась она потом с чрезвычайной быстротой, подскакивая на одной ноге, кружась поднимая в зеркале бурю. (p. 134)[1]

E2: The box of paints, the pencils, a dusty ray of sunlight slanting across the room—all this reminded her of the time when she posed in the nude.   (p. 127)

2. At the beginning of Chapter 26 the Russian version and E1 have a few lines describing the hotel life *à trois*: every night Kretschmar would plead with Magda until eventually he would get what he wanted. Meanwhile Horn, in the room adjoining theirs, would hear Kretscmar's 'roars of delight' (see R, p. 127). None of this appears in E2.

3. Later in the same chapter, when the bath water begins overflowing, R and E1 give details of Magda's hurrying back from Horn's room:

Магда вышла из блаженного оцепенения, поцеловала напоследок Горна в ухо и бесшумно проскользнула в ванную...   (p. 130)

E2 has simply: 'Margot slipped back into the bathroom' (p. 132).

4. In the following chapter, R and E1 mention that Magda takes a bath every night and every morning. (This is her pretext for leaving Kretschmar and making love to Horn.) This is also omitted from E2.

5. In Chapter 36, E2 cuts a particularly graphic description of the blind Kretschmar pleading with Magda to make love. This passage is worth quoting in full:

«Магда, вернись», — умоляюще говорил он, протягивая руку. «Тебе вредно, тебе вредно», — равнодушно отвечала она, поглаживая Горна по его длинной и мохнатой спине. Кречмар не унимался, дергался, яростно протирал глаза. «Я хочу тебя, — говорил он, — Гораздо вреднее, что вот уже два месяца мы не...» (Тут следовал самодельный, так

---

[1] The page reference here is to the Berlin book edition.

сказать, глагол, домашний, ласкательный, из их любовного
лексикона). Горн подмигивал Магде. Она многозначи-
тельно улыбалась, стуча себе пальцем по лбу. Кречмар
продолжал ее звать, словно тетерев на току. (pp. 87–8)

E1 translates part of this passage but omits the reference to
the home-made euphemism. In E2 the entire passage is deleted.

This decrease in the amount of sexual detail gives *LD* a unique
position in Nabokov's English translations. In other translations
the erotic content increases rather than diminishes in successive
versions. The English translation of *Korol', dama, valet* is a
particularly good example of this, as will be shown in Chapter 5.
But is this in fact a 'softening' of treatment as Field maintains?
It must be admitted that even with the deletions the sexual content
of *LD* still remains very pronounced. Nabokov is clearly not
intending to eliminate all erotic allusion. What he is doing is to
lighten the tone of the tale, to purge it of sordid elements, and
to touch it up with comedy. At the same time, he seems not
unaware of the advantages of sometimes leaving something
suggested, but unsaid. By omitting examples 2 (i) and 5 given
earlier (pp. 29, 31) and example 5 above he eliminates the
only tasteless elements from the novel. The omission of some of
the explicatory passages, such as examples 1, 2, and 3 (pp. 49, 50)
allows the reader to draw his own inferences, to imagine the
situation for himself. And there are several more instances in E2
when Nabokov abandons specific detail in favour of inexplicit
allusion. When Kretschmar is bathing Magda, Nabokov describes
her in the Russian version lying in the bath and lifting up a sponge
with her toes:

> Он засмеялся, ничего уже не соображая от предчувствия
> близкого наслаждения, сказал: «конечно, еще бы», — и
> Магда наконец вылезла, он, торопясь, завернул ее в мохна-
> тую простыню, растер и понес в спальню. (p. 137)

In E2, Margot is seen

> amusing herself by standing in the full bath upon her enormous
> sponge (bubbles coming up as in a glass of champagne) . . . He
> laughed and said thoughtlessly, his mind wholly absorbed in other
> pleasant things: 'Of course, why not?' (p. 79)

And that is all. There is no mention of his wrapping her in a
towel and carrying her off to the bedroom. The stylization which is

evident in this short description recurs in other passages describing Margot. When she is lying in her bathing costume on the seashore Nabokov eliminates details of the shape of the costume and the mention of her nipples showing through the fabric. Only the main lines of the picture are retained: tanned young girl, seductive cut-away costume—indeed, 'the perfect seaside poster' (E2, p. 72). Nabokov uses a similar economy to describe Margot's love-making. Compare:

> развязная естественность наготы, точно она давно привыкла бегать раздетой по взморью его снов. Она была подвижна и неугомонна, — жаркое дыхание, акробатические ласки... (p. 114)

with E2:

> Her nudity was as natural as though she had been long wont to run along the shore of his dreams. There was something delightfully acrobatic about her bed manners. (p. 54)

And Albinus's enjoyment of these caresses is described in E2 with a fanciful image:

> a puritan's love, priggish, reserved, was less known in this new free world than white bears in Honolulu. (p. 54)

A comparison of these descriptions with the Russian original gives the measure of Nabokov's increased detachment. His treatment of sex in E2 undergoes the same shift of perspective as his treatment of character and structure. This is not 'softening'—rather it is distancing. Nabokov has fitted his camera with a 'zoom-out' lens. This same detachment is noticeable in many of the changes which Nabokov makes in the style of the novel.

Style

E2 undergoes substantial stylistic elaboration. A number of images and verbal effects lost in E1 are restored, and many more are added. There is also considerably more alliteration and carefully balanced phrasing. Many of the changes help to portray the characters more vividly. The dominant image used in describing Magda in the Russian version is that of a reptile—a lizard or a snake. E2 preserves all these images (pp. 51, 105, 125–6, 181). One is elaborated. Albinus is thinking of Margot and Rex:

> But their sinuous path burned in him like the trace which a foul, crawling creature leaves on one's skin. (p. 182)

Compare:

> он представлял себе... как Магда целует Горна, трепеща жалом, извиваясь среди открытых сундуков... (p. 101)

Some reference has already been made to the images which Nabokov adds in E2 to evoke Albinus's visual perceptions before his accident and his sensations after he goes blind (see pp. 36–7). There are others:

1. For hours on end he lay on his back, silent and motionless, listening to daytime sounds, which seemed to have turned their backs upon him in merry converse with others. (p. 157)

   > он часами молчал, неподвижно лежа на спине и слушая звуки провансальского дня... (p. 79)

2. in the depths of a night which employed the bright small-talk of daylight ... (p. 159)

   > глубокой ночью, полной дневных звуков... (p. 81)

3. Albinus touched the furniture, patted the different objects as if they were the heads of strange children ... (p. 163)

   > Кречмар трогал мебель, ощупывал предметы, старался ориентироваться. (p. 84)

Alliteration is used in a similar way to make the characterization more vivid. The description of Margot's mother combines imagery and alliteration:

> a coarse callous woman whose red palm was a perfect cornucopia of blows. (pp. 15–16)

> Мать, еще довольно молодая, но рыхлая женщина, холодного и грубого нрава, с ладонью, всегда полной потенциальных оплеух... (p. 49)

Alliteration enlivens the description of Elizabeth:

> a willowy, wispy, fair-haired girl with colourless eyes and pathetic little pimples just above that kind of small nose which English lady novelists call 'retroussée' (note the second 'e' added for safety). (p. 10)

> миловидная, бледноволосая барышня, с бесцветными глазами и прыщиками на переносице... (p. 44)

Sometimes these effects can give character and situation an appropriate touch of humour. Rex, for instance:

1. When torturing Albinus he sits

> with his hairy legs crossed and his chin cupped in his hand (rather in the pose of Rodin's *Thinker*) . . .   (p. 177)

> скрестив мохнатые ноги, и подперев подбородок рукой... (p. 96)

2. He first got in touch with Frau Levandovsky

> through two hearty commercial travellers with whom he had played poker on the boat train all the way from Bremen to Berlin. (p. 20)

> С Левандовской он познакомился через двух темперамент-ных комивояжеров, с которыми играл в покер, по дороге из Гамбурга в Берлин, а затем в берлинском кафе.   (p. 54)

3. His curiosity:

> for it was not anything morbid with a medical name—oh, not at all—just cold, wide-eyed curiosity . . .   (p. 91)

> да, это было только любопытство...   (p. 149)

Alliteration and imagery also embellish passages of description. Here Albinus is waiting for Margot:

> The asphalt was drying patchily after a recent shower, the damp still showing in the form of grotesque black skeletons as if painted across the width of the road.   (p. 38)

This image is not in the Russian version. Another example is the description of the ice-hockey game:

> Among catcalls, clappings, and clamour, the players were leisurely gliding across the ice . . .   (p. 97)

> На лед плавно въехали игроки...   (p. 154)

It has already been shown how in the description of the sunny morning in Rouginard Nabokov cuts out specific details of blue villas and cherry orchards and substitutes more striking visual effects—patterns of sun and shade, and the alliterative 'feathery foliage of a mimosa tree' (E2, p. 137; compare R. p. 134). Often, attention is focused on a single object, rather than many. Nabokov sometimes does this for dramatic effect:

1. At Rouginard, after Margot has slept with Rex:

> They sat on the terrace. *A white moth* fluttered round the lamp and fell down on the tablecloth.   (p. 133)[1]

---

[1] My italics here and in the following examples.

они сидели на террасе, вокруг лампы колесили ночницы и падали на скатерть. (p. 130)

Note that in E2 the moth is white. This identifies the image more directly with Albinus.

2. The hotel bedroom at Rouginard after Albinus has learnt the truth about Margot:

The room was dead, the open wardrobe empty; empty, too, the glass shelf above the wash-stand. *A torn and crumpled newspaper lay on the floor.* (p. 149)

Дверь в номер Кречмара была открыта. Пусто, валяются листы газет, обнажен красный матрац на двуспальной кровати. (p. 71)

The same device is used to suggest beauty, particularly Albinus's view of beauty:

1. Albinus gazes at the sky, just before going off to visit Margot:

The sky was still quite blue, with a *single salmon-coloured cloud* in the distance . . . (p. 50)

легкие сумерки оживлялись нежными оранжевыми огнями, небо было еще совсем голубое... (p. 80)

2. Albinus's arrival in Rouginard:

An orange-flushed cloud curled in wisps across the pale-green sky . . . (p. 130)

над окрестными горами линяли лохматые розовые тучи... (p. 127)

3. On the first evening at Rouginard Albinus looks out at the night sky:

There was *a big star* in the plum-coloured sky, the black treetops were perfectly still . . . (p. 131)

Синева, огоньки, черные купы деревьев... (p. 129)

4. When evoking Albinus's sense of the elusiveness of female beauty Nabokov again uses the singular:

they [girls] had just slid past him, leaving for a day or two that hopeless sense of loss which makes beauty what it is: *a distant lone tree* against golden heavens; ripples of light on the inner curve of a bridge; a thing quite impossible to capture. (p. 10)

This last passage is not found in the Russian version. It is strikingly reminiscent of the vision of beauty seen by the main character of the story *Oblako, ozero, bashnya*. This story, first published in 1937, would very likely have been written at approximately the same time as *LD*, and a comparison of the two passages provides an interesting example of cross-fertilization between Nabokov's English and Russian writing.[1]

These examples provide, it is hoped, adequate illustration of the keenness of eye with which Nabokov views character and description in *LD*. The style of this version is more dense, more vivid, and more colourful than the Russian original, and certainly than Winifred Roy's translation. However, the stylistic elaboration can have another and quite opposite effect. It can distance and veil rather than intensify the 'life' of the novel. Brilliant stylistic effects can shift the focus more on to manner than matter, on to the telling rather than what is told. This also happens in *LD*. There are some passages of gratuitous improvisation which border on preciosity. One such example is the description of Margot's ride with the motor cyclist:

> It was a sunny evening and a little party of midges were continously darning the air in one spot.   (p. 18)

> Был солнечный вечер, толклась мошкара.   (p. 51)

Another is the description of Margot's poverty:

> The winter seemed colder than winters used to be; Margot looked about her for something to pawn: that sunset perhaps.   (p. 26)

> Зима была холодная, деньги шли на убыль.   (p. 59)

---

[1] This is the passage from *Oblako, ozero, bashnya*:

Это было чистое синее озеро с необыкновенным выражением воды. Посредине отражалось полностью большое облако. На той стороне, на холме, густо облепленном древесной зеленью (которая тем поэтичнее, чем темнее), высилась прямо из дактиля в дактиль старинная черная башня. Таких, разумеется, видов в средней Европе сколько угодно, но именно, именно этот, по невыразимой и неповторимой согласованности его трех главных частей, по улыбке его, по какой-то таинственной невинности, — любовь моя! послушная моя! — был чем-то таким единственным, и родным, и давно обещанным, так понимал созерцателя, что Василий Иванович даже прижал руку к сердцу, словно смотрел тут ли оно, чтоб его отдать.   (p. 39)

Examples of this sort of gratuitous elaboration are few. However, all the changes which Nabokov makes in the style of the novel have this potentially dual effect. They give life, colour, and move-ment, but at the same time they stylize that life, they freeze and fix the images for the visual and auditive delight of the reader.

This conclusion may be generalized and applied to the changes which Nabokov makes in other areas of the novel—in character and structure, as well as style. Everywhere the revisions have this same dual effect. The structure becomes more tightly knit and dynamic, but at the same time the mechanism of the plot is more openly exposed; the style becomes more brilliant, but more brittle, more self-conscious; the characters are more brightly coloured, but more the puppets of their creator. Action, character, and description are made more vivid, but the involvement of author—and reader—is lessened. It could be suggested that this pattern of alteration arises naturally out of the restrictive con-ditions attending a rewrite. The author can emend, elaborate, improve his earlier work, but he cannot recapture the original creative impulse. The work is already finished, and the author remains outside it. There may indeed be some truth in this hypo-thesis. Nevertheless, this same combination of stylization and lively narration is characteristic not only of Nabokov's revisions of his works, but of much of his original writing in his later period.

Nabokov weaves into *Lolita* (1955) an intricate web of literary allusion and parody. Themes, characters, and style are borrowed from American, English, and European writers, and give relief and literary perspective to the tale of Humbert Humbert and his love for the young Lolita.[1] Yet this conscious deployment of literary artifice does not mean that Nabokov abandons the con-ventional narrative mode. The obscure puns and tantalizing allusions combine with passages of high comedy and high drama in which Nabokov displays a developed narrative skill and a cultivated talent for memorable characterization. Few readers will forget the description of Quilty's murder, or of Humbert's last visit to Dolly Schiller, or his account of life with the bourgeois Charlotte Haze.

The parody of literature and literary conventions is an even

---

[1] Nabokov's use of literary allusion in *Lolita* is discussed by Proffer in *Keys to Lolita*, Chapter 1, and by Appel in *The Annotated Lolita*.

more pronounced feature of *Ada* (1969). In this novel there is an abundance of word-play and literary allusion which at times threatens to swamp the narrative and exhaust the reader's patience. But there are parts of the novel where Nabokov holds his literary expertise in check and where he achieves a blend of narrative and artifice which is as effective as anything to be found anywhere else in his writing. Such is the description of Lucette's suicide in Part Three, Chapter 5. This chapter abounds in multilingual puns and in literary allusion. There are references to Borges ('Osberg'),[1] to *Don Juan*, *Don Quixote*,[2] and to Tolstoy's *Otets Sergey*.[3] There are references to Nabokov's own works—to *Lolita*,[4] *Laughter in the Dark*,[5] and *Spring in Fialta*.[6] And at the very climax of the chapter—Lucette's suicide—the narrator breaks off to make some asides to the reader.[7] However, all this extraneous literary paraphernalia does not dissipate the drama of the whole account. On the contrary, these irrelevancies and digressions slow down the pace and serve to heighten the suspense. They also help convey a sense of Lucette's isolation immediately prior to her death. The reader, occupied by this welter of irrelevancies, is unable to involve himself in Lucette's feelings. Her plight is progressively withdrawn in precisely the way that a person on the verge of suicide withdraws into isolation from society.

[1] 'Osberg's novella', p. 488.

[2] 'The Don rides past three windmills' (p. 489). Van and Lucette are watching a film which purports to be about Don Juan, but which incorporates features of that other Spanish fictional hero.

[3] p. 490.

[4] pp. 488–9. The young gipsy girl in the film is called Dolores. The gipsy theme is also present in *Lolita*. There are numerous allusions to Mérimée's *Carmen*.

[5] pp. 488–9. Van is watching a film in which Ada, his young mistress, plays a leading role. This is a direct echo of the film scene in *LD*, where Albinus watches Margot's performance.

[6] 'Spring in Fialta, and a torrid May on Minataor, the famous artificial island, had given a nectarine hue to her limbs' (p. 477).

[7] 'Now I've lost my next note. Got it.'

'. . . and there was an increasing number, okay, or numbness, in her neck and arms.'

'She did not see her whole life flash before her as we all were afraid she might have done' (p. 494).

4

MAJOR REWORKINGS: *DESPAIR* AND *THE EYE*

Otchayanie was first published in three parts in the journal *Sovremennye zapiski* in 1934,[1] and came out in book form two years later in Berlin. There is evidence, though, that the novel was at least partially completed as early as 1932. On 3 November 1932 *Poslednie novosti* printed an interview with Sirin, 'U V. V. Sirina', signed by Andrey Sedykh. In this interview Nabokov spoke of a new novel he was engaged upon: *Otchayanie*. On the 17th of the same month a brief unsigned notice appeared in the same newspaper: 'Vecher V. V. Sirina'. At this soirée Nabokov had read some poems, the story *Muzyka*, and 'a most interesting extract' from a new novel, *Otchayanie*. On 31 December *Poslednie novosti* published a short piece by Sirin, entitled *Otchayanie*. No indication was given that the story was an extract. It is, in fact, Chapter 1 of the novel. Two more extracts appeared in *Poslednie novosti* in 1933.[2] In 1937, Nabokov's own English translation of the novel, entitled *Despair*, was published in London, and in 1966 a revised edition of this translation was published in New York and in London.

Both these translations stand in a considerably closer relation to *Otchayanie* than do the English *Camera Obscura* and *Laughter in the Dark* to their Russian originals. There is also a much closer connection between the two English versions. Practically all the changes which are introduced in the first translation (E1) are retained in the second (E2). Moreover, the types of alteration made in both versions follow a consistent pattern. Nabokov rarely by-passes E1 and returns to the Russian. The reason for this is clear. Not only is E1 Nabokov's own translation, but it is also indisputably a more imaginative, a more

---

[1] As in the Russian editions of *CO*, there is a mistake in the numbering of the chapters. Two chapters are headed 'Chapter VII'. This affects the sequence of all the following chapters. There is no mistake in the book edition of the novel.

[2] *Still ist die Nacht*, 8 October 1933; *Otezd Ardaliona*, 5 November 1933.

creative translation than Winifred Roy's version of *Camera Obscura*.

Otchayanie is the story of a murder, recounted in the first person by the murderer himself, Hermann Karlovich. While on a business trip to Prague he chances upon a sleeping tramp, Felix, in whom he sees his perfect physical double. Hermann conceives the plan of luring Felix to Berlin, dressing him in his clothes, killing him, and passing off the corpse as his own. His wife, Lydia, would then collect his Life Insurance, and eventually join him in France. The novel describes every stage of the execution of this design. Felix is murdered, and Hermann assumes his identity and leaves the country secretly. In France, he avidly reads newspaper reports of the crime and learns that the plan has misfired—the police have not been deceived by the imposture, and are hunting Hermann as the murderer. Hermann is safe as long as the identity of Felix is unknown. But some weeks later a report appears which states that an object has been found establishing the victim's identity beyond doubt. Hermann thinks back over every stage of his 'perfect crime,' and at last recalls his one fatal mistake—he had left Felix's stick, inscribed with his name and address, in his car. The novel ends as Hermann awaits arrest.

The effectiveness of this tale derives principally from the reader's awareness that Hermann is insane. Without violating the convention of the first person narrative, Nabokov skilfully juxtaposes the real course of events, with events as they are seen through the perverted logic of Hermann's madness. Hermann is blind to the truth of Felix's appearance: Felix, in fact, bears only a very slight resemblance to him. He is equally blind to the nature of his wife's affection for him. He thinks she is completely devoted to him, whereas, in reality, she is openly deceiving him with her cousin, Ardalion. And he is blind to the flaw in his 'perfect' crime. The discovery of the stick finally explodes his belief in his consummate skill as an artist.

It should be stressed that the Russian *Otchayanie* is already a powerful and well-constructed piece of writing. Hermann's style is brilliantly individualized, a blend of vulgar colloquialisms and high-flown conceits, with a wealth of literary allusion. His insanity is underlined by a careful deployment of structural devices and subtle dramatic irony. The changes which Nabokov makes in E1 and particularly in E2 add depth to this 'portrait of a madman', and intensify the dramatic irony.

E1: *Despair*, 1937

E1 is both an accurate and a talented translation. The deletions are few: there are only one or two small cuts, all of which are sustained in E2. Of more significance are the additions, which affect structure, characterization, and style.

Structure

Structurally, E1 makes two important changes, both concerning the stick which is to play such a key part in the plot. In Chapter 2 of *Otchayanie* Hermann gives as an illustration of his wife's stupidity, her interpretation of the word 'mystic'. She conceives of it as a diminutive:

> Мы выяснили как-то, что слово «мистик» она принимала всегда за уменьшительное, допуская таким образом существование каких-то настоящих, больших «мистов», в черных тогах, что-ли, со звездными лицами.   (р. 124)

Since '-ik' does not exist as a diminutive suffix in English, Nabokov compensates in E1 with an equivalent piece of word play: 'We discovered one day that to her the term "mystic" was somehow dimly connected with "mist" and "mistake" and "stick"' (p. 35). This association of 'stick' and 'mistake', which is here purely verbal, will be borne out by the later development of plot.[1] A second structural change is made in Chapter 9, shortly before the murder. E1 here evokes the sound of the car on rough ground with: 'Ick. And once again: ick' (p. 221). (The Russian is *ukh! esche raz: ukh!*—an echo of the chorus from 'The Song of the Volga Boatmen'.) The 'ick' not only recalls the name of the car, Icarus (*Ikar* in the Russian), but the same inescapable *stick* which Felix leaves inside it.

Characterization

A few touches are added to the characterization of Hermann, and more detail is given of his insanity. One example of this occurs

---

[1] Hermann uses the word 'mystic' later on (*all* versions), when talking to Lydia about his fictitious brother: 'You forget that he is a murderer and a mystic.' (See E2, p. 151.)

in Chapter 5, where Hermann is describing his different kinds of handwriting. E1 adds an appropriate grotesque simile:

> then an inclined one, sharp and perky, the scribble of a dwarf in a hurry, with no dearth of abbreviations . . . (p. 110)

The Russian is:

> засим: наклонный, востренький, — даже не почерк, а почерченок, — такой мелкий, ветреный, — с сокращениями и без твердых знаков... (p. 77)

(E2 makes further slight improvements: 'then a fast cursive, sharp and nasty, the scribble of a hunchback in a hurry, with no dearth of abbreviations' (p. 90).)

Style

The Russian original is already rich in imagery. As in *CO*, clusters of images are used thematically in the novel. In *Otchayanie* the predominant thematic images are again images of illusion: the cinema, the theatre, literary creativity, conjuring, and also dreams and nightmares, mirrors, and reflections in water. All these images are retained in E1. Any images lost, and these are very few, are neutral images. For example:

1. убитые камни дороги, движущейся как конвейер... (p. 146)

This becomes:

> the beaten stones of a country road   (p. 71)
> the pebbles and mud of a country road   (p. 61)

2. и господин в пальто, со съехавшим набок механическим галстуком, с беременным саквояжем на коленях, — вероятно ветеринар.   (p. 149)

> and a man in an overcoat, with his ready-knotted cravat askew and a heavy-looking travelling sack on his knees: probably a veterinary surgeon.   (p. 75)

E2: and a man in an overcoat despite the heat, with a heavy-looking traveling bag on his knees: probably a veterinary surgeon.   (p. 64)

E1 also adds several images, many of which embellish Hermann's lunatic style. For example:

1. When Hermann is describing the effects of distorting mirrors:

> a neck bared, no matter how slightly, draws out suddenly into a downward yawn of flesh.   (p. 32)

> малейшая обнаженность шеи вдруг удлиняется.   (p. 123)

2. Before his arrest:

> expecting every minute to hear the guillotinette of the mouse trap in the corner crash down and behead an anonymous mouse . . . (pp. 284–5)

> ожидая, что в углу с треском хлопнет мышеловка, отхватив мыши голову.   (p. 69)

3. The police car which Hermann observes from the bus:

> I saw from my bus two policemen in a fast car which was white as a miller's back . . .   (p. 277)

This is an elaboration of the Russian simile:

> я из автобуса увидел двух ажанов в быстром, словно мукой обсыпанном автомобиле . . .   (p. 64)

There is considerably more alliteration and assonance in the English translation. This is already a feature of Hermann's Russian style, and E1 provides some effective equivalents in translation. However, the number of instances of alliteration is more than doubled. Here is a representative sample of the alliteration which Nabokov adds in Chapter 1 of E1.

1. a languid lady in lilac silk   (p. 8)

> в сиреневых шелках, томная   (p. 109)

2. I trod upon soft, sticky soil   (p. 11)

> я зашагал уже по мягкой, липкой земле   (p. 110)

3. a hill, splendidly steep, sloped up into the sky   (p. 11)

> великолепный холм поднимался стеной в небо   (p. 110)

4. a spot of wild and wonderful beauty   (p. 11)

> какой-то чудной глухой красоты   (p. 111)

5. the red rotundity of that gasometer   (p. 14)

> облый румянец газоема   (p. 112)

6. on the blue background of a breezy May day   (p. 14)

> среди ветренной синевы майского дня   (p. 112)

7. the remarkable qualities of clarity and cohesion   (p. 14)

> необыкновенную ясность и стройность   (p. 113)

8. this slightly marred the marvel   (p. 15)

   чудо слегка замутилось, но не ушло   (p. 113)

9. two forked fingers   (p. 16)

   двумя расставленными пальцами   (p. 114)

10. the vague-eyed vagabond   (p. 18)

    рассеянный бродяга   (p. 115)

11. as if I were the mimic and he the model   (p. 20)

    точно мимикрирующей особью был я, а он — типом   (p. 116)

12. Suddenly I felt limp, dizzy, dead-tired   (p. 21)

    Я почувствовал вдруг, что ослабел, прямо изнемог, кружилась голова   (p. 117)

13. framed in frizzly bronze, Felix awaiting me   (p. 22)[1]

    обрамленный курчавой бронзой, ждал меня Феликс   (p. 118)

Some of these examples combine alliteration and assonance. Here are two other examples of assonance added in E1:

1. seemed to me most rural and alluring   (p. 11)

   показавшийся мне вольным, деревенским, весьма заманчивым (p. 110)

2. thus a breeze dims the bliss of Narcissus   (p. 23)

   так ветер туманит счастье Нарцисса   (p. 118)

Another feature of this version is the successful handling of the word-play which abounds in the Russian version. Ingenious equivalents are found in practically every instance, and in some chapters the verbal humour is elaborated. Two examples of such elaboration are given below:

1. A description of two forked trees:

   A couple of inseparable birches grew there (or a couple of couples, if you counted their reflections) . . .   (p. 46)

   На ней росли две неразлучные березы (или четыре, если считать их отражения) . . .   (p. 131)

---

[1] Not every instance of added alliteration has been included here. Where alliteration seems virtually 'unavoidable', as, for example, in the translation of *na podborodke i shchekakh* as 'with chin and cheeks', it has not been counted. And it is of course true that while the Russian version is less alliterative than the English, it does have other patterns of sound: coincidence of word endings, for instance. (See examples 2 and 7.)

2. Hermann to Lydia:

> 'The chief thing is naturalness of grief. It may not exactly bleach your hair but it must be natural.' (p. 155)

> «Главное — естественность горя. Пускай оно будет не ахти какое, но естественное». (p. 17)

It is this first English version, also, which contains most of the delightful 'Englishing' of Hermann's stilted literary style—the addresses to the reader ('gentle reader', 'dear reader', etc.); the quaint inversions ('Long did I keep toot-tooting'; 'Many a time had I done Lydia's nails'); the poetic vocabulary ('The hamlet where I languish lies in the cradle of a dale'); the metric phrases ('and my will lay limp in any empty world'); the studied rhetoric ('and what is death, if not a face at peace').

E2: *Despair*, 1966

E2 is a more sophisticated and extensive elaboration of the two pre-existing versions. Proffer, in his article 'From *Otchaianie* to *Despair*', has compared this 1966 version with the Russian original. This article contains many interesting and valuable points. Unfortunately, however, some of Proffer's conclusions are undermined by the fact that he has not examined the first English version. Practically all the verbal effects which he quotes as examples of Nabokov's development as a stylist in fact date from as early as 1937, from the first translation. The same criticism applies to some of his remarks on the structure and on the translation of literary allusions. To ignore this early version is to give an exaggerated picture of the distance separating Nabokov's early and later production.

Structure

Nabokov does not make any major structural changes in E2, but all the changes made are valuable improvements. He tidies up the logical development of his narrative and intensifies the dramatic irony by highlighting Hermann's insane delusions. He plants more clues to the importance of the stick in the plot. When Hermann meets Felix in Tarnitz, E2 inserts three more references to this stick:

1. 'A beggar,' he repeated again and again [, now leaning with both hands on his stick and swaying a little]. (E2, p. 85; E1, p. 102)[1]

---

[1] For use of square brackets see Note on References on p. x.

2.   'I'll tell you something,' he went on, laying his stick aside and addressing me with some heat.   (E2, p. 85)

Compare:

'I'll tell you something,' he went on, suddenly addressing me with some heat.   (E1, p. 103)

3.   his poor dusty shoes stood on the floor with toes turned in; his trusty stick had been carefully placed across the seat of the chair that supported his clothes folded with proletarian tidiness.   (E2, p. 108)

Compare:

his poor dusty shoes stood on the floor with toes turned in, whilst on a chair his clothes were folded with proletarian tidiness.   (E1, p. 133)

E2 also adds three more references to the name of Hermann's car, Icarus (pp. 42, 175, 182), which again recalls the stick that Felix leaves inside it. The name occurs only once in the Russian version and twice in E1.[1]

Allusions to Lydia's love affair with Ardalion are multiplied in E2, making Hermann's blindness all the more obvious and comic. 'A wilted tulip' is listed as one of the items to be found in Lydia's untidy chest of drawers (p. 35). The reader remembers this detail when, a few pages later, Hermann describes the subject of one of Ardalion's paintings—'phallic tulips in a leaning vase' (p. 42). (Compare E1, p. 45: 'livid lilac bloom in a leaning vase')[2] As another illustration of Lydia's untidiness, Hermann mentions that 'her lipstick turned up in incomprehensible places such as her cousin's shirtpocket' (p. 36). (This detail is not in previous versions.) Later, in Chapter 5, Hermann looks forward to taking a hot bath, 'though wryly correcting anticipation with the thought that Ardalion had probably used the tub as his kind cousin had already allowed him to do, I suspected, once or twice in my absence' (p. 108). This innocent suspicion is also absent from the

---

[1] The name 'Icarus' (*Ikar*) had already been given to Dreyer's car in *KDV*. It is given later to the car in *Spring in Fialta* (English version only), and to the car belonging to Humbert Humbert in the Russian translation of *Lolita*. (In the English *Lolita* the same car is called 'Melmoth'.) Incidentally, Icarus is also the name of a species of butterfly: *Polyommatus icarus*, the Common Blue. Hermann's car and Humbert Humbert's are both blue. And the name Melmoth while alluding to Maturin's novel and to the name which Oscar Wilde adopted in his last years, is perhaps also not without lepidopteral associations.

[2] The Russian version contained a pun upon Nabokov's surname and his pen-name Sirin: 'malinovoi siren'yu v nabokoi vaze.'

Russian version and E1. In Chapter 6, when Hermann chances upon Lydia half-undressed in Ardalion's room, Nabokov adds the detail that Ardalion has nothing on underneath his smock: 'There was nothing beneath save his silver cross and symmetrical tufts of hair' (p. 116). In previous versions, he is at least wearing underpants! (See E1, p. 142; R, p. 98.) In Chapter 7, when Hermann is persuading Ardalion to go to Italy, he innocently quips: 'An artist cannot live without mistresses and cypresses, as Pushkin says somewhere or should have said' (p. 136). This is also new in E2.

By other small changes Nabokov tightens up the logic of the tale. One incidental character is eliminated. The artist who accompanies Ardalion to the station becomes, in E2, the same 'desperate friend', Perebrodov, to whom Ardalion had lent Hermann's money (p. 146). In previous versions, it is another artist, named Kern, who arrives with Ardalion (see E1, p. 183; R, p. 9). In Chapter 9, as Hermann is driving to the scene of the murder, Nabokov deletes a flashback to the previous summer. In R and E1 Nabokov has:

> Once or twice I struck badly cobbled bits; and hens were already appearing . . . this fowl or that would come running across the road (though it may quite likely be that it took place not then, but in summer).   (E1, p. 215)

It is the parenthesis which is cut in E2 (p. 171). This is one of several instances when Hermann's sense of time becomes momentarily confused. However, in most other instances the jump is forward in time and not back.[1] One such example is Hermann's confusion of the occasion when Lydia is making goggle-moggle and the occasion when she is grinding coffee (pp. 40-1, 153). Another is his confusion of summer and winter on Ardalion's plot of land (pp. 46-7, 173, 175). These devices have a structural importance. They give the reader a glimpse of the future action. The deleted flashback performs no structural function, and it is arguable that Nabokov considered that it constituted an unnecessary break in the action.

Some adjustments are made to Hermann's preparations for the murder and to his removal of the tell-tale evidence afterwards. In E2 Hermann does not neglect to tell his wife where to find his will after his body has been discovered: 'The policy and my

---

[1] In Chapter 4 and elsewhere there are some flashbacks to Hermann's youth in Russia. These, however, have bearing on his character, but not on the plot.

testament are in the middle drawer of my desk' (p. 156). At the
scene of the crime Nabokov mentions how Hermann transfers
that vital weapon, the gun, to the other pair of trousers:

> plucked out of the suit I had shed several things—money, cigarette-
> case, brooch, gun—and stuffed them into the pockets of the tightish
> trousers which I had drawn on . . .   (p. 179)

The gun is not mentioned directly in R and E1:

> plucked out of the suit I had cast off my money and something
> else and slipped both into the pockets of the tightish trousers which
> I had drawn on . . .   (E1, p. 226)

After committing the murder, Hermann is careful not to leave
Felix's comb on the spot:

> I even went so far as to brush the footboard where I had been
> cutting his nails [and to unbury his comb which I had trampled
> into the ground but now decided to discard later].   (p. 182; E1,
> p. 231)

This last added detail shows Hermann coming very close to
making a dangerous oversight. On this occasion, the reader's
fears are quickly allayed, but his attention is drawn to the possibility of a slip-up. Next time, his fears will be justified. This false-
alarm device is a favourite with Nabokov. He uses it twice in
LD—once when a telephone rings (Chapter 4), once when a door-
bell rings (Chapter 11). In *Despair* he uses it again in Chapter
8 (all versions), when Hermann almost decides to take a suitcase
with him, then realizes just in time how imprudent this would be.

Nabokov also introduces a few more thematic links which give
the narrative cohesion and movement. When Hermann first
meets Felix all versions describe the few pale violets drooping
from Felix's buttonhole (see E2, p. 19). In E2, when Hermann
returns to the same spot on the following day, he finds there
'a dead violet' (p. 27). This detail is absent from previous versions.
In Tarnitz, Hermann is reminded of a village on the Volga, and its
'pale sky sick of looking on fisheries'. Consistent with this memory,
Nabokov in E2 transforms Carl Speiss, a baker whom Hermann
had known in this fishing village, into a fishmonger 'who likewise
sold spitchcocks' (p. 78). (Compare E1, p. 94: 'the name of
a baker: Carl Speiss, reminding me of one Carl Speiss whom I
used to know in that Volga village of my past and who likewise

sold buns'.) E2 also makes some additions to the thematic imagery, particularly the imagery of mirrors and of the double:

1. There is an added reference to Narcissus:

> With a condescending grin he offered his hand, hardly bothering to sit up. [I grasped it only because it provided me with the curious sensation of Narcissus fooling Nemesis by helping his image out of the brook.]   (p. 23)

2. A description of the reflections of foliage in water is highlighted:

> Below, on the still surface of the water, we admired the exact replica (ignoring the model of course) of the park's autumn tapestry of many-hued foliage . . .   (p. 72)

Compare E1:

> Below, on the still surface of the water, there was reflected the rich tapestry of brown and rusty-red foliage . . .   (p. 86)

3. The description of mirrors is elaborated. *Zerkalo* is on one occasion translated as 'every speckly psyche' (p. 74). E1 simply has 'glass' (p. 89). Later, *guashevoe zerkalo* is rendered by 'a looking glass with one reflection' (p. 190). E1 has here 'a whitelead mirror' (p. 243). When Hermann gazes at Felix's address in his diary he conjures up his features: 'Looking through that trembling prism' (p. 66). E1 has just: 'Looking through it' (p. 78).

4. In E2, Hermann gives an example of the illusory logic of dreams which when remembered are utterly meaningless:

> 'Besides being silent before tea, I'm silent before eyes in mire and mirorage.'   (p. 118)

This illustration, which is not in R or E1, is by no means meaningless to the reader. It is another insight into Hermann's insane obsessions.

5. The novel ends with an added passage which adumbrates the themes of illusion and delusion. When Hermann sees the people gathered awaiting his arrest he leans out of his window and makes a last insane bid for freedom:

> 'Frenchmen! This is a rehearsal. Hold those policemen. A famous film actor will presently come running out of this house. He is an arch-criminal but he must escape. You are asked to prevent them from grabbing him. This is part of the plot. French crowd! I want you to make a free passage for him from door to car. Remove its

driver! Start the motor! Hold those policemen, knock them down, sit on them—we pay them for it. This is a German company, so excuse my French. *Les preneurs de vues*, my technicians and armed advisers are already among you. *Attention!* I want a clean getaway. That's all. Thank you. I'm coming out now.' (p. 222)

Characterization and Style

In E2, Nabokov fills out the characterization of Hermann with more illustrations of his insanity and sexual obsessions. Since this is a novel written in the first person, many of these changes are embedded in the style—Hermann's style. There are five added references to madness and violent death.

1. Hermann elaborates a simile with the words:

> and scrags of rotting moss stuck out of its earthern walls like the broken springs of decrepit furniture [in a house where a madman had dreadfully died]. (p. 16; see E1, pp. 11–12)

2. Describing his different handwritings, he adds the variation:

> then a suicide's hand, every letter a noose, every comma a trigger . . . (p. 90)

3. Describing his agitation on meeting Felix, he adds:

> I felt hot all over. The wind had died in the madhouse. (p. 83)

E1 has just:

> For some odd reason I was feeling hot all over. (p. 100)

4. Nabokov adds a reference to a film which had been shot at Roussillon. The film was called *Les Contrebandiers*, and a gendarme points out to Hermann 'a scaffold of sorts painted yellow which was all that remained of the scene where one of the smugglers almost got hanged' (p. 219). Roussillon is the place where Hermann is awaiting arrest. The scaffold is an ominous portent of the future course of events.

5. A significant addition is made to Hermann's nightmare, recorded in Chapter 3. In R and E1, only one variation of this dream is described—the discovery of the empty room. In E2 Nabokov adds a further variation. One night a chair appears:

> not as a first item of furniture but as though somebody had brought it to climb upon it and fix a bit of drapery, and since I knew *whom* I would find there next time stretching up with a hammer and

a mouthful of nails, I spat them out and never opened that door again.   (pp. 56–7; see E1, p. 65)

Nabokov also increases the suspense surrounding this nightmare. Not only does he make the description longer and more elaborate, he does not state explicitly *who* it is that Hermann finds there. Earlier versions both reveal that Hermann finds there his double:

and then one unforgettable day finding it empty no more, and seeing my double rise and come out to meet me?   (E1, p. 66)

Compare:

Or was I, perhaps, only making my way along that ordinary corridor of my dreams, time after time shrieking with horror at finding the room empty, and then one unforgettable day finding it empty no more?   (E2, p. 58)

Greater scope is given to Hermann's deranged and grotesque imagination. There are many instances of this in almost every chapter of the novel. The main examples are summarized below.

Chapter 1

1. Felix looking in a mirror:

he pawed at his face, then glanced at his palm, but found neither blood nor bird spat.   (E2, pp. 21–2)

Compare:

he pawed at his face . . . but found neither blood nor dirt.   (E1, p. 19)

2. When Hermann notices Felix pocketing his silver pencil:

A procession of silver pencils marched down an endless tunnel of corruption.   (E2, p. 24)

This is not in R or E1.

Chapter 2

3. When defending his secretiveness in not telling anyone about Felix, Hermann puts forward this analogy:

a child in the womb is not referred to as Tiny Tom or Belle . . .   (E2, p. 41)

This is not in R or E1.

4. In E2, Lydia wakes Ardalion by crying out 'in a trumpet voice'. A window opens and a man looks out 'with a real trumpet in his

hand' (pp. 43–4). In previous versions, Lydia shouts in a 'megaphone voice', and the man who emerges is not holding any trumpet (see E1, pp. 46–7).

Chapter 4

5. Hermann's letter to Felix:

> First of all we must have an eye-to-eye monologue and get things settled.   (E2, p. 69)

Compare:

> First of all we must have an eye-to-eye talk and get things settled. (E1, p. 82)

6. Nabokov adds a stylistic 'beauty and beast'[1] combination when describing the reflection of a leaf in water:

> there would rise towards it, eagerly, its exact [, beautiful, lethal] reflection.   (E2, p. 72; see E1, p. 86)

7. Another grotesque detail:

> A brutal wind was blowing and chasing leaves [— scurry, cripples! —] athwart the street.   (E2, p. 78; see E1, p. 94)

Chapter 5

8. Hermann expands upon his anecdote about the unfortunate guest who unwittingly comes out with the same quotation from Turgenev:

> A few minutes later there arrived one more guest, who, in the middle of the conversation, delivered the very same phrase [, lifted from the program of a concert at which I had noticed him heading for the greenroom]. He, and not I, made an ass of himself, to be sure; still it produced an uncomfortable feeling in me [(though I derived some relief from asking him slyly how he had liked the great Viabranova),] so I decided to cut out the highbrow business. (E2, p. 89; see E1, p. 109)

9. The passing of time elicits the image:

> half a year has suddenly gone—a fall in a dream, a run in time's stocking . . .   (E2, p. 91)

This is not in R or E1.

> [1] The phrase is used by Proffer in 'A New Deck for Nabokov's Knaves': 'In his later works Nabokov loves beauty and beast combinations, proximity of poets and monsters' (p. 306).

10. Felix's account of his cousin's death:

> my aunt broke her heart over him until the day when, thank God, he dashed his brains out by missing a flying swing [and his wife's hands]. (E2, p. 98; see E1, p. 120)

11. Another 'beauty and beast' combination. Speaking of Felix's respect for money Hermann writes:

> The weighty German word for 'money' . . . was mouthed by him with extraordinary reverence, which, curiously, could turn into brutal lust. (E2, p. 101)

Compare:

> extraordinary reverence, which, curiously, turned to lust. (E1, p. 124)

12. An unpleasant memory is described as being 'as sticky as a sheet of flypaper into which one has walked naked in a pitch-dark room' (p. 98). Compare:

> it is as sticky as a sheet of fly-paper into which one has run in a pitch-dark room. (E1, p. 121)

Chapter 6

13. The description of Hermann listening is embellished with an image:

> I kept on sending one ear out to walk up and again up to the door of my flat, though it was much too late now. (E2, p. 122)

Compare:

> I kept on being on the alert though it was much too late now. (E1, p. 151)

Chapter 7

14. Another image is elaborated. Hermann is expressing his unwillingness to post letters:

> It is like diving into icy water or jumping from a burning balcony into what looks like the heart of an artichoke . . . (E2, p. 133)

Compare:

> It is like diving into icy water or parachuting into the void . . . (E1, p. 167)

Chapter 8

15. When Hermann's feet are numb with cold he reflects:

> I wondered if perhaps they would freeze less if I did not give my black shoes such a smart shine: a passing and repassing thought. (E2, p. 141)

This is not in R or E1.

16. Another contrast: Lydia in her leopard's skin coat is seen as 'a lamb in leopard's clothes' as she trots alongside Ardalion's train (E2, p. 147). Compare:

> Lydia trotted alongside the carriage and kept shouting something. (E1, p. 183)

17. Hermann's fictitious twin brother is described with more invention:

> At first we shared a bed with a pillow at each end until it was discovered he could not go to sleep without sucking my big toe, whereupon I was expelled to a mattress in the lumber room but since he insisted on changing places with me in the middle of the night, we never quite knew, nor did dear mamma, who was sleeping where.   (E2, pp. 147–8)

This is not in R or E1.

Touches of grotesque comedy are added to the account of Hermann's reunion with this brother. We learn that 'even the waiters wept' (E2, p. 149), and also that 'a gypsy orchestra in the café drowned part of his speech' (E2, p. 150). The speech is the brother's announcement of his intention to commit suicide! Neither of these details is in previous versions.

18. Another elaborated image: Hermann's thought of the profit he would get by his twin brother's death 'seemed as stupidly matter of fact, as, say, the inauguration of a railway during an earthquake.' (E2, p. 150). Compare:

> seemed as stupidly matter-of-fact, as, say, a lightning rod on the roof of a bank, yanked out of black night by the sudden flash of a thunderstorm.   (E1, p. 188)

Chapter 9

19. Cutting Felix's toe-nails:

> They snapped loud and flew far, those ugly black parings, and in

recent dreams I have often seen them speckling the ground much too conspicuously. (E2, p. 179)

This is not in R or E1.

Chapter 10

20. When Hermann assumes Felix's identity, he asks himself:

> Should I practice doing things with my left hand? (E2, p. 186)

This is not in R or E1. It is the positioning of this question, at the very end of a paragraph, which gives it comic effect.

Hermann's wayward and pretentious literary style is also enriched by added word play. For example:

1. Hermann asks Ardalion:

> 'You have, I suppose, one of those Nansen-sical passports, not a solid German one, as all decent people have.' (E2, p. 138)

This pun—on the Nansen passport—is not in R or E1.

2. Hermann combs his hair 'with a pocket comb of genuine tortoise-shell—not the dirty mock turtle I had seen that bum using' (E2, p. 108). This is not in R or E1.

3. The turkeys at his home:

> and choleric turkeys with carbuncular caruncles (I made a gobbling sound) . . . (E2, p. 93)

Compare:

> and choleric, full-blooded turkeys (E1, p. 114)

4. The cross which Ardalion wears when bathing:

> kept jumping out when he jumped in. (E2, p. 49)

Compare:

> there kept jumping out the cross . . . that he wore next to his skin. (E1, p. 55)

5. The play upon the name Orlovius. In R and E1, the pun connecting Orlovius with 'eagle' (*orel*) is dormant:

> Таких людей, как Орловиус, весьма легко провести... этот подслеповатый осел... (R, p. 7)

> People like Orlovius are wonderfully easy to lead by the nose . . . that purblind ass . . . (E1, p. 179)

In E2, the pun is fully fledged:

> Old birds like Orlovius are wonderfully easy to lead by the beak . . .
> that purblind eagle . . .   (E2, p. 143)

In addition, Turgenev in E2 is addressed as 'Turgy', and Dostoevsky is punned as 'Dusty' and 'Dusty-and-Dusky'. Hermann suggests *Crime and Pun* as a title for his novel, and Dostoevsky's hero becomes Rascalnikov, not Raskolnikov (p. 199). (E1 spells the name 'Raskolnikoff'.) Felix gains a surname, Wohlfahrt, which means 'well-being' and thus pairs nicely with his first name. His home town, Zwickau, occasions the rhyme: 'Felix Wohlfahrt from Zwickau. With his stickau he pointed' (E2, p. 213). E1, here, has just: 'Felix so-and-so from Zwickau. With his stick did he point' (pp. 275–6).

There is also some added alliteration and assonance, though the proportion of additions is much smaller than in E1. Here is a representative sample from Chapter 1.

1. the bus, the motorbus, the mighty montibus of my tale. (E2, pp. 13–14)

Compare:

> the mighty motorbus of my tale.   (E1, p. 8)

2. in a house where a madman had dreadfully died.   (E2, p. 16)

This is added to E1.

3. my vast inward wilderness   (E2, p. 18)

Compare:

> my vast wilderness   (E1, p. 14)

4. but found neither blood nor bird spat   (E2, p. 22)

Compare:

> but found neither blood nor dirt.   (E1, p. 19)

5. the curious sensation of Narcissus fooling Nemesis   (E2, p. 23)

This is not in E1.

6. the rough brown taste tinged with lemon of a large flat veal cutlet (E2, p. 24)

Compare:

> the brown taste of a veal-steak   (E1, p. 22)

7. like an equiradical rhyme   (E2, p. 25)

This is not in E1.

8. nice low benches with backs carved and curved in perfect accordance with the human spine.   (E2, p. 28)

Compare:

> with backs carved in perfect accordance with the human spine. (E1, p. 27)

It remains to consider the extra illustrations which Nabokov gives in E2 of Hermann's sexual obsessions. Most of these have already been pointed out by Proffer in his article on the novel[1] and will only be summarized here.

1. The main addition in E2 is too long to quote. It is a two-page description of Hermann's sexual relations with his wife, and of the dissociation he experiences during the sexual act (E2, pp. 36–9).

2. There is an added reference to a sausage in Felix's pack:

> an opened flap revealed a pretzel and the greater part of a sausage with the usual connotations of ill-timed lust and brutal amputation. (E2, p. 19)

Compare:

> a pear-shaped shoulder-bag with bits of string doing their best to strengthen the straps.   (E1, p. 16)

3. A description of Felix's stool:

> I discovered there . . . that pathetically impersonal trace which the unsophisticated wanderer is wont to leave under a bush [: one large, straight, manly piece and a thinner one coiled over it]. (E2, p. 27)

5. More is learnt of Hermann's premarital sexual experience. He came by his revolver as a result of 'a sordid bet won from a wenching upperformer' (p. 56). His visits to the brothel are described in greater detail:

> At sixteen, while still at school, I began to visit more regularly than before a pleasantly informal bawdy house; after sampling all seven girls, I concentrated my affection on roly-poly Polymnia with whom I used to drink lots of foamy beer at a wet table in an orchard—I simply adore orchards.   (E2, p. 57)

Compare:

> When still at school, in the last form but one, I became a fairly regular visitor at a bawdy house; used to drink beer there. (E1, p. 65)

---

[1] 'From *Otchaianie* to *Despair*'.

The memory of Christina Forsmann is concretized:

> Christina Forsmann[, whom I had known carnally in 1915] . . . (E2, p. 77; see E1, p. 93)

5. The description of the naked Lydia is embellished:

> [frightened] Lydia . . . posed [in the buff and the brown (fat thighs so tightly pressed together she could hardly stand)] for her portrait before Ardalion . . .   (E2, p. 65; see E1, p. 76)

6. Felix naked:

> His back was about as muscular as mine, with a pinker coccyx and uglier buttocks. When he turned I could not help wincing at the sight of his big knobbed navel—but then mine is no beauty either. I doubt he had ever in his life washed his animal parts: they looked fairly plausible as these things go but did not invite close inspection. His toenails were much less abominable than I had expected.   (E2, p. 103)

This is not in R or E1.

7. The bathroom scene (Chapter 6) is more comic in E2, with added references to Hermann's nakedness. He is completely naked, not half-naked, as in previous versions. He opens the bathroom door, not 'an inch wider', but sufficiently for the maid, Elsie, to reply, '"A man" . . . as if commenting on my nakedness'. Elsie is seen 'contemplating with the utmost indifference my pearly armor', and as Hermann rushes out he collides with her in the passage: '"He's gone", she said, politely disengaging herself from my unintentional embrace.' Also, it is only in E2 that we learn the age of this maid—she is seventeen. (See E2, pp. 120–1; compare E1, pp. 148–9.)

8. In Hermann's story of his twin brother there is added homosexual innuendo. This passage is quoted in Example 17, p. 74.

9. Perebrodov, at the station, thrusts out 'as if it held a dirty postcard, an unshakeable hand in my direction' (E2, p. 146). In E1 he is described as 'giving a clammy hand' (p. 183).

There are no comparable additions in E1. In his Foreword to *Despair 2* Nabokov suggests that at least some of the sexual interpolations were already written at the time he was working on *Otchayanie*. He refers to the longest of these added passages as 'an important passage which had been stupidly omitted in more timid times'. (This is Example 1, referred to above, p. 77.) The inference is that the younger Nabokov consciously curtailed the erotic content of his novels in deference to the pressures of public opinion and the tastes of his potential readers. This is not the only occasion when Nabokov alludes to censorship exercised upon his early work. In a prefatory note to the English translation of *Solus Rex* he speaks of the 'restoration of a scene that had been marked in the *Sovremennyya Zapiski* by suspension points'.[1] This turns out to be a graphic description of the Prince's homosexual practices: 'With fat fingers, the prince undid Ondrik's fly, extracted the entire pink mass of his private parts, selected the chief one, and started to rub regularly its glossy shaft.'[2] In another prefatory note to *A Dashing Fellow* Nabokov says that the Russian original of this story—*Khvat*—was rejected by *Rul'* and *Poslednie novosti* as 'improper and brutal'.[3] These statements are not open to question. Some restrictions *were* imposed on Nabokov's publications, and Nabokov himself may well have exercised some private censorship on his own work. But it would seem misleading to generalize from Nabokov's remarks and thereby be tempted to regard *all* the sexual allusions added in *Despair 2* and in other translations simply as 'restorations'. Admittedly, the degree of tolerance of sex in literature is considerably greater today than it was in the 1930s. But the *émigré* literary scene could hardly be described as prudish; indeed, by comparison with its contemporary Soviet counterpart it appears to have been very liberal. It is illuminating in this context to refer to *émigré* reviews of *Lady Chatterley's Lover*, when a Russian translation appeared in 1932. (Nabokov, it will be remembered was already engaged upon *Otchayanie* in 1932.) Adamovich wrote a laudatory article in which he said that whatever criticisms could be made of the literary qualities of the novel, no one could quarrel with the author's intentions; these were irreproachable:

> Давать или не давать эту книгу в руки юным девушкам, — вопрос особый, но нет сомнения, что «Любовник леди Чаттерлей» написан поэтом, которому самое понятие «порнография» было совершенно чуждо.[4]

---

[1] *RB*, p. 147.   [2] Ibid., p. 204.   [3] Ibid., p. 130.
[4] 'O knige Lorensa', 7 April 1932. See also Adamovich's comments in 'O "pafose Moskvy"', 26 May 1932.

Vladimir Varshavsky reiterated these sentiments in his review of
the novel which appeared in *Chisla*, 1932:

> Между тем, мне кажется ошибочным видеть в «Любовнике
> леди Четтерле», только эротическое исследование. Главное
> в книге — это призыв к защите человеческой нежности и
> любви, к защите теплого пламени жизни против мертвящего
> духа сегодняшнего времени...

We also note that Nabokov's early writing in Russian is by no
means free of sexual detail and allusion. The editors of *Sovremennye zapiski* may well have objected to the description of the
Prince's perversions in *Solus Rex*, but they did allow other sexual
allusions in the story to stand. *Khvat* was rejected by two newspapers; but it *was* published—first in Riga in the early 1930s and
later in Nabokov's collection of stories, *Soglyadatai* 1938, on the
press of *Russkie zapiski*. The 'distastefulness' of the story lies not
so much in the inclusion of sexual detail, which is in fact minimal,
as in the brutality of the central character. It recounts a day in the
life of a small-time womanizer. The 'hero', an *émigré*, meets a
woman in a railway compartment. He fantasizes, flirts, proposi-
tions, and seduces—then leaves the same evening to catch another
train, without saying goodbye, and without informing her that
her father is on the point of death. The narration is partly in the
first person, and renders with clinical and telling accuracy the
workings of a crude and callous mind.

We have also seen how the original Russian version of *Camera
Obscura* contained some explicit sexual references which were
toned down in the two English translations. And the original
Otchayanie already contains a reference to masturbation which, to
one little versed in the precise hierarchy of permissiveness, would
seem to be potentially more 'shocking' than the comic account of
Hermann's sexual dissociation:

> Как отрок после одинокой схватки стыдного порока с
> необыкновенной силой и ясностью говорит себе: конечно,
> больше никогда, с этой минуты чистота, счастье чистоты...
> (p. 92. See E2, p. 107)

Nor does it appear that the sexual content of Nabokov's work was
the target of *émigré* criticism. Nabokov was criticized by many
reviewers for coldness and lack of humanity, but few questioned
his moral integrity. Mikhail Tsetlin, in his review of *Korol'*, *dama*,

valet in 1928, likened Nabokov's method to that of the German expressionists with their regrettable 'coarsening' of the material of art.[1] But Adamovich, on the other hand, defended rather than attacked Nabokov's approach. He wrote of *Camera Obscura* in 1934:

> Сирину не свойственна сдержанность, он вовсе не гонится за тем, чтобы его романы могли быть рекомендованы в качестве чтения для юных барышень. Но никому, конечно в голову не придет упрекать его в стремлении к сомнительно-соблазнительным эффектам.[2]

The influence of censorship, while not to be ignored, should not be over-exaggerated. The most severe censorship exercised upon Nabokov's Russian writing was the banning of the chapter on Chernyshevsky in *Dar*—this, for political reasons.[3]

Further to this question of sexual elaboration there remains the evidence of Nabokov's later English production. This increase in erotic content characterizes not only Nabokov's more recent translations, but also his original writing in his later period, following the publication of *Lolita*. *Lolita* secured Nabokov general recognition as a talented writer of English. It also gave him a certain notoriety: the novel was widely described as pornographic. It is not unreasonable to contend that in the wake of *Lolita* Nabokov has deliberately fostered his public image of the so-called 'pornographic' writer, and has accordingly increased the erotic content in his novels. This point will be taken up in more detail towards the end of the following chapter.

It will be clear from this examination of the two English translations of *Otchayanie* that the changes which Nabokov introduces are not as far-reaching as those made in the translations of *CO*. Two reasons can be put forward for this. Firstly, Nabokov's first English translation is already a very competent one, and a good deal superior to the first version of *CO*. Secondly, the very form of the novel, a dramatic monologue, gives less scope for

---

[1] Стремление к выразительности во что бы то ни стало, к подчеркиванию, к заострению и, увы, к огрублению художественного материала — вот методы экспрессионизма.

[2] 'Sirin', 4 January 1934.

[3] The chapter was refused by the editors of *SZ*. It was restored in the second edition of the novel, published in New York in 1952.

elaboration than a novel with not one, but several, fully developed characters and an independent narrative voice. All the changes which Nabokov makes in the English translations are consistent with the restricted viewpoint he has chosen—consistent with Hermann's style and with his character. Nabokov is not overtly present in the work as he is in *LD*. This does not mean, however, that the type of changes made in *Despair* are essentially very different from those made in *LD*. The structure is tightened and made more logical and dramatic. The reader is given a better view of the action and is able to dissociate himself more from Hermann's point of view. The increased distance which Nabokov creates between reader and narrator allows more opportunity for irony and for comedy. Hermann's style maintains its highly individual character, yet here, too, the changes made are characteristically Nabokovian: the rich alliterative texture, the added imagery and word-play, the comedy, the grotesqueries.

The same pattern of alteration occurs in *The Eye* which was published shortly before *Despair 2*.

THE EYE

Soglyadatai was first published in Number 44 of *Sovremennye zapiski* in late 1930. The novel was subsequently included in a collection of thirteen stories, entitled *Soglyadatai*, which was published in Paris in 1938 on the press of *Russkie zapiski*. The English translation, prepared by Dmitri Nabokov and entitled *The Eye*, was serialized in *Playboy* early in 1965 and appeared in book form later that same year. It is a slight work and many critics have classified it as a long story, or a novella.[1] Nabokov, however, has in recent years included it in his corpus of Russian novels, and accordingly it is as a novel that it is discussed in this chapter.[2]

Soglyadatai is a first person narrative, and a study of personality and identity. The narrator is a Russian *émigré* living in Berlin who at an early stage in the novel attempts to commit suicide. The attempt is unsuccessful, but the narrator cannot believe that he is not in fact dead. He feels completely dissociated from his former

[1] See, for example, Field, in *Nabokov*, p. 166. See also Struve in 'Les "romans-escamotage" de Vladimir Sirine', April 1931.

[2] In his Foreword to *The Eye*, Nabokov speaks of 'this little novel'. See also the Foreword to *Glory*, where Nabokov includes it in a list of his Russian novels.

self—an onlooker, a *soglyadatai*. The rest of the novel is taken up with his description of a group of Russian *émigrés* with whom he becomes acquainted, and in particular with a newcomer to the group, one Smurov. Smurov fascinates him and he sets out to discover the 'real' Smurov beneath the many different images he presents to different members of the group. Gradually it becomes clear to the reader that Smurov is merely an objective projection of the narrator's own self, and that he and the narrator are one and the same person. The final confirmation comes at the end of the novel when the narrator meets a character from his pre-suicide life who addresses him by name: *Gospodin Smurov*.

Structure

The English translation makes only minor modifications to the structure of the novel, and these are primarily changes of format. The Russian version is divided into six chapters and subdivisions of those chapters are marked typographically by double spaces and by paragraphing. In the English version Nabokov does away with chapters and instead divides up the narrative using double and treble spaces and paragraphing. (Double or treble spacing is substituted for all the chapter divisions with the exception of the fourth, which is marked merely by a new paragraph.) The effect, in a novel of this size (the Weidenfeld and Nicolson edition is only 90 pages long), is to streamline the narrative and give it greater movement and cohesion. Instead of a series of structural units the novel appears as a continuous narrative, with pauses marking changes in direction and tone. Discounting the chapter breaks, the number of double spaces in the English text is only slightly greater than in the Russian. However, they serve a rather different function. In the Russian version they are there primarily for dramatic effect, to divide up a sequence of actions. The scene where Smurov is thrashed by Kashmarin is punctuated in this way (R, p. 95); so too is the description of Smurov's preparations for suicide (R, p. 99) and of his walk to see his old room (R, p. 148). Practically all the spacings in the English text, on the other hand, indicate changes in the focus of the narrative. They may denote a shift from the particular to the general, from incident to commentary (E, pp. 35, 65, 80, 102) and vice versa (E, pp. 74, 91); or they may mark a change of place or subject (E, pp. 50, 56, 77).

Characterization and Style

More significant changes are made in the actual text of the novel. In the English version Nabokov touches up and elaborates his characterization of Smurov. Added details and added word-play fill out this portrait of a disturbed mentality and an over-active, sick imagination. Smurov's sensual impressions are evoked more vividly. Weinstock's mistress, for instance, is described by him as a 'little pink-faced, red-haired lady with plump little hands, who smelled of eucalyptus gum' (E, pp. 46–7). In the Russian version there is no mention of the gum—the lady is simply *krepko nadushennaya* (R, p. 114). Again, Smurov in the English translation claims that English cigarettes 'always smell of candied prunes' (E, p. 55), whereas in the Russian version he merely says that they smell of honey (R, p. 120). And Uncle Pasha interrogates Evgenia in 'a sprayey whisper' (E, p. 66), instead of a loud whisper (*gromkim shepotom*, R, p. 127).

Smurov's imagination becomes more highly coloured. His fabricated account of his exploits in the Civil War is embellished in the English translation. He mentions the daughter of a dentist who nursed him while he was in hiding (p. 52). He adds circumstantial details of appropriating 'a tin of zwiebacks and a keg of Crimean wine' and setting out 'in the auroral mist' (p. 54). Then again, the dream which he has of a conversation with Khrushchov is more colourful in the English translation. In the Russian version he sees terraces stretching into the distance and a small port with glimpses of blue sea (R, p. 142); the translation is: '. . . the terraces stretched away into the distance, where one seemed to distinguish cascades and mountain meadows' (E, p. 89). The dream which he has of Vanya at the very end of the novel is also more evocative:

> Every other night I dream of her dresses and things on an endless clothes-line of bliss, in a ceaseless wind of possession, and her husband shall never learn what I do to the silks and fleece of the dancing witch.   (E, p. 103)

Compare:

> У меня с нею были по ночам душераздирающие свидания, и ее муж никогда не узнает этих моих снов о ней.   (R, p. 152)

This is one of several images added in the English translation. (There are at least five fully developed new images.) There are many more instances where Nabokov elaborates existing images. One such example of this is the extended simile of the city dweller who visits the country (R, p. 100; E, pp. 26–7), which is expanded as follows:

> I saw now [, as one sees a real turnip field instead of the picture-postcard glens and glades,] how conventional were my former ideas on presuicidal occupations . . .

Another example is Smurov's description of his beating heart:

> It was throbbing like a small animal you want to carry to a safe place [, a fledgling or field mouse] to which you cannot explain that there is nothing to fear . . .   (E, p. 28; see R, p. 101)

Smurov's style is studied and self-conscious. Alliteration and assonance is already a feature of this style in the Russian version.[1] It is an even more pronounced feature of the English translation. For example, the play on the word 'individuum' is preserved in English with the added bonus of alliteration:

> и тогда не сдобровать отдельному индивидууму, с его двумя бедными «у», безнадежно аукающимися в чащобе экономических причин.   (R, p. 105)

> and then woe to the private individuum, with his two poor u's, hallooing hopelessly amid the dense growth of economic causes. (E, p. 35)

In the following example Nabokov modifies his translation in order to include alliteration:

> и руки ее, грубоватые и холодные   (R, p. 131)

Compare:

> and her hands, adolescently clammy and a little coarse   (p. 73)

This same self-consciousness is reflected in Smurov's unusual and pretentious vocabulary. In Russian he already uses elaborate constructions and recherché words such as *perlyustratsiya* and *knigochii* (p. 81). In English, this feature of his language is also more pronounced. Smurov uses 'eidolon' to refer to the impression which Evgenia has formed of him (p. 61). (The Russian here is *obraz* [p. 123].) He speaks of needing time to get 'acclimated'

---

[1] Bitsilli was one *émigré* critic who commented upon the alliterative quality of Nabokov's style in *Soglyadatai*. See his review of *Priglashenie na kazn'* and *Soglyadatai*, 1939.

to Vanya's presence (p. 93). (In Russian this is: *nuzhno bylo nekotoroe vremya, chtoby osvoit'sya s ee prisutstviem* [p. 145].) He tells how the maid 'would . . . somnambule back to the kitchen' (p. 76) (R: *sonno udalyalas'* [p. 133]); and speaks of 'phantasmata' and 'the phantomatic nature of my existence' (p. 35). (R: *prizrach-nost' moego sushchestvovaniya* [p. 105].)

The sexual frustration which is a contributing factor in Smurov's disturbed mental condition is also stressed more in the English translation. There are some added sexual references.

1. There is Smurov's allusion to an affair with the dentist's young daughter which has already been mentioned above (p. 84).

2. Matilda, Smurov's mistress in the opening pages of the novel, acquires more physical presence:

> I would try to change the subject, but this was Matilda's hobby-horse, which she straddled with her strong fat thighs. (p. 16)

Compare:

> Я старался переменить разговор, но это был матильдин конек, на который она садилась плотно и с удовольствием. (p. 93)

3. So too does the maid who succeeds Matilda as Smurov's mistress:

> The maid, casting down her charming dim eyes, would pass through the dining room; slowly and carefully place a bowl of fruit [and her breasts] on the sideboard . . .   (E, p. 75; see R, p. 133)

It is only in the English version that this same maid is described as a 'creamy-haunched wench' (p. 76).

4. Also new in the English translation is Smurov's comment on the aridity of his sexual experience with Matilda:

> The summit of love-making was for me but a bleak knoll with a relentless view. (p. 16)

5. The description of Vanya, whom Smurov loves without return, is more evocative. Her pink chapped lips which in the Russian version seem to call out for the balm of cold-cream (*rozovatost'yu, trebovavshei prokhlady kol'd-krema* (p. 131)), in English seem to need so badly 'the balm of a butterfly kiss' (p. 73). And Smurov's frustrated orgasm is alluded to more explicitly with the added

comment: 'I believe I might have consummated a shiver of oneirotic rapture had I been able to hold her a few seconds longer' (p. 96).

6. Roman Bogdanovich's theory that Smurov is a frustrated homosexual is also stated rather more explicitly in the English text:

> 'It is remarkable that these sexually unfortunate individuals, while yearning physically for some handsome specimen of mature virility, often choose for object of their (perfectly platonic) admiration—a woman—a woman they know well, slightly, or not at all.' (pp. 85–6)

Compare:

> «Замечательно, что такие несчастные в половом смысле, субъекты, часто выбирают себе предмет воздыханий — правда, вполне платонический — среди знакомых, мало знакомых или вовсе незнакомых им дам». (p. 140)

These added sexual allusions, the added alliteration, and the recherché vocabulary are all features characteristic of much of Nabokov's later English production. Here, however, in this translation of an earlier novel, they are successfully incorporated in the characterization of the central hero and narrator; they serve *his* preoccupations, *his* imagination, *his* style. In this respect *The Eye* has very close similarities with *Despair*.

In a first person narrative of this kind, authorial participation is virtually non-existent. Nevertheless, without intruding openly in the novel, Nabokov does introduce into the English text more detachment from the dominant narrator's viewpoint. In the English version, Nabokov makes Mukhin rather more present in the story. Mukhin is Smurov's rival for Vanya's affections, a rival he would willingly overlook. A few added references make the reader more aware of the true state of affairs, namely that Mukhin is a better man than Smurov, *and* that it is Mukhin whom Vanya loves. When Smurov overhears the sisters returning from the theatre, Mukhin is there, saying goodbye to them at the door: 'They were saying goodbye to Mukhin. Wouldn't he come in for a minute? No, it was late, he would not' (p. 63). This exchange is added in the English translation. When Smurov is describing how he danced with the maid to the music of the distant phonograph, Nabokov adds in the English version: 'Mister Mukhin had brought back from London some really lovely records of moan-sweet

Hawaiian dance music' (p. 76). The reader cannot but wonder who, meanwhile, is dancing to the same music in the main part of the house—Vanya and Mukhin? Also, by making Mukhin a former colonel in the White Army, Nabokov underscores the folly of Smurov's boasts about his own—fictitious—exploits in the Civil War. Roman Bogdanovich discloses this piece of information in his letter: 'a certain M. M. Mukhin, one of the youngest colonels in the White Army' (p. 86). The reader, however, has already been prepared for this disclosure by an earlier small detail. When Smurov finishes his account of his military adventures there is silence, a silence which is broken when Mukhin opens his gun-metal cigarette case (p. 55). The adjective 'gun-metal' does not appear in the Russian version, and Roman Bogdanovich refers to Mukhin not as a former officer, but simply as an engineer (compare R, pp. 119, 140). These small additions intensify the ironies of the plot and enable the reader to dissociate himself more from Smurov's point of view.

There are a few other extra details which widen the critical distance between reader and characters. Into this category comes the mention of the book Vanya is reading: 'a pogromystic novelette by a Russian lady in Belgrade or Harbin' (p. 93). Another instance is the elaboration of the details of Roman Bogdanovich's story:

> He was doubtless capable, in a moment of wrath, of slashing a chap into bits, and, in a moment of passion, of carrying a [frightened and perfumed] girl beneath his cloak on a windy night [to a waiting boat with muffled oarlocks, under a slice of honeydew moon], as somebody did in Roman Bogdanovich's story. (E, p. 43; see R, p. 111)

When Smurov is about to read what Roman Bogdanovich has written about him, he looks up at a 'milk chocolate advertisement with lilac alps' (p. 85). The humorous incongruity of this detail prevents the reader from identifying with Smurov's anxiety at this tense moment. There are also intrusions of purely incidental humour. For instance, when Weinstock is asked for a Russian–Spanish dictionary in the bookshop he presents the customer with a Russian–Portuguese one, assuring him that it is 'practically the same thing' (p. 32). This is new in the English version. The conversation between Weinstock and Lenin's spirit is made more ludicrous. To Weinstock's question, 'Have you found rest?' Lenin replies, 'This is not Baden-Baden' (p. 45). The Russian is '*Net. Ya stradayu'* (p. 112). And when Weinstock then asks why Lenin won't tell him of life beyond the grave, Lenin replies: 'Must wait till there is a plenum' (p. 46). The Russian here is simply '*Tam noch*'' (p. 113).

The alterations which Nabokov makes when preparing this English translation are, as has been said, relatively slight. Nevertheless, the pattern of changes is similar to that undergone by successive versions of *Camera Obscura*. The narrative acquires more pace; the characterization is made more vivid. At the same time, added irony and humour distance the reader from the action and enable him to view the characters with more detachment. Even closer similarities exist between *The Eye* and *Despair 2*. Both novels are written in the first person, and both treat a central character who is mentally unstable. The English versions were prepared at approximately the same date. Nabokov's Foreword to *The Eye* is dated 19 April 1965; his Foreword to *Despair* is dated 1 March 1965. As a version, *The Eye* is very much a pendant to *Despair*. It exhibits many of the same features, only on a smaller scale.

5

MAJOR REWORKINGS:
KING, QUEEN, KNAVE

Korol', *dama*, *valet*, Nabokov's second novel, was published in book form in Berlin, in 1928. An English translation, prepared by Dmitri Nabokov and revised by the author, was published in 1968 in New York and London.

As Nabokov says in his Foreword to the English translation, 'this plot is basically not unfamiliar.' Franz, a young man from the provinces, arrives in Berlin and is given a job as a sales assistant in his uncle's clothing store, 'Dandy'. Franz becomes the lover of Martha, his uncle's thirty-four-year-old wife. Martha, who is the dominant partner in the relationship, succeeds in persuading Franz that only by murdering Dreyer can they secure their happiness—and Dreyer's money. Dreyer cannot swim, and Martha hits upon the idea of taking out a rowing boat and engineering his death by drowning. This could so easily be made to look like an accident. All goes according to plan: Franz, Martha, and Dreyer go out rowing. But in the boat, Dreyer casually mentions that he has to return to Berlin to clinch a very profitable business deal. Hearing this, Martha's resolution falters. She decides to delay the murder for a few days and allow Dreyer time to conclude his deal. This delay proves fatal; Martha is taken ill that same night and dies of pneumonia two days later. Dreyer is heart-broken, but Franz, freed at last from Martha's dominant will, feels only relief.

Émigré critics were not slow to point out the deliberate artificiality of plot and characterization.[1] The setting—Berlin in the late 1920s—is realistic enough, but against this background are placed cardboard characters who, like puppets, go through the

---

[1] See Tsetlin's review of *KDV*, 1928:

Но интерес романа не в фабуле. Механичность, обездушенность, автоматизм современных людей хотел показать нам автор... Как бы не доверяя пониманию читателей, автор поясняет замысел символикой. Муж все время занят осуществлением изобретения: двигающихся маннекенов — автоматов.

motions devised for them by their creator. Various symbols underline this dehumanization. There are the three court cards in the title of the book which symbolize Dreyer, Martha, and Franz. (Dreyer, incidentally, means 'threesome' in German.) There are the mechanical mannequins which Dreyer commissions from an inventor. There is Franz's landlord, a conjuror, for whom Franz exists only through the magic of his art. When Franz vacates his room, the landlord dismisses him with the words 'You no longer exist'. Literary allusion and parody also increase the reader's awareness that this is fiction, not reality. The most frequent allusions are to Flaubert's *Madame Bovary*, that other novel of adultery and illusory love. This use of literary models is a device which Nabokov was to use later in *Camera Obscura*[1] and *Otcha-yanie*. Also in *KDV*, as in these other two novels, there is the ever-present image of the cinema—that modern master of the art of illusion. It is this 'revelation of the device', to employ the Formalist formula, which is even more apparent in the English version of the novel.

Structure

In his Foreword to the English edition, Nabokov draws the reader's attention to his 'amiable little imitations of *Madame Bovary*' (p. viii), and in the text itself several of these literary allusions are made more explicit and are openly commented upon. The allusions to Flaubert's *aveugle* in Chapter 1 (the fellow-traveller, pp. 3–4, 16) and in Chapter 8 (the tailor's dummy, pp. 169–70) remain virtually unchanged.[2] So too do the references to Madame l'Empereur, to whom Martha supposedly goes for keep-fit lessons when, in fact, she is visiting Franz.[3] But when Martha becomes

---

[1] In *CO*, Irma has some similarities with Seryozha, Anna's son in *Anna Karenina*. She, too, is interested in trains, and during her illness she listens for 'the friendly rumble of an electric train which emerged from underground very near the house'. Kretschmar shares the same mannerism as Karenin and cracks his finger joints when worried. There is also an actress with the stage name Dorianna Karenina.   [2] See *Madame Bovary*, Part 3, Chapters 5 and 8.

[3] Ibid., Part 3, Chapter 5:

'C'est Mlle Lempereur, n'est-ce pas, qui te donne des leçons? . . . Eh bien! je l'ai vue tantôt . . . chez Mme Liégeard. Je lui ai parlé de toi: elle ne te connaît pas.'

Mlle Lempereur supposedly gives Emma piano lessons. Emma, in fact, is going regularly to Rouen to visit Léon. Nabokov makes use of the same literary parallel again in *Lolita*:

I had permitted Lo to take piano lessons with a Miss Emperor (as we

Franz's mistress, Nabokov in the English translation adds a short passage of comment:

> She was no Emma, and no Anna. In the course of her conjugal life she had grown accustomed to grant her favors to her wealthy protector with such skill, with such calculation, with such efficient habits of physical practice, that she who thought herself ripe for adultery had long grown ready for harlotry.   (p. 101)

The slippers—a present from Franz—which Martha puts on whenever she visits him in his room, elicit the comment: 'for life not unfrequently imitates the French novelists' (p. 102).[1] The allusion remains implicit in the Russian version. When Dreyer, Franz, and Martha go together to see a variety show at the theatre, Nabokov in *KQKn* has the orchestra play extracts from *Lucia di Lammermoor*, adding 'which in the circumstances was pretty apt, though lost on our audience' (p. 116).[2] The details which Nabokov adds of Martha's unkindness to her dog, Tom, make an oblique allusion to Emma's equally capricious treatment of her daughter, Berthe.[3] And in her delirium Martha speaks of a gondola, an object which also figures in Emma's dreams.[4] Added literary allusions furnish ironic comment on the action and in particular on Dreyer's blindness to his wife's adultery. Early in the novel he is seen reading *Dead Souls* (p. 43), and in the final chapter he is reading G. B. Shaw's *Candida* (p. 263).[5] In the Russian version, Nabokov names no book titles. In the reworked version of Martha's death, her last request is for her jewels. This is reminiscent of the death scene in Balzac's *Eugénie Grandet*, where Grandet asks, '*Mets de l'or devant moi*'.

> French scholars may conveniently call her) to whose blue-shuttered little white house a mile or so beyond Beardsley Lo would spin off twice a week. One Friday night . . . the telephone . . . rang and Miss Emperor asked if Lo was coming next Tuesday because she had missed last Tuesday's and today's lessons. (pp. 198–9).

[1] *Madame Bovary*, Part 3, Chapter 5:
même elle disait 'mes pantoufles', un cadeau de Léon, une fantaisie qu'elle avait eue. C'étaient des pantoufles en satin rose, bordées de cygne.

[2] Ibid., Part 2, Chapter 15.

[3] Ibid., Part 2, Chapters 3, 5, 6, 10.

[4] 'We're going to a tombola in a gondola' (p. 256). See *Madame Bovary*, Part 2, Chapter 12: 'Ils se promèneraient en gondole, ils se balanceraient en hamac.'

[5] The situation in *Candida* (husband, wife, young man) has obvious similarities with the plot of *KQKn*. The title, *Dead Souls*, echoes the lifelessness of Nabokov's cardboard characters in the novel.

The thematic imagery is also elaborated in the English translation. The symbol of the playing cards, which in *KDV* occurs only in the title, is integrated into the body of the English text. Franz acquires the surname Bubendorf, *Bube* being the German for 'knave'. *King, Queen, Knave* becomes the title of a play by Goldemar, a film version of which is advertised on the hoardings outside a new cinema near where Franz lives. The première of this film is to be on 15 July. This would appear to be the same day as that on which the novel ends (pp. 172-3, 215-16, 261). The picture on the hoarding shows the King wearing a maroon dressing-gown, the Knave wearing a red turtleneck sweater, and the Queen a black bathing-suit. The reader subsequently learns of Martha buying a black bathing-suit (p. 224), and hears that Franz possesses a 'turtleneck thick red sweater' (p. 250). The characters themselves become partially aware of this symbolism. Dreyer, in his conversation with Erica, recites an old poem: 'I am the page of High Burgundy', which tells of a queen and her page (pp. 173-5). Later, when reflecting upon this conversation, Dreyer thinks of Martha in terms of this poem and he refers to her as a queen: 'Erica with her dyed hair cannot understand that the queen's coldness is the best guarantee, the best loyalty' (p. 176). Franz sees Dreyer as 'a stylized playing card, a heraldic design' (p. 177). (In *KDV* the image is a different one: there Franz sees Dreyer as a cut-out photograph [R, pp. 173-4].) Towards the end of the novel Franz too begins to see Martha as a symbol. He imagines that her bathing wrap is her 'heavy coronation robes' (p. 242). The description of the mannequins is also substantially modified and a closer connection drawn with the main characters. In the English version there are three mannequins in all: two male (one young, one older) and one female (Chapters 11 and 13). The clothes worn by the models closely resemble those worn by their real-life counterparts. The older model, for instance, wears 'a replica of Dreyer's blue blazer' (p. 261). In *KDV* all three mannequins are *male*, and though their clothes do bear a certain resemblance to those worn by Franz and Dreyer (R, p. 210), the identification is not so explicit. Other cinematic allusions are added. In the following example, Franz and Martha are outlining a plan to murder Dreyer:

> The door to the parlor would be open. From its threshold he would fire half a dozen times in quick succession, as they do in American

movies. For appearance's sake, before vanishing, he would take the dead saloonkeeper's wallet and perhaps the two ancient French silver candlesticks from the mantelpiece. (p. 179)

Compare:

> Дверь гостиной будет открыта. Он выстрелит с порога. Заберет для видимости бумажник. И сразу исчезнет. (p. 175)

The café scene in Chapter 6 is described like a film set:

> An unprepossessing sullen little café, not far from where Franz lives. Three men engrossed in a silent game of skat. (p. 110)

Compare:

> Это был неказистый, насупленный ресторанчик на той улице, где жил Франц. Трое мужчин молча дулись в скат. (p. 108)

There are recurrent references to a film called *The Hindu Student*. Martha sees in Franz a resemblance to its hero, played by Hess (pp. 50, 111, 200), while Franz's landlord reminds Franz of the professor in 'the "Hindu Prince" farce' (p. 87).

In open asides to the reader, Nabokov repeatedly stresses how derivative and 'corny' are the actions of his characters. For instance, when Dreyer contemplates returning home unannounced, Nabokov adds:

> Despite his keen sense of humor, Dreyer was too naively self-centered to realize how thoroughly those sudden returns had been exploited in ribald tales. (p. 154)

Martha's conduct at the theatre elicits the comment: 'strictly adhering to every rule of adultery' (p. 115). Her memory of the early days of her affair with Franz is also garnished with a literary image: 'How happy they had been in the rhythm of that earlier novel in those first chapters' (p. 252). There is another authorial digression in Chapter 11:

> That little trip to Pomerania Bay was in fact proving to be quite a boon for everybody concerned, including the god of chance (Cazelty or Sluch, or whatever his real name was), once you imagined that god in the role of a novelist or a playwright, as Goldemar had in his most famous work. (p. 224)

Into the same category of changes comes Nabokov's manner of addressing his characters when he parodies well-established literary conventions. There are addresses such as, 'our lovers',

'Crazy Franz', 'our two farcical schemers', and there are comments such as the following:

> Franz felt envious of that unusual pair, so envious that his oppression, one is sorry to say, grew even more bitter, and the music stopped. (p. 254)

Compare:

> И Франц так позавидовал этой чете, что сразу его тоска еще пуще разрослась. Музыка остановилась. (p. 240)[1]

Nabokov is not content to parody literary convention in his narrative—he himself appears in the novel, thinly disguised under various pseudonyms. There is Goldemar, the author of the play *King, Queen, Knave* (Woldemar/Vladimir?); the photographer at the ski resort is a Mr. Vivian Badlook (p. 153); a certain Blavdak Vinomori stays at the same hotel as the Dreyers at Gravitz (pp. 239, 240, 253). In addition, the happy couple who make Franz so conscious of his own misery become recognizable as the author and his wife. They are introduced in an added passage (pp. 232–3). Butterfly nets are propped up against the wall behind them, and Dreyer wonders: 'What language were they speaking? Polish? Esthonian?' When they reappear at the dance, more details are given of their appearance. The husband is 'slender, elegantly balding, contemptuous of everything on earth but her', and is 'looking at her with pride' (p. 254). And when Franz sees them for the last time on the promenade, we learn that the woman is 'pale-haired' and that—and this is typical Nabokovian self-parody—they perhaps pitied him 'not without some derision' (pp. 258–9). These intrusions by the author increase the impression that *KQKn* is an elaborate game, that the characters are pawns in the hands of their creator.

In the English version, Nabokov not only exposes the mechanism of the plot—he also corrects and adjusts that mechanism. In his Foreword, he mentions the main structural alteration—the improvement of a transition in the last chapter. In *KDV* Dreyer

---

[1] There is already some authorial comment in the original version. For example:

> безотчетно вспоминая подробности хитрых убийств, описанных когда-то в газетке, в грошовой книжке, и совершая тем самым невольный плагиат, которого, впрочем, избежал один разве Каин, Марта предложила следующее... (p. 174)

sends Franz off to Berlin to return a cigarette case to an American businessman. When Franz returns Martha is already dead. In *KQKn*, Nabokov contrives to remove Franz temporarily from the action by a more plausible expedient. Martha is taken to hospital, Dreyer goes with her, and Franz is left alone at the hotel. He is later called to the hospital to bring Martha her jewels. She is already dead when he arrives. (This alteration affects E, pp. 267–71.)

In the rest of the novel Nabokov makes minor changes which tighten the plot's mechanism. The reader is told in advance that Martha has a weak heart, so that her death appears less of a hasty expedient on the author's part to dispose of his heroine. There are three added references to this abnormal heart condition of hers:

> The great Dr. Hertz had told her a couple of years before that her cardiogram showed a remarkable, not necessarily dangerous, but certainly incurable abnormality which he had seen only in one other woman, a Hohenzollern, who was still alive at almost forty ... (p. 198)
>
> What could she care about neuralgia, bronchitis, irregular heart beat? (p. 249)
>
> A pain, of another musical tone than intercostal neuralgia or that strange ache which a great cardiologist had told her came from a 'shadow behind the heart', entered into excruciating concords with the orchestra. (p. 251)

As early as Chapter 8 Nabokov alludes to her carelessness about her health. To please Franz she leaves off her warm, but unbecoming underwear in favour of his 'favorite frills' (p. 165). (The Russian version describes her wearing warm undies, as a precaution against bronchitis.) This new detail anticipates the same carelessness, this time fatal, which Martha shows on the boat trip when she sits shivering in her wet bathing costume. More is learnt about Martha's preparations for the boat ride. Dreyer reflects, 'She liked bets and boats' (p. 236), and, indeed, earlier, she has taunted Franz: 'I bet (she adored bets), I bet you a new sweater that you can't do it again' (p. 104). (Neither of these details is in the Russian version.) Again, we learn that 'Martha, who loved bets but thought them undignified, had asked him [Dreyer] not to tell anybody about their little rendezvous at Rockpoint' (p. 241). Nabokov also gives more explicit details of

Martha and Franz's earlier plans to murder Dreyer. One plan had been to shoot Dreyer in the house, and Nabokov adds a description of Franz and Martha counting out steps in the garden (p. 181). Another plan had involved inveigling Dreyer into a forest. In his English version Nabokov gives more prominence to this little scheme by pointing out more clearly its drawbacks (p. 182). Dreyer's incompetence as a swimmer and his distrust of boats is also underlined. The following passages are added:

1.   'I see you're not only a lecher but also a liar.'
       He suddenly looked worried. 'What do you mean?'
       'I thought', she said, 'you told me—when was that? A year ago?
       —that you were taking lessons at the Freibad, and that you now
       swam like a fish.'
       'An inexcusable exaggeration', he answered, much relieved.
       'A very poor fish, really. I keep afloat for three meters, and then
       I sink like a log.'
       'Except that logs don't sink', said Martha merrily.   (p. 212)

2.   Dreyer, a wretched sailor, could not imagine how he or any other
       tourist would care to go out rowing on that desolate expanse of
       water, when there were so many other things to do at the seaside.
       (p. 232)

3.   'Let's go for a good ramble', suggested Dreyer.
       'Why don't we hire a boat?' said Martha for a change.
       'Count me out,' said Dreyer.   (p. 233)

4. Martha gives this warning to Franz:
       'This is the critical moment . . . He will never get into a boat
       if he does not now. Try to look more cheerful.'   (p. 243)

These additions help build up the suspense of the narrative—the plan might yet be foiled!

There are other small ways in which Nabokov creates more suspense in *KQKn*. For instance, the reader only discovers that the landlord's wife does not exist when Franz vacates his room, at the end of Chapter 11. In the Russian version this is made clear as early as Chapter 5 (see E, p. 229; R, p. 97). The reader is also kept guessing until the very end as to whether Dreyer will die. In the final chapter Nabokov inserts the following ambiguous statement: 'Dreyer . . . remained with an open shirt collar for the rest of his known existence' (p. 262). This *could* mean that Dreyer is soon to die. In fact, 'his known existence' refers to Dreyer's existence within the span of the novel.

Characterization

A very substantial proportion of Nabokov's changes in *KQKn* affect characterization. The main characters are considerably better drawn, their biographies are expanded, and their relationships are shown in more depth.[1] Franz and Martha become distinctly more unsympathetic. Conversely, Dreyer, the victim, acquires a more likeable and interesting personality.

—*Franz*

Franz is identified with Martha in his dislike of animals. These passages are added:

1.   Nostalgically he remembered a nasty old lady's nasty old pug (a relative and great enemy of his mother's pet) that he had managed to kick smartly on several occasions.   (p. 30)

2.   'Where is Mr. Tom today?' he inquired. 'I thought I saw him going for a walk.'

'No, he's locked up in the gardener's shed. He's a good dog but a little neurotic. As I always say, dogs are acceptable pets if they are clean.'

'Cats are cleaner', said Franz.

'Oh, I abominate cats. Dogs understand when you scold them, but cats are hopeless—no contact with human beings, no gratitude, nothing.'

'We shot lots of stray ones back home, a school friend and I. Especially along the river in spring.'   (p. 51)

We also learn that Franz is a petty thief. He packs the landlord's towel before vacating his room (p. 228). The cruel streak in his nature is brought out in his attitude to sex. Here is one of his fantasies about women whom he sees in the streets:

and these girls were accessible, (again that hiss), they were accustomed to avid glances, they welcomed them, and it was possible to accost any one of them, and start a brilliant and brutal conversation. He would do just that but first he had to find a room in which to rip off her dress and possess her.   (p. 47)

Compare:

эти дамочки доступны, они привыкли к жадным взглядам, они рады им, можно, пожалуй, любую остановить, разговориться с ней... Он так и сделает, но только нужно сперва найти комнату.   (pp. 47–8)

---

[1] Proffer describes Nabokov's elaboration of the biographies of the principal characters in his article, 'A New Deck for Nabokov's Knaves', pp. 296–300.

When Martha comes to see Franz and he helps her off with her coat, he notices that 'the silk lining was crimson, as crimson as lips and flayed animals, and smelled of heaven' (p. 95). Compare:

Подкладка была малиновая, шелковая, теплая, пропитанная духами. (p. 94)

It is partly the evil in Martha which Franz finds so attractive: 'She was so sinful and beautiful!' (p. 159). Compare: '*Ona byla tak khorosha*' (p. 156). Franz has a cruel and a dirty mind *but* he is a coward, and Nabokov repeatedly underlines the contrast between his thoughts and his actions. At the Christmas party there is a graphic description of Franz's nausea, nausea which is brought on by his terror of Dreyer. This is followed by an account of Franz's feelings the following morning: he feels strong and well and brave.[1] Nabokov also inserts a direct comment on Franz's cowardice:

> A high-strung and abject coward in matters of feeling (and such cowards are doubly wretched since they lucidly perceive their cowardice and fear it), he could not help cringing when, with a banging of doors in a dramatic draft, Martha and Dreyer entered . . . (p. 105; compare R, p. 106)

The English version brings out another ironic contrast between Franz's squeamishness at other people's physical unpleasantnesses and his own dirty personal habits. First, his squeamishness:

> His recollections of school seemed always to be dodging away from possible, impossible, contacts with the grubby, pimply, slippery skin of some companion or other pressing him to join in a game or eager to impart some spitterish secret. (p. 4)

The Russian version of this passage is less evocative:

> Мутило его и на последнем экзамене, — оттого, что сосед по парте, задумавшись, грыз и без того обгрызанные, мясом ущемленные ногти. И школу Франц покинул с облегчением, полагая, что отделался навсегда от ее грязноватой, прыщеватой жизни. (p. 8)

We learn, too, that Franz could not stand his mother's 'physical

---

[1] See E, pp. 147–8; compare R, pp. 144–5, where the contrast in Franz's feelings is not so sharply drawn.

appearance, mannerisms, and emanations'.[1] At work, he cannot tolerate the B.O. of a blonde assistant:

> At table he sat between the plump blonde and the champion swimmer. Whenever she stretched toward the bread basket or the salt, her armpit flooded him with nausea reminding him of a detested spinster teacher at school. The champion on his other side had another infirmity—that of spitting whenever he spoke, and Franz found himself reverting to his schooldays' system of protecting his plate from the spray with forearm and elbow. (p. 80)

This is new in *KQKn*. However, Franz's own 'sybarite habits of personal hygiene' are described with an unmistakable irony which is absent from the Russian version (compare E, p. 80 and R, p. 80). The following passage is also added in *KQKn*:

> Ruminative, naked, morose, he sniffed one armpit, and tossed his undervest under the washstand. It landed on the floor next to a rubber basin with Martha's rather depressing paraphernalia. He kicked the vest into a corner—she could wash it for him after tomorrow, with the socks, which were still comparatively clean. (p. 166)

Dreyer, who is granted something of the author's vision, comments on one occasion: 'The poor boy stank like a goat. And those long drawers on a day like this!' (p. 185.)

Nabokov also makes important modifications to the development of Franz's personality during his affair with Martha. This he does by a judicious use of flashbacks, and by charting carefully the changes in Franz's sexual appetites. At the start of the novel Franz is depicted as a sexually eager but frustrated adolescent ready to sample all the fabled delights of the capital city. The Russian version already gives some indications of this, but *KQKn* is a good deal more explicit. These are Franz's first impressions of Martha:

> Her face was serious, her eyes cold, a little dark down, the sign of passion, glistened above her upper lip, and a gleam of sun brought out the creamy texture of her neck at the throat with its two delicate transverse lines as if traced with a fingernail across it, one above the other: also a token of all kinds of marvels, according to one of his schoolmates, a precocious expert. (p. 6)

Compare:

> лицо серьезное, холодноватые глаза, легкая тень над губой

---

[1] See expanded passage: 'His love for his mother . . . that dreadful local dainty Budenzucker' (pp. 93-4); compare R, p. 92.

и бархатно-белая шея в нежнейших поперечных бороздках на горле. (p. 10)

Before Franz possesses Martha he masturbates almost nightly, and even contemplates going to a brothel (pp. 22, 60). Neither of these details is in *KDV*. When out walking in the street, he has one thought—girls! Compare, for example:

> He thought he recognised Tom in a dog being walked by a plump but not uncomely housemaid. (p. 46)

> В собаке, гулявшей с горничной, ему показалось, что он узнал Тома. (p. 47)

Compare too:

> He walked slowly shaking his head, clucking his tongue, looking around every moment. The kissable cuties, he thought almost aloud, and inhaled with a hiss through clenched teeth. What calves! What bottoms! Enough to drive one crazy! (p. 46)

> Он шел медленно, болтая руками, поминутно оглядываясь: «Ах, какие дамочки», — почти вслух думал он и легонько стискивал зубы... — «Какие икры, — с ума сойти!..» (p. 47)

At this early stage of the novel, almost all Franz's memories of the provincial backwater where he spent his childhood are unpleasant.[1] His only pleasant recollection is of swimming naked in the river near his home town[2] (p. 32. This is expanded from *KDV*); but even this memory becomes tarnished as he describes it over and over again to Martha.[3] When Martha becomes Franz's mistress in Chapter 5, she completely takes over his personality. He becomes her creature, an automaton, whose conscious mind is entirely subordinated to her will. Martha, for example, notes with satisfaction how unresponsive he is to the charms of the two young girls, Ida and Isolda, who attend the Christmas party:

> She was pleased to note how unresponsive Franz was to the practically naked charms of those two practically identical vulgar young things with revoltingly thin arms, and snaky backs, and insufficiently spanked little popos. The injustice of life—in ten years' time they would be still a little younger than I am now, all three of them as a matter of fact. (p. 142)

---

[1] See E, pp. 3–4. This is an elaboration of *KDV*, pp. 7–8. See also E, p. 83; R, p. 83. See also E, pp. 93–4, which again is an elaboration of *KDV*, pp. 92–3.

[2] p. 32. This is expanded from *KDV*.   [3] E, p. 83; R, p. 83.

This passage is new in *KQKn*. It shows clearly how diminished are Franz's sexual appetites. But underneath this blind submission to Martha's will, Nabokov traces carefully in *KQKn* the growth of Franz's subconscious antagonism to his mistress, so that the reader is better prepared for his callous reaction to her death—for the burst of Gogolesque laughter with which the novel ends (E, p. 272; R, p. 260). Franz's attitude to his childhood undergoes a complete change. Whereas in the early part of the novel Franz has remembered his childhood with distaste, he later recalls it with nostalgia, as a time of young hopes and dreams. When he goes to play tennis with Dreyer and notices two happy young girls on the courts, he reflects:

> All that was in the past, dreams and desires of a boyhood long gone. They blinded him with a blended smile, mistaking him for some- body. (p. 187)

This is expanded from the Russian version, which has just:

> Нет, все это миновало. Все это теперь кончено. (p. 181)

When Martha is indefatigably outlining her murder plans in Chapter 9, Franz thinks back for a moment to the sunny days of his boyhood:

> A girl's voice cried something from a window below, and another girl's voice, still more angelic, responded from a balcony on the opposite side of the street. This was the season of guitar music on the river at home, of rafts gently singing in the shadow of the willows. (p. 198)

This passage is not in *KDV*. It immediately precedes Franz's unconscious reflection that Martha rather resembles a toad (E, p. 198; R, p. 192). In the final chapter, as Martha lies dying, Franz is seen buying a postcard to send home to his sister Emmy (p. 258). This detail is new. And when he tries to will Martha's death, he resorts to a trick which he had used in his childhood during school examinations (see pp. 267–8). In *KDV*, Franz employs a similar trick, with tram numbers, but this does not involve a flashback to childhood (see p. 256). Gradually, Franz is shaking off Martha's influence and assuming his old personality. Towards the end of the novel he begins to show his former interest in girls. In Chapter 12, he is described watching a barmaid sun-bathing:

> Franz opened his window, which faced south with no sea to view, but at least it revealed a small balcony one story lower on which on three consecutive afternoons at the siesta hour he had watched the spread-eagled barmaid sunning herself on a towel. The floor of the balcony was darkly damp. It might dry in time for her siesta if the sun came out before noon. (p. 238)

After the boat trip, Martha finds Franz in conversation with this same barmaid: 'She found him in a corner of the lounge. The barmaid, a skinny artificial blonde, was bothering him with vulgar small talk' (p. 250). On the next to last day, Franz has three or four brandies at the bar, 'vainly waiting for the attractive blonde to get rid of two elderly gentlemen flirting with her, ponderously and obscenely' (p. 269). And on that same day, Franz fulfils a long-cherished dream: he buys himself some plus-fours!

> The day before he had resolved to take advantage of solitude and make a purchase that Dreyer might have ridiculed with his usual wit, and Martha thought frivolous at such a critical time in their lives. It was his old dream of fashionable plus-fours. (pp. 268-9; see also p. 46)

Franz steps out of the novel a free man, tried and tested by his rude apprenticeship in love and crime. Significantly enough, Nabokov, in the English version, gives the reader a glimpse of what Franz will become in later life:

> In those days—which as a very old and very sick man, guilty of worse sins than avunculicide, he remembered with a grin of contempt—young Franz was oblivious to the corrosive probity of his pleasant daydreams about Dreyer's dropping dead. (p. 138)

The tone of this new passage is very reminiscent of *Ada*, Nabokov's English novel, which appeared in the following year, 1969.

—Martha

In the English version, Nabokov gives a fuller picture of the two driving forces in Martha's character, the 'blending of bank and bed'. It is, however, the second element, bed, which predominates in the changes which Nabokov makes. Her domination over Franz is extended to complete sexual domination. She is insatiable, and she unmans him by her incessant demands. The pattern is set from the start of their affair, when it is she who takes charge of the contraceptive precautions. (See pp. 96-7, 102, 220, 225. All the references to contraception are added in *KQKn*.) There are repeated references to her attempts to stimulate Franz: For instance:

1. 'I bet you a new sweater that you can't do it again.' (p. 104)

2. 'Undress quick and hop into my bed. I have a great need.' (p. 158)

3. 'Is he stronger than we? Is he more alive than this, and this, and *this*?' (p. 204)

As the novel progresses, Franz becomes increasingly loath to comply with her demands. For example:

1. Well, to work, old soldier. (p. 166)

Thus reflects Franz, as he undresses for the umpteenth time.

2. He sat down on the edge of her bed, grimly expecting she would command him to fulfill a duty that he had managed to evade since they came here. (p. 258)

Compare:

> Он сел к ней на постель, угрюмо предчувствуя, что сейчас постучится горничная. (p. 243)

Martha's domination over Franz is complemented and explained by what Nabokov tells us in *KQKn* of her sexual relations with Dreyer. Dreyer is the dominant sexual partner, and Martha feels towards him a mixture of fear and disgust. Her defence is frigidity. There are references to the 'dismal surprises of their honeymoon' in Salsborg, 'when he kept pawing and licking her like an animal, in a locked hotel room' (p. 141). Dreyer 'threatened her with a priapus that had already once inflicted upon her an almost mortal wound' (p. 178). Dreyer regrets that Martha 'regarded afternoon lovemaking as a decadent perversion' (p. 38). On one occasion Martha coldly asks her husband: 'And will you please cover your obscene nudity' (p. 39). She later confesses to Franz: 'How can one love a man whose mere touch makes one feel sick' (p. 102), and describes in 'atrocious, disparaging and quite inaccurate terms . . . the dead man's private parts' (p. 156). Her concessions to Dreyer are rare and calculated: on one occasion she submits in order to secure the exclusion of a younger brother from Dreyer's will:

> There was the will he had recently made which had cost her two nights of strenuous love-making but which had completely

excluded, thank goodness, a wayward young brother in South Africa who, she suspected, was very much looking forward to his share. (p. 114)

(See also pp. 62, 75–6, 213, 214.) All these references are new in the English translation.

Nabokov adds life and definition to his characterization of Martha by some perceptive authorial comment and by increasing the proportion of indirect as well as direct speech. There is more banter and more open hostility in her conversation with Dreyer. A good example of this is the conversation which has been quoted earlier (Example 1, p. 97), when Dreyer admits to his wife that he cannot swim. Compare also:

> 'I've telephoned', he answered, and went back to his paper. 'They are soaked. An archeologist has found a tomb in Egypt with toys and blue thistles three thousand years old.'
> 'Thistles are not blue', said Martha, reaching for the coffee pot. 'Have you written about the rooms?' (p. 213)

> «Три дня шел ливень», — ответил он, продолжая двигать глазами по строкам газеты. — «И сегодня — погода неверная. В Египте нашли в гробнице игрушки и розы, — им три тысячи лет...»
> «Ты написал насчет комнат?» (p. 206)

Martha's conversation with Franz becomes more vulgar and crude; the endearments she uses come straight out of trashy novelettes: 'my sweet', 'my treasure', 'poor pet', 'you awkward brutal darling'. Nabokov comments that she preferred 'a trim suburban lawn to the most luxuriant jungle', and adds some amusing illustrations of her 'suburban' mentality. The lace on her bed cover is 'washable, ninety by ninety inches' (p. 40); her social conversation acquires the appropriate dash of foreign locutions, as, for example, in this address to Franz: 'Eat, drink, my lord. We are *chez nous*' (p. 123). Her attitude to servants and to restaurant service is suitably critical. For example, in the train:

> A waiter brought them café-au-lait in bulky cups, and Martha criticized each sip she took. (p. 17)

> лакей принес им кофе в толстых чашках, кофе было скверное. (p. 20)

And in the hotel at Gravitz:

> The two maids she disliked most, one a thief, the other a slut, were busy, too busy, making her room, which she had told them to do always *punkt* at ten, and now it was almost noon.   (p. 249)

This is new in *KQKn*. Her imagination also becomes rather more lurid and sick in *KQKn*. Here, for example, she is telling Franz of her holiday in the Tyrol:

> 'One imagined those mountains might crash down on the hotel, in the middle of the night, right on our bed, burying me under them and my husband, killing everybody.'   (p. 30)

Compare:

> «мне казалось, что эти горы вот-вот рухнут на гостиницу». (p. 32)

Also:

> That morning a cripple walking in front of her had slipped on the bare ice. It was frightfully funny to see his wooden stump erect while he sprawled on his stupid back.   (p. 126)

> Она видела утром, как на голом льду поскользнулась пожилая дама. Очень смешно, когда шлепается пожилая дама...   (p. 125)

—Dreyer

Changes in the characterization of Dreyer follow a similar pattern. There is a greater proportion of inner monologue and of both direct and indirect speech. Dreyer's personal relationships with Franz and Martha are more sharply defined. His sexual frustration is made more explicit (see pp. 38–41 and compare R, pp. 40–3). He is furnished with some new mistresses in addition to Erica who already figures in the Russian version. There is Ida and her twin sister Isolda who turn up at the Christmas party (p. 147). Dreyer has sampled both of them. In *KDV*, there is just a passing reference to *dve gromkikh polugolykh baryshni* who are guests at the party (p. 140). Ida and Isolda reappear on Dreyer's skiing trip (pp. 153–4). In Chapter 9, Dreyer thinks of dating 'Isida' (p. 177); and in the last chapter he rings up Isolda for a brief date (p. 261). His secretary is transformed from a nameless male into the neurotic Sarah Reich (p. 107), who takes sleeping pills (p. 126), and who has an ailing husband (p. 234). Dreyer is persistently teasing Franz about women. For instance, he asks Franz if he is thinking of marriage and offers to find him a 'very amorous bride' (p. 219). And it is characteristic of Dreyer that he should criticize the flat-chestedness of the female mannequin: 'You might have thrown in a little more bosom' (p. 261).

Dreyer owns a clothes shop, and in the English version added indications are given of his professional eye, such as, for example, his criticism of Franz's dinner-jacket (p. 128) and his appraisal of Franz wearing a pair of trousers he had lent him (p. 186). Dreyer is a businessman by profession, but he also has something of an artist's vision. He is an artist *manqué*, 'a happy and healthy failure', and Nabokov puts a good deal more emphasis on this side of his character. He replaces an account of Dreyer's business affairs with a biographical summary of his frustrated ambitions:

> He was a bachelor with a beautiful marble wife, a passionate hobbyist without anything to collect, an explorer not knowing on what mountain to die, a voracious reader of unmemorable books, a happy and healthy failure. (p. 224)

Dreyer in *KQKn* is endowed with a more fantastical and whimsical imagination. On the station platform he notices not a bicycle with its pedals wrapped in paper, but an 'old sewing machine with its arthritic pedal wrapped up in brown paper' (p. 15; see R, p. 19). The scarred and disfigured face of a fellow passenger reminds him not of a 'baby child', but of a 'baby monkey' (p. 16; see R, p. 19), and we later learn that he had presented his bride-to-be with a monkey (p. 66). In *KDV* he gives her a squirrel (p. 66). Dreyer relishes the coincidence of Franz having sat in the same railway compartment and this gives rise to another anecdote:

> In the no-time of human thought he also recalled . . . how an acquaintance once had rung him up while he was taking a tumultuous shower, and Martha had shouted through the bathroom door: 'That stupid old Wasserschluss is calling'—and five paces away the telephone receiver on the table was cupping its ear like an eavesdropper in a farce. (p. 33)

Nabokov makes situations involving Dreyer a good deal more comic than in the Russian version. Especially good examples of this are the tennis game in Chapter 9 (pp. 185–90), the visit to the museum in Chapter 10 (pp. 205–9), and all sessions with the inventor (Chapter 5, pp. 88–91, 108–9; Chapter 10, pp. 192–5;

Chapter 11, pp. 217–19; Chapter 13, pp. 261–3). All these passages are considerably reworked.

The greater emphasis which is placed on Dreyer's artistic perception is matched by a greater emphasis on his blindness to everyday affairs. It is only in the English version that the inventor is depicted as a charlatan.

> '. . . have you approached anyone else with that offer?'
>
> 'Well,' said the inventor with perfectly mimicked sincerity, 'I confess this is the first time. In fact, I have just arrived in Germany. This *is* Germany, isn't it?' he added, looking around.   (p. 90)

In *KDV*, there is no indication that Dreyer is being taken in:

> «...вы уже обращались к кому-нибудь с такими предложениями?»
>
> «Нет», — сказал изобретатель. — «Это первый раз. Я только-что сюда приехал».   (p. 89)

Dreyer's blindness to Martha's unfaithfulness is also underlined. Erica's remarks are more pointed: she not only bets that Martha is deceiving Dreyer, she adds: 'You're not the best witness in the world. . . . You never knew I deceived you until his fiancée rang you up' (p. 175). Dreyer even misinterprets Martha's very last words: 'Frieda, why is the dog here again? He was killed. He can't be here any more.' Martha, unbeknown to Dreyer, had given orders for the dog to be destroyed before she left for Gravitz. But Dreyer interprets this as a flash of second sight: 'And the fools say second sight does not exist' (p. 271). The contrast which Nabokov stresses here in *KQKn* between Dreyer's keen artistic perception and his blindness in love recalls the characterization of Albinus in *LD*, and the exposure of blindness in the 'man of perception'—the art connoisseur.

—Minor characters

The minor characters play a more prominent part in *KQKn* than they do in the original Russian version. Characters who are just mentioned in passing in *KDV* are given names and, in some cases, identities. Ida and Isolda have been mentioned above, and so has Sarah Reich. Another example is Martha's sister from Hamburg. She acquires a name, Hilda, and at least four or five lovers, instead of the three she had in the Russian version (p. 84; see R, p. 84).

The first of these lovers, we learn, was a man who taught Martha's monkey to light matches (E, p. 66). Franz's landlord becomes 'old Enricht', with the stage name 'Menetek-el-Pharsin', instead of Menetekelfares. Several of the added names introduce word play in German. Franz's athletic fellow salesman acquires the name Schwimmer—and peculiarities. He is a homosexual, and has an effeminate Swedish friend 'with embarrassing manners' who comes to work at the store. It seems highly likely that they are the same two young men who assist the inventor with his demonstrations: they work in the store, their names are Max and Moritz (recalling the popular heroes of Wilhelm Busch's illustrated children's tales), and they are described as 'giggly'! (See Chapters 11 and 13.) In *KDV* the inventor has no such assistants. The two fellow-residents at Gravitz, the dancing master and the student, become Schwarz and Weiss, who, quite appropriately, are seen playing chess outside the hotel (pp. 252, 260).[1] The American who shows interest in buying the mannequins is a Mr. Ritter—and a more sympathetic character than his counterpart in the Russian version (E, p. 261; R, p. 246). The doctor who attends Martha at Gravitz is a Professor Lister of Swistok (punned by Dreyer as 'Professor Klister of Swistok'), and a much more formidable and forthright character than his forerunner (E, pp. 264-5; R, pp. 250-1). New characters are added. To mention just a few, there is a tennis coach, Count Zubov (p. 188); a tailor, Kottmann, who resembles a cat's whiskers fish (p. 104); a heart specialist, Dr. Hertz; a customer, a Mrs. Steller of Robbe Avenue (p. 202), who not too surprisingly purchases the face of a rubber sea lion. And there are many more. These extra minor characters, with the exception of Ida and Isolda, add nothing to the plot. Like the authorial intrusions they are intentional irrelevancies, in the margins of the action, put there for the entertainment of the reader.

Style

KQKn undergoes marked changes, not only in structure and characterization, but also in style. Here, Nabokov's customary ornamental devices—imagery, word-play, and alliteration—are very much in evidence. Since the pattern of these stylistic changes

---

[1] The description of the chess game is also new in *KQKn*. See added passage: 'The two young fellows . . . whose position was desperate.' (p. 241).

is similar to that followed in *LD*, *Despair*, and *The Eye*, only a brief summary will be given here.

Nabokov's English style is richly alliterative. He adds a great many alliterative effects in the new version, while at the same time preserving many examples of alliteration which are already present in the Russian. Few images are lost from the Russian. Less than ten examples have been found of deleted or contracted images and none of these is strikingly original. One example of a deleted image occurs in the last chapter:

> Мелькнул велосипедист, как отпущенный конец резины. (p. 249; see E, p. 264)

An example of a contracted image is found at the beginning of Chapter 4: 'Everything that lay between those two live oases was a *terra incognita* blank' (p. 67). Compare:

> Все, что лежало между этими двумя живыми оазисами, было неизведанным туманом, так что образ столицы в его сознании напоминал те первые карты, на которых географ, еще не остывший после странствий, начертал все, что открыл, обдав остальное облачной синевой и поразив суеверные умы размашистой «Терра Инкогнита». (p. 67)[1]

Another small number of images are changed in translation. Some dead leaves, for example, which in *KDV* are likened to old leather gloves (R, p. 52), become 'claw-like crisp leaves' (E, p. 51). More frequently, Nabokov elaborates upon existing images. Franz's guileless method of calculating happiness is described in *KDV* with the simile:

> точно так же, как ребенок, любящий шоколад, воображает страну, где горы из шоколада: гуляешь и лижешь. (p. 137)

This becomes 'the way a greedy child imagines a country with chocolate-cream mud and ice-cream snow' (p. 138). More frequently still, Nabokov *adds* new similes and metaphors. The majority of these added images relate to the three principal characters; some are *ot avtora*, others are adapted to the perceptions of the characters themselves. Here are some examples of 'authorial' similes:

1. Franz, talking to Dreyer:

> Franz made the gesture of a clown's stooge when presented with a conundrum. (p. 219)

[1] *Terra Incognita* reappears as the title of a story, first published in 1931.

2. Martha:

> She had now thrown the pink shawl over her shoulders and, like a woman in some old fashioned romance, gazed at him fixedly from the far corner of the settee. (pp. 86–7)

Compare:

> Она, накинув розовый платок, из дальнего угла пристально смотрела на него. (p. 86)

Here are some examples of 'internalized' imagery:

1. Franz: his horror of Dreyer:

> On the court, with the thoroughness of an executioner preparing the block, Dreyer was already measuring the height of the net with his racket. (p. 187)

2. Martha: her cheap notions of romance:

> Because he wore glasses even for love-making, he reminded her of a handsome, hairy young pearl diver ready to pry the live pearl out of its rosy shell as in that Russian ballet they had seen together, or that picture of conches facing the last page in volume M. (p. 166)

3. Dreyer: his poetic fantasy, describing Martha to Erica:

> 'She does not make love on a bench in the park, or on a balcony like a swallow.' (p. 175)

In all, Martha gains about a dozen images, Dreyer over twenty, and Franz nearer thirty.

Most of the word-play which is added in the English version is included in the main narrative rather than put in the mouths of the characters. Examples of this sort of word-play are the anagrammatic versions which Nabokov introduces of his own name, and the puns he makes on the names of some of the minor characters. Nabokov does, however, give some word-play to Dreyer, the one character endowed with a sense of humour. For instance, when endeavouring to remember the punch-line of a story, Dreyer exclaims: 'I've got the beginning and middle. My emporium for the end!' (p. 210.) He also comes out with a smart rejoinder when Mr. Ritter outlines a project for providing musical tap water in hotels:

> 'Water made to produce recognizable tunes. The music of water in a literal sense. . . . Wash your hands in a barcarolla, bathe in *Lohengrin*, rinse your silver in Debussy.'
>
> 'Or drown in a Bach', punned Dreyer. (p. 263)

It remains to say something more about the added sexual references in the English version. It has been seen that many of the additions clarify the motivations of the three main characters—motivations which are primarily sexual. The explicit and detailed references which Nabokov gives to the sexual preoccupations of Franz and Martha repel and disgust while at the same time contriving to be highly comic. The effect is analogous to the effect of the added authorial comment and the added symbolism. The reader's distance from the characters is increased. Franz and Martha are clockwork characters with but one driving-force—sex.

Nabokov's sexual additions, however, are not confined to the central characters. The entire narrative is spiced with added sexual allusions. Tucked into the margins of the tale are allusions to homosexuality (pp. 92–3), to incestuous lesbianism (p. 154), to necrophilia (p. 192). Nor are the other physical functions neglected. Franz throws up once in the Russian version (R, p. 144; E, p. 146). He will vomit twice more in *KQKn* (pp. 147, 229–30). And there are a full dozen more references to lavatories (*passim*), as well as one reference to a brimming chamber pot! The tone of the English novel is altogether more ribald, more blatantly, if humorously, vulgar. It is a tone which Nabokov recaptures in many passages of *Ada*. It is his bold parody of pornography, his nod to modern literary fashion.

It will be clear from this analysis that Nabokov's revision of *KDV* has very close similarities with his revisions of *CO*, *Soglyadatai*, and *Otchayanie*. The structure is altered less than that of *CO*, but the changes are of the same kind: logical flaws are corrected, and pointers to the development of the plot are added. The use of artifice is more extensive and overt. Considerably more changes are made to characterization in *KQKn* than in the other translations, but, again, they are of the same order. The motivations of the main characters become clearer, their expression becomes more colourful. At the same time, authorial humour and irony continually intervene to expose their weaknesses and deflate their dreams. There is, indeed, sufficient kinship between characters such as Rex and Dreyer (both have a keen eye and a keen sense of humour, though Rex's humour is certainly more cruel), Dreyer and Albinus (their blindness in love), and even Martha and Margot (their 'cinematic' view of life), for some of the elaboration to take strikingly similar forms. Nabokov's demonstration of authorial control extends to the intrusion of the author into the narrative. In *LD* Nabokov remakes Udo Conrad in his own image. In *KQKn*, several minor characters become his namesakes, and Nabokov even makes a personal appearance—Hitchcock fashion—at the very end of the novel.[1]

There are, then, close similarities between Nabokov's method of revision in his early period, in the 1930s, and his method in his later period, in the 1960s. Certain features do, however, make it possible to distinguish between an earlier and a later translation. The preference which Nabokov shows in *LD* for the singular noun in natural descriptions is (see above p. 56) a feature which recurs in other stories written at the same time, notably in *Oblako, ozero, bashnya*, 1937. It is not characteristic of his later revisions. On the other hand, 'beauty and beast' combinations are more characteristic of Nabokov's later period.[2] Many features of *KQKn* also appear in *Ada*, the novel which Nabokov was engaged upon at the time when he reworked his translation. *Ada*, for instance, has a profusion of minor characters most of whom have comic, or meaningful names. The names are sometimes paired: the sisters Aqua and Marina recall the siblings Ida and Isolda in the translation. There is a wealth of literary allusion and parody, and some of the discussion on literature and art is reminiscent of passages which Nabokov adds in *KQKn*.

Another feature which characterizes Nabokov's later writing is his prodigal and humorous treatment of sex. The original version of *CO* already contained a good deal of explicit sexual reference, but it was not comic. Nabokov, in his translation (*LD*), went some way towards stylizing the sexual descriptions. He eliminated some of the 'naturalistic' detail and added more touches of humour. In later translations, in *The Eye*, *Despair 2*, and *KQKn*, Nabokov carries this process still further. He adds much *more* sexual detail, but the presentation is highly stylized and highly comic.

---

[1] This is not the only appearance which Nabokov makes in his works. It is one of his favourite literary conceits. See, for example, *Ada* (passim) and *Pnin* (Chapters 5, 6, 7). The story *Tyazhelyi dym* contains a reference to one of Nabokov's novels, and an 'Adam von Librikov' turns up as an incidental character in *Transparent Things* (p. 75). See also the references to Vivian Bloodmark and Sirin in *Speak, Memory* (pp. 218, 287).

[2] In 'A New Deck for Nabokov's Knaves' (pp. 306–7) Proffer lists some examples of 'beauty and beast' combinations added in *KQKn*.

The danger inherent in a study of this kind is that exclusive concentration on the alterations made can give a distorted picture of the relation of the translations to their originals. In conclusion, therefore, it should be emphasized that the changes which Nabokov makes to his novels—however extensive—are nevertheless in keeping with the original design. As was pointed out in Chapter 4, the Russian originals were already conceived as novels of pattern and plot, in which the characters were manipulated with a cool ironic detachment. And it has been seen in the examination of the translations how carefully Nabokov preserves the main thematic devices, including the thematic imagery, altering it only to render it more telling. A fitting comment on this is given by the young Nabokov in *KDV*:

> Так художник видит лишь то, что свойственно его перво-начальному замыслу.   (p. 104)

Translated by an older Nabokov, in 1968, this becomes: 'Thus an experienced artist sees only that which is in keeping with his original concept' (p. 106).

The difference between original and translation is a difference of degree, not of kind. It is, nevertheless, an important one: Nabokov dresses up his characters in bright costumes, teaches them to project their voices, he burnishes the set until it glitters; he then takes his reader, sits him in the upper balcony and hands him a pair of opera glasses—the reader has become a spectator.

It has been left to the end of this chapter to discuss more fully the question of sexual elaboration and to expand the point made earlier in the section on *Despair* that Nabokov, in the wake of *Lolita*, has deliberately fostered his public image of the so-called pornographic writer.

It is well known that *Lolita* created a literary sensation when it was first published by the Olympia Press in Paris, 1955. Nabokov, as he states in his Afterword to *Lolita*, had previously submitted his manuscript to four American publishers but all refused to publish it. The theme of the novel, allied to the somewhat scabrous reputation of the publishing house itself, provoked many critics into accusing the author of pornographic writing. The defence of the novel was conducted with no less vigour. In 1956, Nabokov wrote a short piece defending his intentions, 'On a Book entitled

Lolita', which was appended to all subsequent editions of the novel, English and Russian. And in 1957, the Olympia Press brought out a collection of essays entitled: *L'Affaire Lolita — défense de l'écrivain*.

Whatever view is held of the novel—and I consider that *Lolita* is in no sense a pornographic work, but rather parodies the conventions of pornography[1]—it cannot be disputed that it was the notoriety of the novel which ensured its instant popularity with the reading public, and brought world-wide recognition for its author. Time may well correct this judgement, but today at least Nabokov is remembered by the general reader as the author of *Lolita*, 'that novel about the little girl and the dirty old man'. But what is especially interesting, particularly in view of Nabokov's vigorous denial of the charge of pornography, is that in his English production since *Lolita* he has done nothing to curtail the sexual and erotic content—rather the reverse. Incest is but one of the erotic themes treated in *Ada* (1969), while the commentary in *Pale Fire* (1962) fairly bristles with homosexual allusion and scatological detail. And in *Transparent Things* (1972), a much slimmer tome, the sexual content is no whit diminished; onanism, erotic dreams, the fads and fantasies of intercourse, and numerous allusive puns are trimly fitted within its one hundred pages. This development in Nabokov's later writing would not deserve so much attention were it not for the evidence of the translated novels. The interpolation of sexual detail into early novels shows beyond doubt that this increase in erotic content is both conscious and intended.

A partial explanation of this added emphasis on sex can no doubt be found in the greater tolerance which prevails in contemporary fiction. *Lolita*, which roused such a storm of protest in the mid-1950s, would, had it appeared a decade later, have been met with a good deal more equanimity. Nor can the monetary incentive be discounted entirely. A writer who has once 'hit the jackpot' with a certain type of novel can be expected to want to make capital out of his success. It would, however, be absurd to assert that a novel such as *Pale Fire*, even with all the homosexual

---

[1] This view is shared by other critics of Nabokov. In his article '*Lolita*: the Springboard of Parody' Appel comments: 'The subject matter of *Lolita* is in itself a bravura and "delusive opening move"—a withdrawn promise of pornography.' (p. 123). See also Dupee, 'A Preface to *Lolita*'.

allusions, was in any sense written for a 'popular' market. In form it mimics the scholarly edition; its subject is the complex interweave of one man's poetry with another man's fantasy. And the casual reader of *Ada*, stimulated by Nabokov's colourful résumé on the dust cover to embark on this considerable tome, would as like as not persevere no further than the first two or three chapters! Nabokov cannot be said to be fashioning his novels for the bestseller market.

Even allowing some validity in both these explanations, there is a third which invites consideration, namely that Nabokov is deliberately stepping up the erotic content of his novels not to ape pornography, but to parody it, and to parody the image of himself as a pornographic writer. It is his bold answer to the hostile and, in Nabokov's view, misguided critics of *Lolita*. In case this explanation seems unnecessarily far-fetched, it should be added that this is not the only occasion when Nabokov has used parody as a weapon against critics. There are, for example, the parodies of Freudian theory contained in several of his novels. Nabokov's scorn of psychoanalysis dates right back to the start of his career as a novelist. As early as 1931, he wrote a hilarious send-up of Freud in *Novaya gazeta*, 'Chto vsyakii dolzhen znat''. But this article did not prevent several *émigré* critics from misreading Nabokov's intentions in his novels and criticizing the author for an overindulgence in psychoanalysis. Yury Terapiano, for example, had this to say in his review of *CO* in 1934:

> Мне кажется я не ошибусь, если скажу, вспомнив мелкие рассказы того же автора, печатавшиеся в «Последних новостях», что склонность к сомнительному германскому открытию — психоанализу — основной грех Сирина.

Nabokov's reaction to this criticism was not to change his approach, but to make his parodies of Freud more telling and more blatant, and set more traps for the unwary reader. There is hardly a Foreword in the recent English translations of his novels which does not contain some gibe against the 'Viennese witch-doctor'.

Another amusing example of Nabokov making sport out of his critics is the 'Vasily Shishkov' hoax of 1939. This also involves parody. Nabokov's poetry was never particularly well received by *émigré* reviewers, certainly by comparison with his prose.[1]

---

[1] For a particularly damning criticism, see Georgy Ivanov's review of *SZ*, No. 33, 1927, in which he discusses Nabokov's *Universitetskaya poema*. See

Adamovich was one of the most critical, and in 1939 Nabokov took his revenge. The workings of this 'revenge' can be summarized as follows:

1. In *Sovremennye zapiski*, No. 69, Nabokov publishes a poem, *Poety*, under the pseudonym 'Vasily Shishkov'.[1]

2. On 17 August 1939, in *Poslednie novosti*, the poem is enthusiastically reviewed by Adamovich, who speculates on the identity of this unknown V. Shishkov:

> кто это Василий Шишков? Откуда он? Вполне возможно, что через год-два его имя будут знать все кому дорога русская поэзия.

3. On 12 September 1939, Nabokov publishes in *Poslednie novosti* a short story entitled *Vasily Shishkov*, under his usual pen-name V. Sirin. The story describes a few meetings between Shishkov and an anonymous narrator, an *émigré* writer and critic. At one of these meetings Shishkov volunteers his opinion of the narrator's own writings. The judgements which Shishkov makes are a virtual pastiche of criticisms made of Nabokov's work by Adamovich. The praise which the narrator has for Shishkov's work also echoes Adamovich's praise for *Poety*.

4. On 22 September 1939, Adamovich guesses the truth. Perhaps, he writes in *Poslednie novosti*, Vasily Shishkov does not in fact exist? Perhaps Nabokov has invented the whole thing? This possibility he views with regret. He would like to hear more from Vasily Shishkov:

> Каюсь, у меня даже возникло подозрение: не сочинил ли все это Сирин, не выдумал ли он начисто и Василия Шишкова, и его стихи?.. Было бы очень жаль, если бы беглец Шишков оказался «существом метафизическим»...

5. In *Sovremennye zapiski*, No. 70, Vasily Shishkov makes a final appearance. He signs another poem, entitled *Obrashchenie*.[2]

also Weidlé's comment in 'Russkaya literatura v emigratsii: novaya proza', 1930: 'khoroshikh stikhov u Sirina i vovse net'. In all fairness it should be added that Nabokov's poetry did get some good reviews. See, for example, Struve's review of *Universitetskaya poema*, 1927.

[1] Shishkov is actually the name of a branch of the Nabokov family. See *SM*, pp. 54, 56, 62.

[2] *Poety* and *Obrashchenie* were included in the collection *Stikhotvoreniya: 1929–1951*, and later in *Poems and Problems*, where Nabokov alludes to the Shishkov hoax in a note (p. 95).

There is, of course, more to the Shishkov episode than an elaborate literary joke. The two poems and the story were written very shortly before Nabokov left for the United States, and all treat the theme of departure. In the disguise of the unknown Vasily Shishkov Nabokov is bidding farewell to his identity as a Russian writer, and to the Russian language. Nevertheless, Nabokov's sensitivity to criticism is something which cannot be ignored in an interpretation of his work: it frequently acts as a stimulus to creation.

6

MINOR REWORKINGS

NOVELS

IN the translation of the four novels examined in the previous
chapter, Nabokov's interests are clearly not confined to making
a faithful and accurate reproduction of the original. He is also
interested to revise, elaborate, and update that original. There is
a consistent pattern in the revisions he makes. The structure is
tightened, there is added humour and added verbal effects, more
imagery and vivid detail, and more sexual allusion. While the
changes made do not run counter to the initial design of the novels,
they do affect the relationship between the reader and the narrative. They foster in the reader a more detached and, in some cases,
a more critical attitude to characters and events.

In these translations Nabokov is making no claims to literalness. In his Forewords to both *Despair* and *KQKn* he readily
acknowledges that he has made changes and even enumerates some
of them.[1] However, there remain another six novels, the translation
of which Nabokov clearly did intend to be 'literal'. One of these
novels, *Lolita*, Nabokov translated himself in 1967; the remaining
five were entrusted to other translators and only revised by the
author. They are: *Priglashenie na kazn'* (*Invitation to a Beheading*,
1959), *Dar* (*The Gift*, 1963), *Zashchita Luzhina* (*The Defence*,
1964), *Mashen'ka* (*Mary*, 1970), and *Podvig* (*Glory*, 1971). In the
Forewords to all but two of these novels Nabokov comments upon
the accuracy of the translation.[2] In the Foreword to *IB* he writes

---

[1]. 'For the present edition I have done more than revamp my thirty-year-old
translation: I have revised *Otchayanie* itself'—(*Despair*, p. 8). 'I foresaw having
to make a number of revisions affecting the actual text of a forty-year-old novel
which I had not reread ever since its proofs had been corrected by an author
twice younger than the reviser. Very soon I asserted that the original sagged
considerably more than I had expected. I do not wish to spoil the pleasure of
future collators by discussing the little changes I made' (*KQKn*, p. vii). The
Foreword to *The Eye* contains no discussion of the translation. *LD* has no
Foreword.

[2] The two exceptions are the Forewords to *The Gift* and *The Defence*. However, Scammell, who translated these novels, recalls that Nabokov made it

that he 'found with relief that there was no devil of creative emendation for me to fight'.[1] This same devil of emendation put up more of a fight in his work on the Russian *Lolita*:

> лишь тем горжусь, что железной рукой сдерживал демонов, подбивавших на пропуски и дополнения.[2]

The translation of *Podvig*, he maintains, is 'meticulously true to the text',[3] and he writes of the translation of *Mashen'ka*:

> I realized as soon as my collaboration with Mr. Glenny started that our translation should be as faithful to the text as I would have insisted on its being had that text not been mine. Revampments of the lighthearted and highhanded order that I used for the English version of, say, *King, Queen, Knave*, could not be envisaged here.[4]

A close comparison of these translations with their originals puts some qualification on Nabokov's affirmations. While it is true that the translations adhere very closely to their originals, it is not true that Nabokov succeeds in suppressing completely the creative urge. There *are* modifications in every one of the translations. What is more, these modifications reveal many of the same features as Nabokov's major revisions. The extent of the alterations varies from novel to novel. *IB* suffers the least changes in the process of conversion;[5] there are rather more alterations in *The Gift* and *The Defence*, and more again in *Lolita R, Mary*, and *Glory*.

Structure

In all the novels there are very few deletions or additions. *Lolita R* contains the only deletion of some length. It is a passage twenty-one lines long which describes an occasion when Humbert Humbert is stopped in his car by the police: 'Another jolt I remember . . . as she mimicked limp prostration' (*Lolita E*, pp. 167–8). It is conceivable that Nabokov decided that the incident was repetitious. A similar police scare had been described a few chapters earlier (see *Lolita E*, p. 113).

---

clear before he started work on the translation that what was required was an accurate, faithful rendering.

[1] p. 6.   [2] *Lolita R*, p. 299.
[3] *Glory*, p. ix.   [4] *Mary*, pp. xii–xiii.
[5] The same view is expressed by Hughes in 'Notes on the Translation of *Invitation to a Beheading*': 'Of all the translations of Sirin-Nabokov's works— by various hands, but always quality-controlled by Nabokov himself—this novel seems to have suffered least change in the process of conversion' (p. 285).

Small structural changes are made in some of the novels. In *Glory* Nabokov joins two chapters together to make Chapter 39.[1] In the same novel he also bridges some logical gaps in the narrative and adds a few more pointers which clarify the development of the plot. The Russian translation of *Lolita* exhibits similar features. Some of the clues and cryptic allusions are more explicit in the second version. For instance, when Lolita is confessing to Humbert Humbert about her affair with Quilty, Nabokov illuminates the past course of events with more explicit retrospective detail. Compare:

> Did I know he had seen me and her at the inn where he was writing the very play she was to rehearse in Beardsley, two years later? (p. 266)

> Знал ли я, что он заметил меня и ее в той гостинице каких-то охотников, где он писал *ту самую* пьесу — да «зачарованных», — которую она репетировала в Бердслее два года спустя? Что он ей говорил невозможные вещи внизу в холле? (p. 253)

In Chapter 35 Nabokov introduces another minor alteration which improves the logic of the narrative. Humbert Humbert has just commented upon a difference between old and new houses: in old houses, he says, not just the bathroom, but all the upstairs bedrooms can be locked. In *Lolita R*, Nabokov follows this remark with a reference to Humbert locking the bedroom doors. Compare:

> The house, being an old one, had more planned privacy than have modern glamour-boxes, where the bathroom, the only lockable locus, has to be used for the furtive needs of planned parenthood.
>   Speaking of bathrooms—I was about to visit a third one when master came out of it . . . (p. 287)

> Дом, будучи старым, давал больше возможности уединения, чем дают современные элегантные коробки, где супружеской паре приходится прятаться в уборную — единственный запирающийся уголок — для скромных нужд планового детопроизводства.
>   Кстати, об уборных. Я собрался запереть третью спальню, когда хозяин вышел из соседнего клозета... (p. 273)

In several of these translations Nabokov adds references to times and dates. This is a feature of *Glory* and *Lolita R*, and also of *Mary*

---

[1] See *Glory*, p. 166. The chapter break in *Podvig* comes in the paragraph beginning: 'At the kiosk of the Lausanne station'. The *SZ* edition of *Podvig* contains a misprint in the numbering of the chapters: there is no Chapter 11.

and *The Defence*. Clearly these additions are designed to place the narrative back in time. This is particularly necessary when the gap separating original and translation is as much as forty years. The action of *Mashen'ka*, which was contemporary in 1926 when the novel was first written, is history in 1970. At the same time, however, the dates lend an authenticity to the narrative and, more important, enclose the novels in a very definite temporal framework. In this they perform a structural function.[1]

Characterization

Changes in characterization are also minimal. No characters are added, no new dimensions of character are explored. But again, the translations of *Lolita* and *Podvig* in particular add a few touches to the portrait of the main hero. In *Glory*, some new details underline the acuteness of Martin's vision and his sensibility. Some of the colour epithets are more vivid. Here, for instance, is Martin putting on his Cambridge blazer: 'The celestial blazer buttoned snugly over the white V-necked sweater' (p. 109). Compare:

> На белый, с треугольным вырезом, свэтер тесно налезла голубая куртка.   (р. 98)

Here is Martin's evocation of Tenerife: 'Tenerife—God, what a lovely, emerald word!' (p. 83.) Compare:

> Тенериффа — Боже мой! — какое дивно зеленое слово! (р. 125)

(In this example, Nabokov was presumably also guided by rhythmic considerations in his choice of the polysyllabic adjective 'emerald'.) Nabokov emphasizes Martin's fastidiousness when taking a bath in the lavatory of a train. Martin spreads newspaper over 'its sickening floor' (R: *na polu*), and he avoids coming in contact with the 'filthy fixtures' (R: *stenki*). And when commenting on how Martin could not manage without this morning bath, Nabokov adds a parenthetical imaginative flourish: 'but Martin could not manage without his morning bath [(in the sea, in a pond, in a shower, or in this tub)], which represented, he thought, a kind of heroic defense . . .' (E, p. 182; compare R, p. 109).

The Russian *Lolita* contains a few extra sexual references which

---

[1] See *Glory*, p. 131 (R, p. 118); p. 135 (R, p. 122); p. 136 (R, p. 123); p. 152 (R, p. 81); p. 172 (R, p. 100). See *Lolita* R, p. 128 (E, p. 143); p. 168 (E, p. 182); p. 181 (E, p. 195); p. 189 (E, p. 204); p. 213 (E, p. 227); p. 234 (E, p. 247); p. 232 (E, p. 245). See *Mary*, p. 5 (R, p. 12); p. 31 (R, p. 50); p. 88 (R, p. 131). See *The Defence*, p. 23 (R, pp. 38–9); p. 61 (R, pp. 86–7).

throw still more light on Humbert Humbert's unfortunate passion. Here are two representative examples. An added association of a gynaecological couch intrudes upon Humbert's dreams of the lost Lolita:

> Эта Лже-Лолита (и Лже-Валерия) вяло приглашала меня разделить с ней твердый диванчик, или просто узкую доску, [или нечто вроде гинекологического ложа,] на котором она раскидывалась... (p. 234; compare E, p. 248.)

In Chapter 33, when Humbert Humbert is telling Mrs. Chatfield how Charlie Holmes used to debauch the young girls at Camp Q, *Lolita R* substitutes explicit detail for a humorous quip. Compare:

> 'For shame', she cried, 'for shame, Mr. Humbert! The poor boy has just been killed in Korea.'
>
> I said didn't she think '*vient de*', with the infinitive, expressed recent events so much more neatly than the English 'just', with the past? (p. 282)

> «Стыдно!», крикнула миссис Чатфильд, «как вам не стыдно, мистер Гумберт! Бедного мальчика только-что убили в Корее».
>
> «В самом деле», сказал я (пользуясь дивной свободою свойственной сновидениям). «Вот так судьба! Бедный мальчик пробивал нежнейшие, невосстановимейшие перепоночки, прыскал гадючьим ядом — и ничего, жил превесело, да еще получил посмертный орденок». (p. 269)

Style

All the novels, with the exception of *IB*, contain one or two examples of added or elaborated images. Alliteration is also a feature of the translations. It must be said, however, that in two novels—*IB* and *Lolita R*—more alliterative effects are lost in translation than are gained. This is equally true of the word-play in these two novels. Nevertheless, the fact remains that the translations do gain—Nabokov does elaborate. Not even his closest translations are free of some embellishment. Two examples from *IB* will illustrate this point. Compare:

1. говорить за обедом с тем или другим ее любовником, казаться веселым, щелкать орехи, приговаривать... (p. 72)

   to talk at dinner with one or another of her lovers, appear cheerful, crack nuts, crack jokes . . . (p. 57)

2.   и чем больше двигаюсь и шарю в воде, где ищу на песчаном
     дне мелькнувший блеск...   (p. 100)

and the more I move about and search in the water where I grope
on the sandy bottom for a glimmer I have glimpsed . . .   (p. 85)

As well as adding colour to the narrative, Nabokov brings out
the potential comedy of situations. In *Glory* the description of
Martin's fight with Darwin is rather more comic. Martin does not
simply fall down on the grass—he sits down heavily 'on a pebbly
patch' (E, p. 124; R, p. 112). In the same novel, the maid's intrusion
upon Martin's farewell scene with Sonya acquires a touch of farce.
Compare:

Влетела горничная, забрала чемодан.   (p. 106)

As in a farce the maid dashed in and took the suitcase.   (p. 117)

In *Lolita R*, Humbert prefaces a lie about Lolita's age with the
comment:

Долорес продолжала расти...   (p. 221)

And when Humbert summarizes the contents of John Farlow's
letter, he follows up the news of John's broken leg with the cryptic
remark:

К письму был приложен цветной снимок Джона, еще
целого...   (p. 246)

The English version has simply: 'He enclosed a snapshot of himself . . .' (p. 259).

There has been no attempt here to do more than summarize the
different sorts of elaboration which Nabokov allows himself in his
'literal versions'. A full account would risk becoming repetitive
and tedious. Yet, a few selected details cannot convey adequately
the nature and the full extent of the changes which Nabokov
makes. For this reason a more detailed examination will be made of
Nabokov's practice in one translation, *Mary*, which he prepared in
collaboration with Michael Glenny in 1970.

MARY

In assessing Nabokov's part in the preparation of this English
translation it is of great value to be able to compare the version
submitted by Glenny with the final printed text. Nabokov subjects
Glenny's version to close critical scrutiny. While quick to pick up

any inaccuracies, he has praise for Glenny's inventiveness and the naturalness of his English. In a letter to Glenny he has this to say of the translation of the first eight chapters: 'Much of the stuff is very well translated, in natural and ingenious language, but not all is correct.'[1] Nabokov does make a great number of changes. The majority affect single words or small groups of words, but there are passages which are entirely reworked. The frequency of the alterations varies from a minimum of three or four alterations per printed page to the rewriting of whole pages. What sort of changes are these? It is true, as Nabokov claims, that there are no significant deviations from the Russian text. Moreover, many of the changes are designed to bring the English closer to the original in meaning and in style. But it is clear that Nabokov is concerned not only to correct Glenny's rendering, but to improve upon it and to make it more completely his own—a process which at times involves an elaboration of the original Russian.

At the lower end of the scale of changes comes the correction of the occasional mistranslations—'howlers', as Nabokov terms them, with characteristic forthrightness. These 'howlers' can be a misunderstanding of an elliptic piece of conversation, confusion of related word forms, or a mere slip of the pen. Nabokov is never other than direct in his criticism of this sort of mistake, but he reserves especial severity for any hint of compromise with the original, for any approximate equivalence. This can be seen in his meticulous correction of the translation of material objects, of 'things'. *Umyval'nik*, he points out in a letter to MG, is a washstand, not a washbasin (see *Mary*, p. 6). *Podokonnik*, he asserts, 'is always "window ledge" in Russian. The sill is outside, not inside.' (See *Mary*, pp. 46, 62. On p. 50, however, Nabokov leaves two references to 'windowsill' unaltered.) The care which Nabokov takes over the translation of gestures and facial expressions is also indicative of this concern to convey the exact meaning of the original. He is not satisfied with the dictionary translation of *morshchit'sya* as 'to frown'. He prefers 'to grimace', and substitutes this every time the word is used. He comments to MG: '*Morshchit'sya* is not "to frown" as dictionaries think, but "to make a grimace (denoting some kind of emotion)" ' (see *Mary*, pp. 98, 104). He is not satisfied with an approximate translation of *razvel rukami*, and gives instead a description of the gesture:

[1] Letter to Glenny, 3 February 1970.

'Alfyorov spread out his hands in a gesture of helplessness . . .'
(p. 15). (MG: 'Alfyorov gestured briskly . . . .')[1]

Nabokov is equally concerned to preserve the stylistic individuality of the original. He does not allow MG to introduce any
different images into the text. There are two instances of this:

1. Describing a jacket hung untidily on a chair:

> Другой стул... исчезал под черным пиджаком, павшим на
> него словно с Арарата, так он тяжело и рыхло сел.   (p. 39)

> MG: The other chair . . . had disappeared under a black coat which
> lay there so clumsily and untidily that it might have been a piece of
> flotsam.

> VN: The other chair . . . had disappeared under a black jacket whose
> collapse seemed as heavy and shapeless as if it had fallen from the
> top of Mount Ararat. (p. 23)

2. Describing some neon adverts:

> Ярче, веселее звезд были огненные буквы, которые высыпали
> одна за другой над черной крышей, семенили гуськом и
> разом пропадали во тьме.   (p. 43)

> MG: Brighter and gayer than the stars were the letters of fire which
> broke out like a rash [Glenny is presumably thinking of *syp'* here]
> above a black roof, paraded in single file and vanished all at once
> in the darkness.

> VN: Gaudier, gayer than the stars were the letters of fire which
> poured out one after another above a black roof, paraded in single
> file and vanished all at once in the darkness. (p. 26)

He consistently reinstates images which have been glossed over or
lost by his translator. In a description of the protruding air vents
on the roofs of railway carriages, Glenny abandons Nabokov's
metaphor, *such'i soski*, and settles for the more cautious and
explanatory 'ventilators'. Nabokov reacts like a man betrayed:
'There are no "revolving ventilators" in my text. *Such'i soski* are
"dog nipples".' His final version reads: 'olive-drab carriages with
a row of dark dog-nipples along their roofs' (p. 10). Nabokov also
refuses to allow any attenuation of the imagery in this description
of Lyudmila:

[1] This precision in the translation of Russian gestures features in several
others of Nabokov's translations. And Timofey Pnin, it will be remembered,
was also a 'veritable encyclopedia of Russian shrugs and shakes' (*Pnin*, pp. 41–2).

она летучим каким-то голосом — не тем прежним носовым шепотком — молила, вся улетала в слова... (p. 22)

MG: and begged him in a *fluttery* voice quite unlike her usual nasal whisper, putting all she had into the words . . .

VN: and begged him in a *fluttery* voice quite unlike her usual nasal whisper, her whole being seeming to *fly* into words . . . (p. 12. My italics here and in the following example.)

This is how MG renders another image: 'Like a dry leaf her tiny wrinkled hand would now and then *rise* to the dangling bell knob and then, yellow and faded, would flutter back again.' Nabokov substitutes 'flit up' for 'rise', thus conveying the full force of the Russian verb *vzletala k...* (*Mary*, p. 13).

The same concern to restore the 'full flavour' of the original can be seen in Nabokov's choice of epithets. A typical example is his translation of *nezhnyi* in emotive contexts. On two occasions he replaces 'soft', which is MG's suggestion, by 'tender':

1. как апрельские облака по нежному берлинскому небу.
   (p. 53)

   MG: like the April clouds across the soft Berlin sky.

   VN: like the April clouds across the tender Berlin sky. (p. 33)

2. Рядом с кабачком был гараж; пройма его ворот зияла темнотой, и оттуда нежно пахнуло карбидом. (pp. 102–3)

   MG: Alongside a pub was a garage and from the gaping maw of its entrance came a faint whiff of carbide.

   VN: Near the beer-hall there was a garage and from the gaping gloom of its entrance came a tender whiff of carbide. (p. 66)

The context of this second example makes it clear why Nabokov makes this change. The smell of carbide has tender associations for Ganin:

И этот случайный запах помог Ганину вспомнить еще живее тот русский, дождливый август, тот поток счастья, который тени его берлинской жизни все утро так назойливо прерывали. (p. 103)

Elsewhere, *legkoe shosse* is nicely rendered as 'light-hearted road' (p. 100) (MG had merely 'beautiful road'); *dva blednykh stikha* become 'two pallid verses' (p. 110) (MG: 'two pale verses'); and a hint of personification turns *temnoe zerkalo* into 'bleary mirror' (p. 5) (MG: 'dim mirror').

Some of the changes which Nabokov makes in the vocabulary of MG's version do, however, go further than restoration of the original; they extend to an elaboration of that original. Nabokov frequently opts for a more unusual combination of words in his English translation. Note, for example, his translation of *ukradkoi* in the following sentence:

> Колин, украдкой, отбивал такт, искоса посматривая на Алферова. (p. 29)

Kolin here is silently mocking Alfyorov's garrulity. Glenny renders *ukradkoi* as 'surreptitiously', but Nabokov substitutes 'stealthily', a word usually encountered in a more sinister context: 'Glancing sidelong at Alfyorov, Kolin was stealthily beating time to him' (p. 16). The slight incongruity is humorous. It is with similar humorous effect that Nabokov, again describing the effeminate Kolin, translates the phrase *s drozhashchei ostorozhnost'yu* as 'with tremulous care', in preference to MG's 'with trembling care': 'Kolin, on his left, passed him a plate of soup with tremulous care, giving him such an ingratiating look and such a smile with his strange veiled eyes that Ganin felt uncomfortable' (pp. 13–14). Note, too, Nabokov's choice of 'daintily' when speaking of Klara's parlour romanticism:

> то огромное и всегда праздничное, что зовется смазливым словом «мечта». (p. 23)

MG: that powerful and always delicious sensation that is delicately referred to as 'longing'.

VN: that enormous, always festive sensation that is daintily called 'reverie'. (p. 12)

When describing the one private interview which takes place between Klara and Ganin (Klara adores Ganin from afar), Nabokov adds an incongruous detail which deflates the potential romanticism of the situation. Klara has reproached Ganin with theft. Ganin suggests that they go to Klara's room to talk. Klara consents: 'She detached herself from the wall and with head bowed led him to room April 5' (p. 36). This comic reminder of how the doors in the *pension* were numbered with pages torn off an old calendar is absent from the original version. The characterization of Lyudmila, Ganin's mistress, undergoes an analogous deflation. Her cheap sex-appeal is accentuated by garish alliterative effects. Her *smuglo-vataya pudra* and *shelkovye chulki poros'yachego tsveta* become: 'sultry face powder and piggy-pink silk stockings' (p. 11; R, p. 21). (MG: 'pale-tan face powder and pigskin-coloured silk stockings'.) Nabokov restores the full value of the alliteration in the translation of this phrase:

> прижиматься без страсти к пурпурной резине ее поддаю-щихся губ   (p. 21)

> MG: to press himself, devoid of passion, to the mauve rubber of her proffered lips

> VN: to kiss without passion the painted rubber of her proffered lips   (p. 11)

These last few examples show Nabokov adopting a more ironic attitude to some of his characters—the mistress, the homosexual, the unmarried maiden. The changes made are slight (the Russian version is already ironic), but they are sufficient to nuance the characterization. More important, these changes are consistent with the general development in Nabokov's later production towards a more stringent humour, faintly grotesque, faintly cruel, and very verbal.

The alliterative quality of Nabokov's style, while marked in the Russian version, is an even more distinctive feature of his English translation. There are several instances, as in the example just quoted, where he restores an alliteration abandoned by MG. But he adds many more. Some of this alliteration is comic. For example:

1. Kolin:

> в потрепанных ботинках на босу ногу   (p. 97)

> MG: tattered shoes on bare feet

> VN: battered boots on bare feet   (p. 63)

2. Kolin and Gornotsvetov:

> Горноцветов и Колин залились тонким смехом.   (p. 28)

> MG: Gornotsvetov and Kolin burst into giggles.

> VN: Gornotsvetov and Kolin dissolved in mannered mirth.   (p. 16)

3. Alfyorov's clichés:

«Да, вы правы, нежнейший цветок...»   (p. 28)

MG: 'Yes, you're right, a most delicate flower . . .'

VN: 'Yes, you're right, a most fragile flower . . .'   (p. 16)

In descriptive passages Nabokov uses alliteration to intensify auditive and visual impressions:

Sound:

1. The description of the lift:

вся загудевшая, поплывшая вверх клетка   (p. 11)

MG: the creaking, rising cage

VN: the humming and heaving cage   (p. 3)

2. Riding a bicycle in the dark:

вдавливая в шелестящую пустоту упругие педали   (p. 73)

MG: pressing down springy pedals into a rustling void

VN: pressing resilient pedals into a rustling void   (p. 47)

Sight:

1. Ganin's memory of his nurse waving goodbye out of the carriage window:

и ветер трепал косынку   (p. 55)

MG: and the wind flapped her headdress

VN: and the wind worried her wimple   (p. 34)

2. White dresses showing up in the darkness:

поплыли, празднично и зыбко белеясь, дачницы...   (p. 72)

MG: the gay crowd of holidaymakers, in a flutter of white dresses, drifted away . . .

VN: the crowd of fair vacationists, in a festive flutter of white frocks, drifted away . . . (p. 46)

In the description of Ganin and Mary's love Nabokov makes sensitive use of alliteration and rhythm to evoke the intensity of feeling. Compare, for example, the following passages:

Ветер напирал из тьмы тяжело и влажно. Машенька, сидя рядом на облупившейся балюстраде, гладила ему виски холодной ладошкой, и в темноте он различал смутный угол ее промокшего банта и улыбавшийся блеск глаз.
(p. 104)

MG: Wet and strong, the wind blew from the darkness. Sitting beside him on the peeling balustrade, Mashenka caressed his temples with her cold little palm, and in the darkness he could just distinguish between the blurred end of her wet hair-ribbon and the smiling gleam of her eyes.

VN: Out of the darkness a humid and heavy pressure of gusty air reached the lovers. Mary, now perched on the peeling balustrade, caressed his temples with the cold palm of her little hand and he could make out in the dark the vague outline of her soggy hairbow and the smiling brilliance of her eyes.   (p. 67)

It will be clear from this analysis of *Mary* that Nabokov here is working within strict self-imposed limitations. He wants an accurate translation of his Russian original, and he commissions an outside translator to provide a literal version. In the corrections which he makes to the version submitted by his translator the Russian original is never lost sight of. There is barely an image added or an image lost. Even so, without making any major changes, Nabokov stamps the novel with the characteristics of his mature writing: the vivid visual and auditive effects, the rich alliterative texture, touches of humour and irony in characterization.

The same conclusions can be extended to all six of these novels. The creative writer remains active even in the minor reworkings. However, while the changes are of the same order as the full-scale revisions discussed in the previous chapter, they are not sufficiently far-reaching to alter the reader's relationship with the characters. It cannot be said that Nabokov is increasing the narrative distance in these translations. But then these novels differ from *LD*, *Despair*, *The Eye*, and *KQKn* in that they are not purely novels of pattern and plot. Certainly, there is patterning and stylization in all of them, but they also contain a measure of sentiment, they invite the reader's emotional participation and involvement with the hero. And this is true as much of *The Defence* and *Lolita*, where the hero is a mad chess genius or a sexual pervert, as of the other novels where the heroes are all recognizably 'normal'. In *IB*, the very crime of which Cincinnatus stands convicted is the crime of being human in a society of tyrannical and tyrannized shadows. The characters are still 'galley slaves',[1] but we *can* see their faces.

It should be added that this view of Nabokov's production is not unanimously shared by Nabokov's critics. *Émigré* reviewers of *Zashchita Luzhina*, for example, were very divided in their opinion of Luzhin. While some saw him as a human, sympathetic character, others considered the novel to be an arid cerebral exercise. The sympathetic viewpoint is well represented in a review signed by Novik which appeared in 1931:

> Лужин не беззащитная жертва писательского вивисектор-
> ства, а живой человек, дышащий, двигающийся и, пожалуй,
> уже независимо от автора, создающий свои личные отно-
> шения с читателем.[2]

Adamovich, in his review of the novel, voiced the different opinion:

> Это — выдуманный, надуманный роман, но выдуманный
> отлично, как давно уже у нас не выдумывали... У него все
> по внешности, в блестящей полировке...[3]

Quentin Anderson in a review article written in 1966 also divides Nabokov's production into two categories. He contrasts the group of 'patterned' novels with those novels containing what he terms 'naturalist strands'.[4] But in Anderson's scheme of things *Lolita* and *The Defence* belong in the first group, the group of patterned novels. This variance of critical opinion is understandable. We are dealing here with subjective judgements. What is more, the 'human interest' in these minor reworkings is only *relatively* greater than in the rest of Nabokov's production. Nabokov is never, except perhaps in parts of his autobiography, a 'sentimental' writer. But it is interesting in this context to consider Nabokov's own judgement. It is these novels, the minor reworkings, about which he speaks with most warmth. When asked in interview, in 1966, which novel he held in most affection or esteemed above all others, Nabokov replied: 'The most affection, *Lolita*; the greatest esteem, *Priglashenie na kazn'*.'[5] In an earlier BBC television

---

[1] See Nabokov's interview with Herbert Gold, 1967: 'My characters are galley slaves.'

[2] Novik is the pseudonym of German Khokhlov. Another expression of this view is contained in Struve's article, 'Tvorchestvo Sirina', quoted in Appendix E, p. 237.

[3] Review of *SZ*, No. 41, 13 February 1930.

[4] 'Nabokov in Time', 1966.

[5] 'An Interview with Vladimir Nabokov', conducted by Appel, 1967.

interview, recorded in *The Listener*, he spoke of *Dar* as 'the best and the most nostalgic of my Russian novels'.[1] In his Foreword to *Mary* he confesses: 'I feel no embarrassment in confessing to the sentimental stab of my attachment to my first book.'[2] And he has this to say in his Foreword to *The Defence*: 'Of all my Russian books, *The Defense* contains and diffuses the greatest "warmth"— which may seem odd seeing how supremely abstract chess is supposed to be.'[3]

It remains to comment on one more feature of these minor reworkings—that is, the virtual absence of sexual elaboration. *Lolita R* is the only translation in which Nabokov adds any erotic detail. Of the other novels, *Mary*, *Glory*, and *IB* all contain some sexual episodes, but none of these is embellished in English translation. This puts an important qualification on the conclusions made in the previous chapter. Nabokov does not impose erotic detail indiscriminately on all his later novels, but only on those in which the sexual impulse is already central to the characterization. It has been shown how central it is to the characterization in *LD*, *Despair*, *The Eye* and *KQKn*, and it is equally of Humbert Humbert in *Lolita*. In all these novels the sexual urge has become warped and completely governs the character. In the other novels, the sexual urge is either suppressed, as with Cincinnatus or Luzhin, or takes perfectly normal forms, as with Ganin, Martin, or Godunov-Cherduntsev. This conclusion could be extended to all Nabokov's post-*Lolita* production. Thus *Pale Fire*, *Ada*, and *Transparent Things* contain much sexual detail, while *Pnin* contains virtually none.

SHORT STORIES AND DRAMA

It remains to consider Nabokov's practice in the other prose genres—in the short story and in drama. To date twenty-nine stories and one play have been translated from Russian into English with Nabokov's collaboration. Three of the stories were published in the 1940s (*Cloud, Castle, Lake*, *The Aurelian*, and *Spring in Fialta*); the rest of the stories have appeared in the 1960s and 1970s, and the play, *The Waltz Invention*, was published in 1966. A list of these translations, together with their dates of appearance, is given in Appendix A.

[1] 22 November 1962.   [2] p. xii.   [3] p. 9.

The degree of literalness of these translations varies. Some of them are indeed, as Nabokov claims, 'acrobatically faithful to the original'. Others undergo rather more substantial alterations. None, however, may be classed as a major revision. In one or two of the stories Nabokov introduces small structural modifications. In *The Potato Elf* (the 1973 version) he makes eight sections instead of seven. In *The Aurelian* he divides up a continuous narrative into four sections and, by some judicious pruning and well-placed detail, tightens the plot and increases the build-up. In *Lips to Lips* he highlights a piece of structural parallelism which links the opening and concluding episodes of the story. The main character of this tale, Ilya Borisovich, is a middle-aged businessman with literary aspirations, who is engaged in writing a rather mediocre novel. The reader is made aware from the start of the limitations of Ilya Borisovich's talent. In an opening scene of his novel Ilya Borisovich describes how a theatre cloakroom attendant hands his hero, Dolinin, a cane. But in bestowing this cane upon his hero, the author forgets how 'painfully it would demand mention' when Dolinin later is to carry his loved one across a 'vernal rill'. The story concludes with a 'real-life' parallel to this. Ilya Borisovich is attending a theatrical production and overhears some scornful criticism of his novel. He makes a hasty exit, only to discover that he has left his cane behind in the cloakroom—another instance of forgetfulness, another occasion of embarrassment. Nabokov in his English version makes this identification between Ilya Borisovich and Dolinin more explicit by adding two more references to a cane.[1] Echoes of *Despair* and the highlighting of Hermann's fatal mistake—the forgotten stick!

In a few stories, *The Aurelian, Lik, The Circle, The Potato Elf,* Nabokov adds dates which serve to place the action back in time and provide a temporal framework for the narrative.[2] In *The Aurelian* he also indulges in his predilection for 'fatidic', or significant dates: he situates Pilgram's death not simply on a 'grey,

---

[1] *RB*, pp. 57, 58.
[2] The first appearance of *Kartofel'nyi El'f*, as recorded by Field in his Bibliography, was in 1924. Nabokov in a prefatory note to his translation states that the story was written in 1929 and published in *Rul'* that year (*RB*, p. 220). Nabokov here would appear to be mistaken: the story was written several years earlier and the *Rul'* publication is a reprint. This misapprehension affects the dates which he adds to the story in his English version: Fred was born in 1900 and his death can have taken place no earlier than 1928.

damp April day', as in the original Russian, but on 'a certain first of April, of all dates'. It will be remembered that Hermann's day of reckoning, the day of his arrest, falls on the very same day.

Several anonymous characters are fitted out with names, some of them humorous and some meaningful. The Freudian doctor in *Ultima Thule* becomes Dr. Bonomini. Falter's sister in the same story becomes Eleonora, with a husband, Mr. L. In *Lips to Lips* Ilya Borisovich is given the surname Tal (this underlines his identification with Dolinin), while in *The Potato Elf* Fred's doctor becomes Doctor Knight (Fred plays chess with him), and a French acrobat is dubbed Blondinet. None of the stories is entirely free of descriptive and stylistic elaboration. This is often slight: an occasional example of alliteration, or a 'rich rendering' which fixes a detail more vividly in the reader's imagination. One word can be enough, as, for example, in the description of the bath-house in *The Circle* where the Russian version has a stepped path, 'with a toad on every step' (*s zhaboi na kazhdoi stupen'ke*), and in the English this becomes 'with a toad on every other step'.[1] In the Russian original of *Spring in Fialta* a little toddler is trying to carry three oranges at once, 'but invariably dropping one' (*neizmenno odin ronyaya*). In English this is rendered as 'continuously dropping the variable third'.[2] The picture is immediately brought to life.

In some of the characterizations there is a familiar added touch of astringency. In *The Circle* a 'grey-haired servant' (*sedoi lakei*) is translated as 'a senile flunkey', while the gardener, 'a deaf hunched little old man' (*glukhoi sutulyi starichok*), becomes 'a deaf little hunchback'.[3] And compare these descriptions of an unknown guest in the same story:

некрасивая девица в воздушном платье, пахнувшая потом от волнения...

an ethereal but ugly damsel whose shyness expressed itself in onion sweat . . .[4]

There are also added examples of word play and humorous detail, but these tend to be localized in those works which already contain playful or parodic elements: in *Lips to Lips*, *An Affair of Honor*,

---

[1] *RB*, p. 259.   [2] *Nabokov's Dozen*, p. 2.
[3] *RB*, p. 261.   [4] Ibid., p. 264.

and especially in the play, *The Waltz Invention*. *The Waltz Invention* also contains more humorous sexual references. In the stories, on the other hand, sexual and scatological additions are minimal, although the inferences are often more explicit: the detail of the 'dashing fellow' relieving himself in the kitchen sink, for instance.[1] The only noteworthy addition Nabokov tells us is in fact a restoration of a passage omitted from the original edition of *Solus Rex*. This is the description of the Prince's homosexual practices which has been quoted earlier (p. 79).

The evidence of the stories and the drama merely confirms and enlarges upon the conclusions drawn from an examination of the novels. The changes made are of the same order, if not on the same scale. Nabokov's practice does not vary when he is dealing with a different prose medium.

REWORKING IN ENGLISH

In this discussion of Nabokov's revisions the focus up to now has been on translation. However, as the analyses of *Despair* and *Laughter in the Dark* have shown, Nabokov continues to rework his material in successive English editions. *Laughter in the Dark* and *Despair 2* provide the two most prominent examples of reworking in English, and Nabokov makes it clear to the reader in his prefaces to these translations that changes have been made.

Changes are also made in several other re-editions of his work which are not acknowledged by Nabokov and which have not attracted the attention of his readers. Many of the alterations are very slight: small changes in detail, phrasing, and vocabulary. Others are more considerable. Nabokov's English story, *The Assistant Producer*,[2] appears in its third edition shorn of two rather laboured concluding paragraphs of speculative distancing. *Symbols and Signs*,[3] another English story, was reissued under a slightly different title, *Signs and Symbols*, and with a more dramatic and vivid narrative. The reworking of *Pnin* is a particularly

---

[1] *RB*, p. 140.

[2] The story was first published in *The Atlantic Monthly* in 1943, and then collected in *Nine Stories*, 1947, and in *Nabokov's Dozen*, 1958.

[3] The story was first published in *The New Yorker* in 1948, and collected in *Nabokov's Dozen*.

interesting example. Prior to the publication of the novel in 1957
four of its chapters appeared in *The New Yorker* as separate
stories.[1] Nabokov has been asked in interview about the composition of the novel and has confirmed that the design was complete in
his mind when he composed the first chapter.[2] The *New Yorker*
stories do, however, differ quite considerably from the corresponding chapters in the finished novel. A comparison of the texts
demonstrates Nabokov's skill in the adaptation of his material,
and at the same time provides further illustration of some of his
characteristic processes of revision.

Each story stands complete in itself, but when it takes its place in
the novel it adapts to a larger design. Nabokov alters many of the
dates to fit with the time-span covered by the whole novel. He also
rearranges and expands the description of Pnin's circle of friends
and acquaintances: his students, university colleagues, landlords
and landladies. In the dimension of the short story these figured
merely as background to a portrait of Pnin. In the context of the
novel they require more depth and continuity. The isolated
episodes from Pnin's life also require and acquire greater resonance within the framework of the novel. In Chapter 6, for example,
Nabokov introduces more details about the termination of Pnin's
appointment which prepare for the finale in the following chapter
—Pnin's departure from Waindell. Another structural link which is
present in the novel but not in the separate stories is the 'fascinating lecturer', a long-standing acquaintance of Pnin's, who enters
the action both as participant and narrator. This narrator provides
a link between Pnin's past and present life and neatly contrives the
hero's exit from the pages of the novel when, in the last chapter, he
appears to usurp Pnin's place at Waindell. In Chapter 6 several
references are made to this narrator which prepare for his
appearance. None of these references is in the *New Yorker* edition.[3]
This last change, while explicable in terms of the structural
requirements of the novel, is at the same time very reminiscent of
Nabokov's authorial interventions in reworkings of his novels in
translation. It also, incidentally, gives some clarification and

[1] 'Pnin' (Chapter 1), 28 November 1953; 'Pnin's Day' (Chapter 3), 23 April
1955; 'Victor meets Pnin' (Chapter 4), 15 October 1955; 'Pnin gives a Party'
(Chapter 6), 12 November 1955.
[2] See 'An Interview with Vladimir Nabokov', conducted by Appel, 1967.
[3] *Pnin*, pp. 140, 148, 169–70.

perspective to critics' speculations on the different narrative voices in the novel.[1]

There are many other changes which are not directly attributable to the requirements of the novel form. There is another authorial intrusion in the allusion added to a character from *Laughter in the Dark*—Dorianna Karen—who is described as a 'famous movie star of the twenties', and an 'old Lesbian'.[2] Nabokov also heightens the dramatic effect of certain scenes by some familiar 'structuring'. For example, it is only in the novel that it becomes clear that the events described in Chapter 3 take place on Pnin's birthday, Tuesday 15 February.[3] His departure from Waindell, we note, also takes place on his birthday. There is more play with the idiosyncrasies of Pnin's English[4] and more fun poked at psychiatrists and American academic standards. Dr. Rudolph Aura and her finger-bowl test make their first appearance in the novel.[5] Also absent from the *New Yorker* version is Professor Blorenge's horrified reaction to the suggestion that Pnin could perhaps be allowed to teach a French course: 'You mean . . . he can *speak* French? . . . In that case . . . we can't use him in First-year French.'[6]

Features of the development of *Pnin* are more fully illustrated in Nabokov's Autobiography which forms the subject of the next chapter. Again there is reworking in English. Again separate stories are combined in a larger structural unit. However, Nabokov's relation of his own experiences is not contained solely in the successive versions of the published Autobiography. In common with other writers he has made considerable use of autobiographical material in his fiction. These fictional variants when viewed in conjunction with the factual accounts provide further evidence of the evolution of Nabokov's narrative technique.

[1] See Lokrantz, *The Underside of the Weave*, pp. 21–7; see also Field, *Nabokov*, pp. 131–40.

[2] *Pnin*, pp. 159, 166.

[3] Ibid. In Chapter 1 a reference is added to 'February 15 (his birthday)' (p. 21). In Chapter 3 there are two additions: the parenthetical 'thirteen—no, twelve days late' (p. 67), and the aside to the reader, 'and this was Tuesday, O Careless Reader!' (p. 75)

[4] Ibid., p. 11, 66, 151.　　　　　　[5] Ibid., pp. 138–9.　　　　　　[6] Ibid., p. 142.

7

THE AUTOBIOGRAPHY

Raisins of fact in the cake of fiction are many stages
removed from the initial grape.[1]

OF all Nabokov's production the Autobiography has undergone the most systematic reworking. The successive
versions span his 'middle' English period (1940–55) and
his 'late' post-*Lolita* period (1955 onwards). The complete
Autobiography covers thirty-seven years of Nabokov's life, from
1903 to 1940, and comprises fifteen chapters. These chapters
were, however, first published separately as autobiographical
stories. The first story in the series was written originally in French
in 1936, while Nabokov was still resident in Europe. This was
Mademoiselle O, an account of his Swiss governess, which later
became Chapter 5 of the Autobiography. An English translation
of the story, prepared by Nabokov with the assistance of Hilda
Ward, appeared in the January edition of *The Atlantic Monthly*,
1943. The remaining fourteen stories were written originally
in English, and were published in American journals between
1948 and 1951. In 1951, Nabokov collected these fifteen stories
together and published them in book form under the title
Conclusive Evidence: a Memoir.[2] Thirteen years later, in 1954,
he brought out a Russian translation of this memoir, entitled *Drugie berega*. Then, in 1966, he published a new
revised English edition: *Speak, Memory: an Autobiography
Revisited*.

In his Foreword to *Speak, Memory*, Nabokov comments in
some detail on the changes which he made in his Russian edition
and in this last English version. What he does not mention,
however, is that in preparing *Conclusive Evidence* he had already
made a good many alterations to his first versions—the stories

---

[1] Interview with Nabokov conducted by Allene Talmey in *Vogue*, 1969.
[2] This edition was also published in London the same year under another
title: *Speak, Memory*. This was the same title as Nabokov was to give later to
his revised English version, published in 1966.

published in journals.[1] This effectively gives *three* English versions of every chapter: E1, the journal edition; E2, *Conclusive Evidence*; E3, *Speak, Memory*.[2] To this should be added a Russian version of all but one of the chapters: Nabokov omitted Chapter 11 from *Drugie berega* 'because of the psychological difficulty of replaying a theme elaborated in my *Dar* (*The Gift*)'. And then there is *Mademoiselle O*, Chapter 5, which has gone through not two, but three language changes: from French to English, from English to Russian, and finally back again into English. A list of the versions of all the chapters, together with their dates of publication, is given in Appendix C.

In considering these versions, it should be said at the outset that there are important, if obvious, differences between the re-working of an autobiography and the reworking of a piece of imaginative writing. A new version of a work of fiction refers to the first literary expression of that fiction. However, in rewriting an autobiography the writer can refer not only to the first written expression of his reminiscences, but to hitherto unformulated memories, his own and other people's. A new version furnishes the opportunity to correct erroneous facts and to fill in gaps in the narrative, as well as to swell that narrative with more information and more remembered detail.

In his Forewords to *DB* and *SM*, as well as in the Bibliographical Note to *Nabokov's Dozen*, Nabokov emphasizes his desire for greater accuracy in the successive editions. Between the Russian version and E3 came his return to Europe and with it the opportunity to consult many of his relatives. This resulted in the correction of several details of date and circumstance and also brought to light new information relating to the past history of his family and to people referred to in the memoir. All this he incorporated in *Speak, Memory*. Nabokov refers, too, in his Foreword to *SM*, to the tremendous effort of memory he made when preparing both the Russian and the final English versions—an effort which was

---

[1] In his Bibliographical Note to *Nabokov's Dozen*, Nabokov does, however, mention making certain changes to *Mademoiselle O* when he incorporated it into *CE*. See also Author's Note to *CE*.

[2] Only one chapter of *CE* is identical with its journal edition, bar punctuation and paragraphing. This is Chapter 13. Another one, Chapter 14, is altered only in two points of vocabulary and one small point of detail. These two stories, it will be noted, were published in 1951, very shortly before *CE*.

sometimes rewarded by a more complete recall of his past. He says this of his preparation of *DB*: 'I discovered that sometimes, by means of intense concentration, the neutral smudge might be forced to come into beautiful focus so that the sudden view could be identified, and the anonymous servant named' (*SM*, p. 12). It is interesting to note that it is *DB*, and not *SM*, which has the greater increase in remembered details of this kind. Although Nabokov gives a good deal more information in *SM*, he adds comparatively few new 'spontaneous' memories. This lends support to the hypothesis that it is the reversion to Russian, the language in which these memories were originally experienced, which prompts Nabokov's recall of his past. Here language can be seen assuming a compositional role.

Another feature which distinguishes the hybrid genre of autobiography from fiction is that time here is not just a vehicle for artistic development; it is also in the very real sense historical time. The fifteen or more years which separate the first and final versions of the chapters bring many changes in the circumstances of the author and of some of the people he is describing. Some people mentioned in the memoir have died in the interval; this has to be recorded. Nabokov himself, when he writes *SM*, has left America and moved back to Europe. More important, he has acquired fame as a writer. Whilst he remained a relatively unknown writer, in the 1940s and early 1950s, the reminiscences were chiefly notable as memoirs, as a representative account of the life of one Russian intellectual before and after the Revolution. But today's reader, knowing *of* him, is doubly interested to read *about* him. Thus, in *SM* the focus shifts from memoir to autobiography; the writer's family history, his hobbies, his writing habits, even his insomnia and his dreams are all good copy. In this respect, *DB* again stands outside the development of the successive English versions. Nabokov had already established a reputation as the most significant young writer of the emigration by the novels and short stories which he wrote in Europe before the war. This Russian version of the Autobiography, therefore, written before Nabokov became well known as an American writer, already contains a considerable amount of personal detail.

It is not proposed to go into any detail here about these strictly 'autobiographical' changes made in the successive versions, interesting as some of the examples are. The main concern of this chapter is to examine how Nabokov, even in his Autobiography, continues to function as a creative writer. Many of the changes which he introduces are dictated by literary and not by autobiographical considerations, and as such have close similarities to his practice in reworkings of his fiction. There are certain features of the reworkings, however, which can be seen to perform both a literary and an autobiographical function. These will be considered first.

One such feature is the inclusion of a great many more dates in later versions. While these references to historical time clearly reflect Nabokov's desire for greater precision and accuracy, at the same time they provide a framework for the description of events and help to bind the succession of chapters into a cohesive whole. Here they can be said to have a structural role. It was seen earlier in Chapter 6 (pp. 121-2) that this type of change coincides with Nabokov's practice in translations of much of his fiction. Another feature of this kind is the greater attention which is focused in later versions on the incidental characters who appear in the margins of the narrative—in particular, the servants of the Nabokov household. Although servants are alluded to in E1 and E2, they are often not mentioned by name. In *DB*, Nabokov provides names for many of these minor characters and fills out their characterization with more descriptive detail and anecdote. E3 incorporates many, but not all, of these additions, and adds several new details. In *DB* and E3 Nabokov also introduces cross-references in the text in an attempt to link the recurrent appearances of each servant. This gives a greater coherence to the characterization. In consequence, the servants cease to be just shadowy presences and anonymous stage hands; some of them acquire individuality and personality. They become little miniatures. This point is well illustrated by Nabokov's treatment of Ustin, the janitor of the St. Petersburg house.

Ustin makes only two appearances in the first two English versions—in Chapter 6 and in Chapter 9. The first appearance is in the country, at Vyra. There he catches a beautiful Swallowtail butterfly for the young Nabokov. The second appearance is in St. Petersburg, where he is described sharpening pencils for committee meetings held in the Nabokovs' town house. It is also mentioned that later the family learned that he had 'got in touch with the Tsar's secret police'. In E1 his name is given only once: 'Justin, an agile footman'. In E2, he is not named at either appearance, and no connection is made between the two occasions. In *DB*, by contrast, Ustin makes four major appearances. The two episodes already described are retained, but circumstantial details are added. In Chapter 6, Nabokov comments on how unusual it was for Ustin to be with the family at the country home, but he cannot recall how he came to be there:

> тот самый Устин, который был швейцаром у нас в Петербурге, но почему-то оказался тем летом в Выре... (p. 112)

In Chapter 9, Nabokov mentions that Ustin had a wife, a fat Estonian woman (pp. 171–2). In Chapter 11, Ustin makes a further appearance (Chapter 12 in E3). Here Nabokov tells how, when he played truant from school, he would bribe the janitor to say that he was unwell (pp. 202–3). Earlier, in Chapter 4, in the description of the layout of the St. Petersburg house, Nabokov adds a reference to Ustin's treachery in 1917, when he led representatives of the Soviets to the room where Mme Nabokov's jewels were kept hidden (p. 77). This piece of information is retained in E3. However, Nabokov places it not in Chapter 4, but, more appropriately, in Chapter 9, following the account of Ustin's dealings with the secret police. In this chapter of E3, Nabokov also explains why Ustin had spent the summer of 1906 at Vyra: he had been engaged to spy on Nabokov's father, and had accordingly asked to be taken with him to the country as an extra footman (*SM*, p. 187). The sinister side of Ustin's character is thereby amplified and given continuity. Having remembered this detail Nabokov can emend the earlier reference made in Chapter 6 of *DB*: 'Agile Ustin, our town-house janitor, who for a comic reason (explained elsewhere) happened to be that summer in the country with us' (*SM*, p. 120). He also points a thematic connection between Ustin's catching of the Swallowtail in 1906, and his theft of the jewels, eleven years later:

> and it was he, omnipresent Ustin, who in the winter of 1917–18 heroically led representatives of the victorious Soviets . . . to the niche in the wall, to the tiaras of colored fire, which formed an adequate recompense for the Swallowtail he had once caught for me. (*SM*, Chapter 9, pp. 187–8)

Finally, in E3 Nabokov elaborates upon the physical description of Ustin and his family which he had given in *DB*. He mentions not just the wife, but two young children—twins. Compare:

Этот не раз мной упомянутый Устин казался — как столь многие члены нашей многочисленной челяди — примерным старым слугой, балагуром и добряком; женат он был на толстой эстонке, которая с пресмешным отрывистым шипом звала его из подвальной квартирки («Устя! Устя!»), откуда тепло пахло курицей.   (p. 171)

For years he had been the tritest type of 'faithful retainer' imaginable, full of quaint wit and wisdom, with a dashing way of smoothing out, right and left, his mustache with two fingers, and a slight fried-fish smell always hanging about him: it originated in his mysterious basement quarters, where he had an obese wife and twins—a schoolboy of my age and a haunting, sloppy little aurora with a blue squint and coppery locks . . .   (*SM*, p. 187)

It will be clear from this illustration that memory plays an active role in the additions made in *DB* and *SM*. But not only memory: Nabokov artistically unifies Ustin's various appearances to constitute a finished portrait. This feature of the Autobiography is reminiscent of the English translation of *KQKn*, where Nabokov breathes life into incidental characters who hover on the fringe of the main narrative. It is also reminiscent of *Ada*, the novel which follows *SM* and *KQKn*, in which there is such a proliferation of minor characters, many of whom are servants.

Apart from instances such as those just described, where the intentions of Nabokov the autobiographer overlap with his intentions as an artist, there are other cases of reworking which clearly have an exclusively 'literary' function. There are, first of all, the structural changes which Nabokov makes when incorporating the fifteen separate short stories into the larger structural unit of a book. Nabokov states in his Foreword to *SM* that although the chapters had been composed in erratic sequence, 'they had been neatly filling numbered gaps in my mind which followed the present order of chapters. That order had been established in 1936' (p. 10). Even so, in preparing *CE*, Nabokov did find it necessary to make several structural adjustments, and this process continues in *DB* and *SM*. The larger context of the book entails the deletion of some redundant explanations. For example, in E1, when describing his schooldays, he writes:

They accused me of not conforming to my surroundings, of 'showing off' (mainly by peppering my Russian papers with English and French terms, which came naturally to me, as I had been tutored in those languages) . . . (*My Russian Education*, p. 31)

In E2 (Chapter 9) Nabokov omits the final phrase in this sentence, since Chapters 4 and 5 have already described his early English and French education. Some inconsistencies of detail also have to be corrected. For instance, in *My English Education* Nabokov states that he composed his first poem in one of the lavatories at Vyra. This does not tally with the evidence of a later story, *First Poem*, and accordingly, when the two stories are included in *CE*, the statement is changed. Compare:

and it was there that I composed my first poem. (*My English Education*, p. 26)

and it was there that, later, I used to compose my youthful verse. (*CE*, p. 51)

A good deal of the material is rearranged; details and descriptions are placed in a more fitting context. One interesting example of rearrangement of material is the description of his father catching a rare butterfly. This is first included in *DB*, in Chapter 6, quite appropriately, when Nabokov is relating how it was only his parents who really understood his passion for lepidoptery (*DB*, p. 119). However, in *SM* Nabokov includes it in Chapter 9, in a passage evoking the fear he had felt as a schoolboy when his father was involved in a duel (*SM*, pp. 192–3). There Nabokov speaks of the tender friendship which underlay his respect for his father and recalls some cherished memories. The butterfly episode is one of these. In this context, it functions not just as an anecdote, as it does in *DB*—it has a strong emotional impact.

Successive reworkings of the Autobiography also establish a system of cross-references inside the book—links between the various appearances of characters—links, too, with past and future events. *SM* takes this process so far as to provide an index of names and principal themes. In *DB*, he already introduces a number of thematic pointers. In his Foreword to this edition he makes the following statement of his intentions regarding his memoir:

Ее цель — описать прошлое с предельной точностью и отыскать в нем полнозначные очертания, а именно: развитие и повторение тайных тем в явной судьбе. Я попытался дать Мнемозине не только волю, но и закон. (p. 7)

Underlying many of the revisions is Nabokov's evident intention to reveal the pattern behind his life, the shape of his destiny. He uses the motif of the butterfly in this way as a unifying link. His love of lepidoptery dates back to his early childhood in Russia. It is an interest which he has pursued throughout his adult life, in the many different countries where he has taken up residence: Germany, England, France, America, and Switzerland. References to butterflies are multiplied in successive editions of the Autobiography. In *CE*, Chapter 12, he inserts three new references to butterflies into his description of his love affair with Tamara. There he even turns the butterfly into a symbol of this short-lived love when he speaks of 'a Camberwell Beauty, exactly as old as our romance, sunning its bruised black wings . . . on the back of a bench in Alexandrovski garden' (*CE*, p. 174; see also pp. 168, 182). This anticipates the image which concludes all English versions of Chapter 12: a comparison of Tamara's lost letters to 'bewildered butterflies set loose in an alien zone, at the wrong altitude, among an unfamiliar flora' (*SM*, p. 251).[1] In *DB* he draws an explicit thematic connection between the first catches which he makes at Vyra and his discovery of a new species of butterfly in Utah, 1943 (p. 128). This link is retained in *SM*, where the 'butterfly chapter', Chapter 6, is also considerably expanded. The thematic importance which Nabokov accords to butterflies in his autobiography helps explain the many references to lepidoptera in his fiction. In his later life it becomes a personal motif, and it is significant that it is his later fiction and his recent translations of his novels which contain the greater proportion of allusions.[2]

Other thematic links which Nabokov forges in *DB* and *SM* extend beyond Nabokov's own life-span back into history. In *SM* he links his discovery of the new species of butterfly with the discovery of a river made by his great-grandfather in the early nineteenth century:

> One of these, Nabokov's Pug . . ., which I boxed one night in 1943 . . . in Utah, fits most philosophically into the thematic spiral that began in a wood on the Oredezh around 1910—or perhaps

---

[1] *DB* does not have this image.

[2] *KQKn* contains several added references to butterflies. Butterflies abound in *Ada*: the heroine is a collector. For references to butterflies in *Lolita*, see Appel, *The Annotated Lolita*, p. 8 n. 1.

even earlier, on that Nova Zemblan river a century and a half ago.
(*SM*, p. 126. See also Chapter 3, p. 52)

He also draws a parallel between the occasion in 1917 when
Kerensky asked Nabokov senior to lend him a 'getaway' car
and the Varennes episode of 1791, when an ancestor lent Louis
XVI and family her carriage in which to escape from Paris across
the frontier. The parallel is hinted at in *DB*, where Nabokov first
describes these two episodes (Chapter 3, p. 47; Chapter 9, pp. 166,
167). In *SM*, the two episodes are reworked and the connection
made more explicit:

> and if I treasure the recollection of that request . . ., it is only from
> a compositional viewpoint—because of the amusing thematic echo
> of Christina von Korff's part in the Varennes episode of 1791.
> (*SM*, p. 183. See also p. 56)

This restructuring which can be discerned in the main framework of the Autobiography is active also in the smaller unit of the
individual chapter. A comparison of the five successive versions of
Chapter 5—the chapter devoted to Nabokov's French governess—
provides a fairly representative illustration of this 'unit' reworking.

MADEMOISELLE O

The general development from the original French version is
towards the replacement of the discursive, the descriptive, the
anecdotal by the concise, the tightly structured. The sequence of
events is preserved in broad outline, but successive versions
bring many deletions and rearrangements of material. The main
structural changes are completed by E2, with subsequent modifications in *DB* and E3.

The French version is not divided into sections. It begins with
Mademoiselle's arrival in Russia and ends with her departure to
Switzerland; then, appended as an epilogue, is the account of
Nabokov's visit to her in Switzerland ten years later. In E2 and
following versions Nabokov deepens the awareness of historical
time. More dates are added and Mademoiselle's stay is placed in
a historical framework between the 1905 Revolution and the First
World War. The seven years of her stay are evoked in the French
version with a gentle flow of associations which prompt description and anecdote. In the revisions Nabokov imposes a more rigid

structural pattern on these reminiscences. He first of all introduces sectional divisions. In E1 five sections are made; E2 and E3
have seven, while DB has eight. As a result, several discursive link
passages are eliminated. One link passage is lost by the division
made in E1 between the description of winter morning drives in
St. Petersburg and the account of Mademoiselle's hypersensitivity
(E1, Sections 3/4; E2, E3, Sections 6/7). In the French version
Nabokov had led on from an account of Mademoiselle's exaggerated fears whenever the driver had been drinking, to a general
comment on the fun made of her overdramatization, and thus to
an account of her sensitivity to mockery in general:

> Il arriva deux ou trois fois que le cocher avait bu et j'entends
> Mademoiselle, sitôt rentrée de la promenade, qui raconte à ma
> mère: «Figurez-vous mon horreur, Madame, quand je vis l'homme
> vaciller sur son siège, j'étais glacée d'effroi, je pressais les enfants
> contre moi, contre mon pauvre corps pantelant, — que pouvais-je
> de plus, Madame?» Cette manière un peu extravagante de s'ex-
> primer eut vite fait de devenir un divertissement gratuit pour nous,
> les enfants, car nous étions d'une cruauté raffinée et allègre qui
> tournait brusquement à une sorte de compassion féroce, lorsque
> apparaissaient les ravages que nous avions causés. (MO, p. 163)

In omitting this link passage, Nabokov does not sacrifice coherence.
He replaces this link with another, implicit one. In E1 he rearranges the description of the morning drives and places the
detail of the hat Mademoiselle is wearing—an elaborate affair,
decorated with an exotic bird—not in the middle of the description
as it is in the French, but at the end (see E1, p. 73; compare MO,
p. 162). And in E2, E3, and DB it is no longer just the wing of
the mock bird but a bloodshot eye which attracts his attention.
Compare:

> L'aile moirée d'un oiseau exotique au chapeau de Mademoiselle...
> (MO, p. 162)

> the ruffled exotic bird with one bloodshot eye on Mademoiselle's
> hat. (CE, p. 72; SM, p. 111)

The prominence which is given to this detail in the later versions
lends it something of the value of a symbol—a symbol of Mademoiselle's pathetic vulnerability. It anticipates the comparison
made in the epilogue between Mademoiselle and an aged swan:
'a large uncouth, dodo-like creature' (See SM, pp. 116–17),

and, therefore, provides a fitting preface to an account of her sensibility.

Corresponding roughly to the divisions of the sections, Nabokov contrives an alternation of interior and outdoor scenes combined with a rotation of seasons. This change is virtually completed by E2. In E2 the first section is set out of doors and describes Mademoiselle's arrival in winter. In Section 2 the scene changes to an interior, the same day. Section 3 describes an incident which took place a day or so later; it is still winter, but the setting is once more out of doors. This episode, involving the Great Dane, is the only anecdote which is substantially expanded in the English and Russian versions. (It is alluded to briefly in the French version, p. 158.) It replaces a description of Nabokov's annoyance when Mademoiselle told him off for drinking cold milk on hot days (*MO*, p. 155). Both these anecdotes are meant to illustrate the children's resentment at the changes which the new governess brought in their daily routine. However, the Great Dane episode, which took place very shortly after Mademoiselle's arrival, furnishes a more appropriate illustration of this than the milk-drinking episode which obviously took place in summer. Section 4 of E2 follows with an interior scene. Section 5 shifts to summer and readings outside on the veranda. In the same section Nabokov moves on to a description of interior scenes and winter evenings. This is followed by the description of spring drives in the streets of St. Petersburg. *SM* adds here: 'in another month we shall return to the country' (p. 111). This prepares the reader for the change of setting in Section 6. It is early summer in the country and lilies of the valley are in bloom.[1]

A further change which Nabokov makes to the French version is to dispense with the dramatic representation of the events leading up to Mademoiselle's departure. In *MO* her departure is shown to be the direct consequence of her feud with the new tutor Pétrov (called Orlov in E1; Lenski in subsequent versions). This feud is developed through a succession of incidents, beginning with an occasion when Pétrov drinks from the finger-bowls, and ending when Mademoiselle finds Pétrov in her room and accuses him of being a thief (*MO*, pp. 168–70). The English and Russian versions all mention Mademoiselle's dislike of the tutor, but they do not make this the only reason for her leaving the household. Instead,

[1] In *DB*, Nabokov makes two sections out of E2, Section 5.

her departure takes its natural place in the inevitable passing of time. The children are growing up; they are outgrowing their governess. When Mademoiselle's room is first described, it is situated next door to Nabokov's own bedroom: 'Although next to ours, when we were small, it did not seem to belong to our pleasant, well-aired home.' (See *SM*, pp. 107, 108–9. This detail is in all versions.) Later, after the tutor's arrival, E1 and all subsequent versions mention that her room was no longer next to the children's: ' "The brute! The cad! The Nihilist!" she sobbed later in her room —which was no longer next to ours though still on the same floor' (E1, p. 72). And when Nabokov describes the long letters of resignation Mademoiselle wrote to his mother the room is even further away—it is by this stage 'remote': 'From her remote room she would write a sixteen-page letter to my mother' (E1, p. 72). In *DB*, this detail is given even greater prominence:

> Из глубины как бы все удалявшейся комнаты своей, она писала матери письма на шестнадцати страницах... (p. 107)

Here, the increased distance of Mademoiselle's room becomes symbolic of her alienation from the household. Nabokov has again substituted an implicit device for explicit description. His intention is to convey a representative synthesized 'memory-picture' rather than incidental reminiscences. Thus, a long anecdote of the times when Mademoiselle was stranded in the lift (*MO*, pp. 163–4) is telescoped in E1 and following English versions into a parenthesis:

> If Orlov happened to come tripping downstairs while, with an asthmatic pause after every ten steps or so, she was working her way up (for the little hydraulic elevator would constantly, and rather insultingly too, refuse to function), Mademoiselle maintained that he had viciously bumped into her . . . (E1, p. 72)

And the lengthy account of Mademoiselle's fondness for the French Classics is also telescoped into two passing allusions: to Jézabel in *Athalie* and to Madame de Rambouillet. (E1, pp. 70, 72. See *SM*, pp. 108, 114; and compare *MO*, pp. 167–8.)

This structural development is clearly tied up with a change of perspective in Nabokov's description of his childhood. In later versions he takes a longer look at his past. At the same time as he abandons the anecdotal mode of narration he also ceases to describe his childhood through the eyes of a child. The little world of crimes and punishments fades: the smacks and pensums which Mademoiselle handed out assume less prominence. There is no longer any reference to the fun the children poked at her name, or to the way Nabokov would evade heavy reading duty by choosing the confidante's role in the French tragedies. In later versions Nabokov assumes more often the distance of adult judgement. He tends to analyse, to appraise, and not merely to describe. Compare the criticism in the following passages:

> Il faut bien noter que, malgré l'emphase de son langage et la naïveté de ses idées, le français de Mademoiselle était divin. (*MO*, p. 166)

> And, really, her French was so lovely! Ought one to have minded the shallowness of her culture, the bitterness of her temper, the banality of her mind, when that pearly language of hers purled and scintillated, as innocent of sense as the alliterative sins of Racine's pious verse? (*SM*, p. 113)

It is in the English versions that Nabokov exposes the inaccuracy of Mademoiselle's sentimental recollections of Russia. The parenthetical comments in the following extract are all new in the English version:

> 'Ah', she sighed, 'didn't we love each other! Those good old days in the château! The dead wax doll we once buried under the oak! (No—a golliwog in red pants!) And that time you ran away and left me stumbling and howling in the depths of the forest! (The grove just beyond the old tennis court!) My, what a spanking you bad boys got! (Not I—*I* managed to escape and find Mother!) And the Princess, your aunt, whom you struck with your little first because she had been rude to me! (I don't remember.) And the way you whispered to me all your childish troubles! (Never!) And the cozy nook in my room where you loved to snuggle because you felt so warm and secure!' (E1, p. 70. See, *SM*, p. 107; compare *MO*, p. 158)

This change in perspective cannot but affect the portrait of Mademoiselle herself. The over-all effect of these changes is to make the characterization noticeably less sympathetic.

It must be added, however, that here *DB* stands slightly apart from the linear E1–E2–E3 development. There is a reappearance of anecdote. Some descriptions, the description of the lift for example, are partially restored (p. 107) and more are added. It could be inferred that the renewed impulse of memory brought by the change of language is perhaps the cause. Whilst this is of course an intangible, it is significant that anecdotal additions in *DB* often follow passages of exclusively Russian reference. There is, for example, the opening of Section 7 (Section 6 in E2 and E3), where Nabokov expands the 'uncles and aunts and cousins' into a roll-call of relatives, giving their names and the places from where they have come. These names were presumably considered superfluous for an English edition and are not carried over into E3. However, the roll-call is followed in *DB* by many more vivid details: there is Vasily Martynovich adjusting his white silk tie in the mirrors; cornflowers appear tied with a scarlet ribbon, and Nabokov adds that lilies of the valley and cornflowers were his mother and father's favourite flowers. And once the 'poor relative', Nadezhda Il'inichna, is allowed a name, she acquires a personality, she can move. There follows the delightful description of her walking towards Mademoiselle along the paths of the Vyra grounds (*DB*, pp. 103–4).

Nabokov's reworking of his Autobiography affects style as well as structure, and here too the changes made are characteristic of changes made in his versions of fiction. *Mademoiselle O* will again serve as a representative example.

In style there is a marked development through the English versions, independently of *DB*. On many occasions, irrespective of any modifications in the Russian version, E3 reverts to E2. There is in the English versions an increase in the examples of alliteration. E1 introduces a good number. Considering merely the physical description of Mademoiselle herself, E1 has 'the jelly of her jowl quaking' (p. 67), where the French speaks of *le tremblotement de ses bajoues*; 'prodigious posterior' (p. 67), where the French is *sa croupe monstrueuse*; 'stupendous and sterile bosom' (p. 69) where the French is *son sein monstrueux et infécond*; and 'Buddha-like bulk' (p. 69), instead of *tout son ensemble ample et immobile*. More instances are worked into *CE*. For example,

1. E1: as the heavy sleigh is wrenched out of its world of steel, fur, flesh, to enter a frictionless medium where it skims along a ghostly road that it seems barely to touch. (p. 67)

E2 substitutes 'spectral' for 'ghostly', thus reinforcing the alliteration on 's'.

2. E1: I can hear and see Orlov unflinchingly going on with his soup . . . (p. 72)

E2: I can hear and see Lenski Frenchlessly and unflinchingly (= E3) going on with his soup . . . (*SM*, p. 114)

Examples of the same process are still to be found in E3. There, talking of Mademoiselle's photograph, Nabokov replaces 'noble frame' by 'fancy frame' (*SM*, p. 108). And in this sentence: '. . . causing some little glass object which had been secretly sharing my vigil, to tinkle in dismay on the shelf' (E1), Nabokov changes 'tinkle' to 'vibrate', thus contriving an alliteration on 'v' (see *SM*, p. 110).

The imagery is also elaborated in successive English versions. A number of images are added to the description of Mademoiselle: for example, 'froggy gloss' (E1), 'dodo-like creature' (E2), 'rock of grim permanence' (E2). It is not quantitatively, though, that this development is significant. The number of images added after E1 is, in fact, minimal. It is qualitatively, in the modification made to existing images, that this development is most apparent. It is rare to find a progressive elaboration through all three English versions, but reworkings occur with practically equal frequency in E2 and E3. One example of a modification made in E2 occurs in the description of the view through the different coloured panes of glass on the veranda. E1 has: 'The yellow one led to Cathay and tea-colored vistas' (p. 70). In E2 this 'tea' image becomes implicit, and more effective: 'The yellow created an amber world infused with an extra strong brew of sunshine' (*CE*, p. 68; *SM*, p. 106). The modifications made in E3 tend to be more fanciful and far-fetched. There is, for instance, Nabokov's description of the pictures he drew with his green pencil. Compare:

MO: Le vert qui crée, en tourbillonnant, un arbre ébouriffé... (p. 154)

E2: The green one, by a mere whirl of the wrist, could be made to produce a ruffled tree, or the chimney smoke of a house where spinach was cooking. (*CE*, p. 62. This is practically identical with E1.)

E3: The green one, by a mere whirl of the wrist, could be made to produce a ruffled tree, or the eddy left by a submerged crocodile. (*SM*, p. 101)

The stylistic elaboration which the English versions undergo compensates, in some measure, for the loss of vivid incidental detail. Whilst in the French version anecdote and quotation combine to form a vivid visual and auditive compound, the English versions substitute the auditive and the visual effects of alliteration and imagery.

   DB, at a stage when the major alterations in structure and subject matter have already taken place, loses a significant number of the English images and verbal effects. This version does, however, introduce some new images, not one of which goes forward into E3. A number of these images have specifically Russian reference. There is, for instance, the comparison of Zakhar to Peter the Great (p. 87); the resemblance of the porcelain monkey to A. F. Koni (p. 89); the description of Mademoiselle's pince-nez as 'Chekhovian' (p. 95). See also this description of Mademoiselle and Nadezhda Il'inichna:

> они очень напоминали те два пузатых электрических вагона, которые так однообразно и невозмутимо расходились посреди ледяной пустыни Невы.   (p. 104)

Most of the other images which Nabokov adds are visual images and some can conceivably be attributed to a renewed stimulus of memory.

   There are two general points arising out of this discussion of *MO* which deserve emphasis. The Russian version of this chapter stands in a much less close relation to the English versions than do Nabokov's translations of fiction (English and Russian) to their originals. In structure as well as in style *DB* exhibits many independent features. A reason for this has been suggested: a Russian childhood is perhaps more completely evoked in the language in which it was lived—in Russian. Nabokov himself provides an illuminating commentary on this point in the Foreword to *DB*, where he speaks of the trouble he had in writing *CE*:

> Книга «Conclusive Evidence» писалась долго (1946—1950), с особенно мучительным трудом, ибо память была настроена на один лад — музыкально недоговоренный, русский, — а навязывался ей другой лад, английский и обстоятельный. (p. 8)

A second point concerns the development of the English versions. It has been seen that the restructuring and the lengthening of perspective affected the characterization of the French governess. The final portrait in *SM* is more telling perhaps, more humorous, but less sympathetic, less endearing. Such a development certainly coincides with Nabokov's practice elsewhere in some revisions of his fiction. However, it would be wrong to apply this judgement to the Autobiography as a whole. The 'longer look' which Nabokov takes of his past in later versions sometimes, as here, makes for a more critical, detached, and humorous appraisal of character and event. But, at the same time, this lengthening of perspective brings with it more understanding and more nostalgia. Compare, for example, these passages from Chapter 12. Nabokov is describing his nocturnal rendezvous with Tamara. The version in *SM* is more stylized, but also more nostalgic.

E1: As I reached the top, my pale light would flit across a six-pillared white portico at the back of my uncle's silent, shuttered house. . . . I would put out my lamp and go up the slippery steps. In the restless night, centenary limes that surrounded the house would creak and heave. (*Tamara*, p. 35)

E3: As I reached the top, my livid light flitted across the six-pillared white portico at the back of my uncle's mute, shuttered manor— *as mute and shuttered as it may be today, half a century later.* . . . I would put out my lamp and grope my way toward her. *One is moved to speak more eloquently about these things, about many other things that one always hopes might survive captivity in the zoo of words* —but the ancient limes crowding close to the house drown Mnemosyne's monologue with their creaking and heaving in the restless night. (*SM*, p. 233)[1]

In the reworkings of the Autobiography an increase in sentiment coexists with an increase in humour and critical distance. In Nabokov's revisions of his fiction, sentiment does not play an active part. Nabokov does not increase the sentiment when revising his more 'sympathetic' works, he merely refrains from introducing a greater measure of irony and detachment. This active intrusion of personal feeling is yet another instance where the dictates of autobiography naturally differ from the dictates of imaginative writing.

The principal concern here, however, has been to emphasize the many points of similarity between the development of Nabokov's

---

[1] My italics.

autobiography and the development of his fiction. This fact in itself is not particularly unusual or remarkable. Autobiography, though perhaps not a 'pure' literary genre, none the less undoubtedly possesses many 'literary' features. But with Nabokov the interrelation of fact and fiction is more complex. He is a writer who has made extensive use of autobiographical experience in his fiction. Very many other writers have, of course, done this; and generally it may indeed be said that imaginative writing is to a very large extent founded upon memory—upon conscious or unconscious recollections from a writer's past experience.[1] But what is extremely rare is for an author to present his personal experience— the *same* personal experience—to his public in both forms: as fiction and as autobiography. This Nabokov has done. There are many sections in the Autobiography which adhere very closely to descriptions in his early Russian fiction. Moreover, in many cases, despite the fictional disguise, it is the earlier version which seems to contain a greater measure of 'raw' experience. Nabokov himself endorses this view in respect of *Mashen'ka*, his first novel:

> I am fascinated by the fact that despite the superimposed inventions (such as the fight with the village rowdy or the tryst in the anonymous town among the glowworms) a headier extract of personal reality is contained in the romantization than in the autobiographer's scrupulously faithful account. At first I wondered how that could be, how the thrill and the perfume could have survived the exigency of the plot and the ostentation of fictional characters . . . , especially as I could not believe that a stylish imitation should be able to vie with plain truth. But the explanation is really quite simple: in terms of years, Ganin was three times closer to his past than I was to mine in *Speak, Memory*.[2]

In a sense, therefore, it is possible to view parts of the first English edition of the Autobiography as a revision, in a different language, of a yet earlier fictional version. Nabokov himself disclaims consulting his early works of fiction when writing autobiography. In his Foreword to *Mary* he writes: 'I had not consulted *Mashenka* when writing Chapter Twelve of the autobiography a quarter of a century later.'[2] This does not, however, preclude the

---

[1] Nabokov has made this point himself in interview: 'I would say that imagination is a form of memory. Down, Plato, down, good dog. An image depends on the power of association, and association is supplied and prompted by memory.' 'An Interview with Vladimir Nabokov', conducted by Appel, 1967.

[2] *Mary*, p. xii.

possibility of an *unconscious* recollection of an earlier piece of writing, and all the evidence points to this. In the Autobiography Nabokov strips away the fictional trappings and adds a good deal more circumstantial detail. At the same time, he introduces a greater sense of perspective and judgement and restructures, restyles the narrative. The alterations reflect maturity not just in years, but also in literary technique and in style. Successive versions carry this process of artistic synthesis still further, until finally some of the very same themes re-emerge in his recent fiction. The most complete illustration of Nabokov's reuse of the same material in fiction and in autobiography is the description of his teenage affair with Tamara.

TAMARA

This love-affair is described in Chapter 12 of the Autobiography, and forms the main subject, too, of Nabokov's first Russian novel, *Mashen'ka*. But the first literary expression of the theme is contained in the poems which he wrote at the time of the affair, in 1915–16. The sixty-eight poems published in St. Petersburg in spring 1916 are almost all love poems 'to her, for her, about her', to quote Nabokov's own words in *Speak, Memory*.[1] The tone of the whole collection is intensely personal, the emotion unrelieved by any touches of humour. The poems are not arranged in any very definite order but it is possible to trace a pattern of development running through the collection. The sequence of poems reflects the successive stages of the relationship and follows, roughly, the progression of the seasons: summer and autumn in the country, winter in St. Petersburg, spring the following year. The intense happiness expressed in some of the initial poems is succeeded by a mood of increasing uncertainty and doubt, which in turn gives way to

---

[1] p. 237. Nabokov is very critical of these poems. In *SM* he speaks of them as 'juvenile stuff, quite devoid of merit', and in an interview which appeared in *Vogue* in 1969, he said: 'The versification is fair, the lack of originality complete.' He has never reissued the collection which was privately published in a limited edition of 500 numbered copies. One or two of the poems have, however, appeared in English translation. Copies of this Russian edition are rare, though not perhaps as inaccessible as Nabokov would have his readers believe. The copy which exists in the Lenin Library in Moscow is listed in the main catalogue and was not difficult to obtain. See *SM*: 'a copy . . . still exists, alas, in the 'closed stacks' of the Lenin Library, Moscow' (p. 238). Field lists only sixty-seven poems in this collection. He omits the thirty-ninth poem: *Gore segodnya i glubzhe i proshche*. See *Nabokov: a Bibliography*, Item 0002.

despair and regret as the poet realizes the love is over, lost. Underlying the development of the poet's feeling, there is a recurrent
elegiac note which sounds throughout the collection. The poet,
even at an early stage in the relationship, speaks of sadness and
parting and looks back on the first moments of happiness, question-
ing whether it will be possible to recapture that intensity of bliss.
In the later poems in the collection, this question deepens into a
certainty, and the poet then evokes the first summer with all the
pathos of lost happiness. The retrospective distance which
Nabokov adopts here in many of these poems is conventional and
romantic. It is none the less significant that he retains the retrospective mode of narration in all subsequent versions of the theme,
not only in the Autobiography, but also in *Mashen'ka* and in *Ada*.
It is because these poems set a literary precedent for the manner of
narration in the prose accounts which follow that space has been
given to them here.

It is *Mashen'ka* which most closely resembles the autobiographical account. The novel is set in Berlin in a Russian *émigré*
boarding-house. One of the lodgers, Alfyorov, has learnt that his
wife has obtained an exit visa and will shortly be arriving from
Russia to join him. Ganin, a fellow lodger and the hero of the
novel, discovers that Alfyorov's wife is the same Mashen'ka with
whom he had been in love before the Revolution. The news that
she is coming reawakens Ganin's affection for her and in the next
few days he succeeds in reliving in memory the whole course of
their relationship. He does this so completely, in fact, that on the
morning when Mashen'ka's train is due to arrive in Berlin he
abandons his plan of abducting her from her husband. He realizes
that the act of memory has fulfilled all the possibilities that this
love contained for him. It is now well and truly over. Here the
novel ends.

In this novel as in the Autobiography it is memory which dictates the description of this early love. The account itself tallies
with the autobiographical account not only in the main outline, but
in many points of circumstance and detail. The historical setting
corresponds exactly, though many fewer dates are given in the
novel. The country setting of the action is clearly recognizable
as the Nabokov and Rukavishnikov estates. The near-by village
where Mashen'ka's parents have a villa is called Voskresenskoe
(compare Rozhestveno in the Autobiography), whilst the name of

the local river, the Oredezh, remains unchanged. The protagonists are the same age in both accounts, and physically Mashen'ka very closely resembles Tamara. The sequence of events and the shifts of locality are practically identical. Five stages of the relationship are described: (1) an idyllic summer in the country; (2) a less satisfactory winter in St. Petersburg; (3) a second summer in the country; (4) a last meeting in a train the following summer; (5) finally, an exchange of letters, while Nabokov (Ganin) is resident in the Crimea.

There are, however, some clear differences which reflect Nabokov's differing aims in autobiography and fiction. To begin with, the hero, Ganin, cannot be identified completely with Nabokov himself. Ganin wrote no poetry as a young man; Ganin campaigned in the Civil War, while the young Nabokov only dreamed of going off to join the army. The construction of the novel also differs: it is dramatic, and the actions are psychologically motivated. The first summer of the affair progresses in clear stages from Ganin's first glimpse of Mashen'ka (at a concert), to their first meeting (in the pavilion), to the first day spent together (on the river), to Ganin's declaration of love. Then follows a succession of nocturnal rendezvous which culminate in a dramatic incident on the eve of Ganin's departure for St. Petersburg. That night the lovers are surprised by a peeping Tom, the watchman's son, and Ganin has a fight with this intruder. This episode is viewed as a portent of future disaster. The description of the winter in St. Petersburg lays stress on Ganin's increasing sexual frustration, a frustration which leads to his impotence the following summer when Mashen'ka offers herself to him. This is the only meeting between the lovers that second summer and brings the relationship to an end. Ganin believes he has fallen out of love. The final encounter in the train forms a psychological pendant to the previous scene, for it is then that Ganin realizes that he had never really stopped loving Mashen'ka.

The Autobiography abandons both the psychological framework and the dramatic highlights. There is no fight with a voyeur which portends disaster; there is no unhappy tryst which causes the lovers to part. In *Tamara* (E1) Nabokov presents a more natural flow of events, with less emphasis on individual episodes. The first meeting and the final parting in the train are the only two episodes which Nabokov describes—the rest of the narrative is a synthesis of whole periods of time. Nabokov cannot even recall how he parted from Tamara the second summer: 'no matter how I worry the screws of memory, I cannot recall the way Tamara and I parted' (*Tamara*, pp. 36–7). The leisurely undramatic mode of auto-biography can allow for digressions, and Nabokov includes in *Tamara* a description of the journey south with his family and an account of life in the Crimea during the Civil War. Later versions of the Autobiography add a good deal more personal digression. *CE* adds a description of the poems Nabokov wrote about Tamara and a description of the activities of the chauffeur, Tsiganov. *SM* adds a description of the society Nabokov frequented in Yalta.

However, the successive editions of the Autobiography not only increase the autobiographical content—they rework, they comment, they elaborate upon their primary literary source, *Mashen'ka*. When the mature Nabokov looks back on his early production, he sees that in these early works he had covered much of his genuine personal feeling with a layer of superficial romanticism. He perceives this element of romanticism in the poems he wrote at the time and he sees it persisting in his first novel, in *Mashen'ka*. At several points in his autobiographical account Nabokov comments on and criticizes his early literary ventures. In *Tamara* these allusions remain veiled; in later versions they become more explicit. In E2 he adds the discussion of his love poetry, and in *DB* he openly alludes to a piece of literary romanticism contained in *Mashen'ka*. In the novel, the final meeting between the two lovers on the train is followed by a description of the sun setting over peat bogs. Ganin, as he sits down in the compartment, feels that all this has already happened once before:

> и странные мысли приходили в голову, словно все это уже было когда-то, — так вот лежал подперев руками затылок, в сквозной, грохочущей тьме, и так вот мимо окон, шумно и широко, проплывал дымный закат. (p. 114)

In *DB* Nabokov comments on this passage from the novel, pointing out the allusion to Blok which it contains. He speaks of the sunsets which Blok recorded in his diary at the time, and adds:

> Всем известно, какие закаты стояли знаменьями в том году над дымной Россией, и впоследствии, в полуавтобиографической повести, я почувствовал себя вправе связать это с воспоминанием о Тамаре; но тогда мне было не до того; никакая поэзия не могла украсить страдание. (p. 209)

In E2 and E3 the comment is substantially the same, but the allusion to *Mashen'ka* is only implicit:

> It can be proved, I think, by published records that Alexander Blok was even then noting in his diary the very peat smoke I saw, and the wrecked sky. There was later a period in my life when I might have found this relevant to my last glimpse of Tamara . . . but today no alien marginalia can dim the purity of the pain. (*CE*, p. 176; *SM*, p. 241)

Another passage which represents a commentary on *Mashen'ka* is the description of the mountain scenery in the southern Crimea. In the Autobiography Nabokov juxtaposes two perspectives—the perspective of the mature man and the perspective of the youth. He speaks of the exaltation he experienced at this first taste of exile, an exaltation which he concedes was very possibly influenced by Pushkin's romantic lyrics. In E2 and E3 he writes:

> but though some prompting may have come from his [Pushkin's] elegies, I do not think my exaltation was a pose. Thenceforth for several years, until the writing of a novel relieved me of that fertile emotion, the loss of my country was equated for me with the loss of my love. (*CE*, p. 179; *SM*, pp. 244–5)

That novel was, of course, *Mashen'ka* (in *DB*, Nabokov mentions it by name, p. 213), and the romanticism which Nabokov comments upon is the romanticism which persists in *Mashen'ka* itself. The description of the Crimean scenery in *Mashen'ka* resembles closely the description given in the Autobiography, but in the novel it is a piece of subjective impressionism which furnishes the subject of Ganin's first letter to Mashen'ka. This passage from *Mashen'ka* is reproduced in Appendix D, together with the corresponding passage from *SM*.

Nabokov's treatment of the correspondence he conducted with Tamara can also be read as a retrospective commentary on *Mashen'ka*. The letters which Ganin receives from Mashen'ka, his replies, the description of his feelings, are given fully and directly in the novel. There are quotations from five of Mashen'ka's letters, letters filled with jingles, snatches of poetry, and allusions to the past (*Mashen'ka*, pp. 133–9). Nabokov comments on these letters in the Autobiography and acknowledges that *Mashen'ka* is his source: 'Happy is the novelist who manages to preserve an actual love letter that he received when he was young within a work of fiction, embedded in it like a clean bullet in flabby flesh and quite secure there, among spurious lives' (*Tamara*, p. 39). In the English versions, Nabokov gives two short quotations from these letters:

1. 'Why did we feel so cheerful when it rained?' she asked in one of her last letters . . . (*Tamara*, p. 39)

This appears in Mashen'ka's second letter:

«Почему тогда не было грустно в худую погоду?» (*Mashen'ka*, p. 134)

2. 'Where has it gone, all that distant, bright, endearing world?' (Tamara, p. 39)

This quotation is from Mashen'ka's fifth letter:

«Боже мой, где оно, — все это далекое, светлое, милое...» (*Mashen'ka*, p. 139)

(*DB* omits the first quotation, but reproduces the second virtually word for word.[1]) This is all the direct speech given in the Auto-biography. The rest is a synthesized description of Tamara's letters, and an evaluation of their style: 'Tamara's letters were a sustained conjuration of the rural landscape we knew so well. Just how, I can't be sure, but her high-school-girlish prose could evoke with plangent strength every whiff of damp leaf, every autumn-rusted frond of fern in the St. Petersburg countryside' (*Tamara*, p. 39). When placed alongside the texts of the letters given in the novel, this reads as a commentary upon them. But it is a commentary which is noticeably more evocative than the original. Here, Nabokov is condensing and thereby intensifying his earlier account.

This is not the only instance where Nabokov reworks and synthesizes a more circumstantial description given earlier in *Mashen'ka*. Another example is the presentation of his heroine. Mashen'ka is first pointed out to Ganin by a student at a village concert in a barn (p. 69) and it is from this same student that Ganin later learns her name (p. 75). In *Tamara* Nabokov cuts out

---

[1] Nabokov, revising Glenny's English translation of *Mashen'ka*, is careful to make the wording of this quotation correspond exactly to the wording in *SM*. See *Mary*, p. 93: 'Goodness, where has it gone, all that distant, bright endearing . . .' (MG: 'Goodness, where is it now, that dear distant past . . .'). Compare *SM*, p. 249.

the concert and the external agent, the student. Instead, Tamara's arrival on the scene of the action is heralded by her name. The young Nabokov finds it carved or scrawled on trees, benches, and gates at Vyra and on his uncle's estate: 'as if Mother Nature were giving me mysterious advance notices of Tamara's existence' (p. 35). *First Poem*, which becomes Chapter 11 of the Autobiography, contains another advance notice: Nabokov finds the inscription 'Dasha, Tamara and Lena have been here' inside the pavilion of the Vyra park (see *SM*, p. 216). Inscriptions and carvings are mentioned in *Mashen'ka* (at the meeting in the pavilion (p. 87) and on the boating trip (p. 89)), but they do not forewarn Ganin of Mashen'ka's existence. They are only incidental, 'non-functional' details. This new method of introducing his heroine which Nabokov adopts in his Autobiography is unquestionably neater and more evocative. Moreover, Nabokov contrives a unity of place: Tamara appears only in the park, the park which is to be the setting for all their summer meetings.[1]

Aside from this reordering and synthesizing of descriptions, there are a few intriguing instances in later versions of the Autobiography when Nabokov takes up again and elaborates some of the elements which were very much part of the *fictional* framework of *Mashen'ka*. This he does particularly in *SM*. There is, for example, his handling of the theme of voyeurism. In *Mashen'ka* the first hint that the lovers are being watched is given when they find a *khuliganskaya nadpis'* scrawled on the garden table (p. 91). On their last meeting that summer, this peeping Tom is discovered: he is the son of the watchman and a fight develops between him and Ganin:

оба они успели узнать рыжеватые вихры и выпученный рот сына сторожа, зубоскала и бабника лет двадцати, всегда попадавшегося им в аллеях парка.   (p. 105)

---

[1] Nabokov's English novel, *Pnin*, provides an interesting sidelight on this episode of 'first meeting'. In Chapter 7, the narrator (who has certain similarities with Nabokov himself) recalls a performance he attended in a barn on his aunt's estate. It is at this performance that he first sees, and is attracted by, 'a pretty, slender-necked, velvet-eyed girl'. This is Mira Belochkin, Timofey Pnin's lost love. The details and the whole context of this description differ considerably from *Mashen'ka*. Nevertheless, the recurrence of the same elements—the barn, the amateur performance, the first meeting with a girl—lend support to the supposition that perhaps they have a common origin in Nabokov's own experience. See pp. 177-9.

In *Tamara* and E2, as has been noted earlier, this dramatic episode does not figure. The only person who spies on the lovers is Nabokov's tutor, and Nabokov puts a stop to his interference by complaining to his mother (see *Tamara*, p. 35). The Russian version is substantially the same as E1 and E2, except that the tutor's name is given as Volgin,[1] and a new character makes his appearance— Evsey, his uncle's steward. It is he who lets Nabokov know that Volgin is spying on him. In *SM* Evsey gives place to a different servant, Apostolski. He is introduced as follows:

> but in his turn, one day, the peeper was observed by my uncle's purple-nosed old gardener Apostolski (incidentally, a great tumbler of weeding-girls) who very kindly reported it to my mother. (*SM*, pp. 231–2)

And a little later on, Nabokov nicknames him 'Priapostolski' (p. 232). The same version also sees the reappearance of the hooligan from *Mashen'ka*, with a reference to 'village-idiot scrawl':

> I remember the coarse graffiti linking our first names, in strange diminutives, on a certain white gate and, a little apart from that village-idiot scrawl, the adage 'Prudence is the friend of Passion', in a bristly hand well-known to me. (*SM*, p. 232)

(The 'bristly hand' referred to here is obviously that of Nabokov's tutor.) Here autobiography is taking over what had up till then been the sole property of fiction. However, Nabokov's treatment of voyeurism is entirely different. In *Mashen'ka* the peeping Tom is a sinister character and a portent of future unhappiness. In *SM*, voyeurism is treated in a wholly comic vein.

This, however, is not the end of Nabokov's reworking of this theme. In *Ada* some of the elements of *SM* are taken up and elaborated still further, with the humour giving place to fantasy and farce. In this novel, there are virtually as many peeping Toms as there are lovers; voyeurism is practised by the locals as well as by the hero and heroine's own family. There is Sore, the night-watchman, obviously a successor to Apostolski:

> the lovers could steal out into the deeper darkness and stay there until the *nocturna*—a keen midnight breeze—came tumbling the foliage '*troussant la raimée*', as Sore, the ribald night watchman expressed it. (p. 211)

---

[1] In *CE* and *SM* this tutor is named Lenski. Both names are fictitious.

('Tumbling' echoes the phrase in *SM*: 'a great tumbler of weed-ing-girls'.) There is Blanche, the maid, who is constantly interrupt-ing the lovers' trysts; and not least there is 'Kitchen Kim', who spies on Ada and Van with his camera. Then, in the forefront of the action, there is Lucette, Ada's younger sister, whose jealous love for Van leads her to pursue the pair of lovers to all their summer haunts. It is even possible to see the germ of Lucette's characterization in the following sentence which was added in *SM*: 'And another time, as we emerged onto a turn of the highway, my two little sisters in their wild curiosity almost fell out of the red family "torpedo" swerving toward the bridge' (*SM*, p. 233). Although *Ada* bears no textual relation to *SM*, Chapter 12, the resemblances both of tone and of theme are indisputable.

The development of the Tamara theme is indeed a complex one. First expressed in poetry, it passes through fiction to autobio-graphy and back again into fiction. It crosses and recrosses the frontier of language, from Russian to English and back again. Each change of genre, each shift of language leaves a different stamp. But through these changes of genre and language there is a con-sistent pattern of development. The development is in Nabokov's handling of the raw material of his art, his own experience. In the poems and in *Mashen'ka* there is a wealth of circumstantial detail, an intensity of personal emotion which is thinly disguised in con-ventional poetic usage and in a dramatic fictional framework. In the Autobiography Nabokov, as an older man, strips away the romantic trappings and seeks to distil the 'essence' of Tamara. At the same time, as a mature artist, he stylizes and condenses the narrative and frees it from the exclusively personal perspective of nostalgia and pain. He introduces other viewpoints, and humour. In *Speak, Memory* this digestion process is complete. The Tamara theme, though still very much a part of an autobiographical account, has gained literary independence. Finally, in *Ada*, the theme reappears in fiction. Tamara's ghost is set free—free to haunt the park in a fantasy land.[1]

The earlier chapters of this book have emphasized Nabokov's use of translation as a vehicle for development. However, in this analysis of Nabokov's use of autobiographical material, the

[1] Further illustration of Nabokov's reworking of autobiographical material is given in Appendix D.

question of revision assumes a wider dimension. Reworking can be seen as an essential feature of Nabokov's art. It functions not only across languages, but across genres, and within a single language. Nabokov is an infinitely inventive, if not an infinitely creative, writer. As one critic has expressed it, he 'ingeminates'.[1] Themes, characters, and settings are continually reappearing in different disguises, in different contexts. This analysis of Nabokov's transmutation of experience into art forms a complement to an examination of his artistic development through translation. Taken together, they present 'conclusive evidence' of the unity of Nabokov's production whether in Russian or in English.

[1] Lubin, 'Kickshaws and Motley', p. 187. Some examples of this reduplication of material have been noted above. See p. 25 n. 2 and p. 66 n. 1. When asked in interview whether he was consciously aware of 'repeating himself' in his works, Nabokov replied: 'Derivative writers seem versatile because they imitate many others, past and present. Artistic originality has only its own self to copy.' (Interview conducted by Gold, 1967.)

8

TECHNIQUE OF TRANSLATION

> . . . it is written in Russian and not all is translatable,
> and—well, to be frank, I am rather particular about my
> literary coloratura and firmly believe that the loss of
> a single shade of inflection would hopelessly mar the
> whole.[1]

THE last five chapters have demonstrated Nabokov's continuing preoccupation with artistic considerations in the
translations which he has made or supervised. Every translation contains some emendations or elaboration; where the
translations differ is simply in the extent of the changes made. In
making these alterations Nabokov is, as has already been pointed
out, simply exercising his prerogative as an author. It would be
meaningless and irrelevant to lay the charge of *otsebyatina* against
a translator who intervenes in his own creation. The author's
rights are absolute.

But if it is understandable that an author should wish to alter
and improve his own work, it is equally understandable that he
should wish the individuality, the stylistic quality of the work, to
be adequately conveyed in translation. And in these translations it
is very evident that Nabokov is concerned not only to rework, but
to conserve his original. The conscientious translator coexists with
the creative artist. The balance between these opposing forces of
conservation and revision is different in every translation. Some
novels are rendered more closely than others. But *all* the translations, even those which incorporate substantial revisions, such as
KQKn, reveal Nabokov operating as a scrupulous and painstaking
translator. It is because Nabokov faces squarely the difficult task
of translation and does not introduce changes simply to side-step
awkward problems of transposition that his practice merits serious
examination. Does it conform to any consistent pattern? Does it
evolve or develop? Does it relate to his theories of literalism?

[1] *Despair 2*, pp. 167–8.

Two aspects have been singled out for consideration here because of the special problems they pose for the translator. There is, firstly, the problem of 'cultural translatability'.[1] How does Nabokov render those situational features which are absent from, or alien to, the culture in the other 'target'[2] language? More generally, how does he adapt the original in order to render it comprehensible to readers having a different culture, a different history, a different literary tradition? Secondly, there is the problem of translating formal stylistic effects, such as word play, alliteration, and assonance. How concerned is Nabokov to convey an equivalence of 'sound' as well as of 'sense' in the translation of his own work?

CULTURAL REFERENCE

Nabokov's translations of other writers vary considerably in their approach to the problem of cultural reference. We have, on the one hand, his early translation of *Alice in Wonderland*, in which he favours the method of transposition. There he transposes the entire setting from England to Russia, changing names, places, historical and literary allusions. On the other hand, we have his later practice in *Eugene Onegin*, where he eschews any transposition or even explanatory description. All explanations are reserved for the notes. In both these translations Nabokov adheres fairly consistently to his chosen approach. However, his translations of his own works reveal neither the same extremism nor the same consistency of method. He does not set out to transpose the setting and anglicize or russify his narrative; nor does he rely on notes to convey his full meaning. A good deal of explanation is incorporated in the text, and he sometimes abandons the original reference and substitutes an equivalent drawn from the culture of the 'target' language. In no translation does his practice appear to be governed by rigid principles. His methods seem rather to be dictated by the value in context of each individual example.

As an illustration of Nabokov's method we can consider the different ways in which he translates *lapta*, the name of a Russian ball-game. In the following example from *KQKn* he transposes the allusion from *lapta* to baseball and cricket. During the farcical

---

[1] The term is used by Catford in *A Linguistic Theory of Translation*.

[2] Catford employs the terms 'source language' and 'target language', to denote the original and the translation.

tennis game between Dreyer and Franz, Franz at one point sends his ball soaring high above the pavilion. In the Russian version Dreyer beckons his inexperienced partner to the net and quietly explains: «Друг мой... мы не в лапту играем» (p. 183). In English translation, this becomes: 'We are not playing American baseball or English cricket' (p. 189). This is certainly not a literal rendering, but in this context, where Dreyer is simply commenting on Franz's unorthodox play, the reference to baseball or cricket is just as appropriate. Besides, such a remark is not incongruous in the mouth of Dreyer, who is himself German, not Russian, and who does know some English. In other specifically Russian contexts, however, Nabokov does not transpose. On occasion he retains *lapta* in transliteration, and adds an approximate equivalent in parenthesis. This he does in *The Defence*: 'the mathematics master would get a hard little ball in the ribs as he made a run in *lapta* (Russian baseball)' (p. 19).[1] On other occasions he invents an English translation which conveys some idea of the type of game being referred to, without invoking the different American and English variations. In *Glory*, he has 'tag-bat' (p. 175), and in *Mary* he has 'bat-and-tag' (p. 40). (Glenny, in this last example, suggested *lapta*).

There is variation, too, in Nabokov's translation of proper names. His usual practice is to leave the names unchanged, that is, apart from the omission of the Russian patronymic in narrative passages of English. (The patronymic is often retained when it is used in conversation as a form of address.) However, he does alter names when he is striving after a particular effect. In *LD*, as was seen earlier, he changes the names of the principal characters in order to reinforce the symbolism in the novel. In other works he makes alterations when he wishes to convey an equivalent semantic or affective value in translation. When, for example, Russian names are used in their diminutive forms, he sometimes adapts them in English to give an appropriate nuance of endearment or familiarity. In *Despair*, Lydia addresses Ardalion as 'Ardy dear', where the Russian is *Ardalionchik*, and Ardalion in his turn calls her 'Lyddy', where the Russian is *Lidusha* (*Otchayanie*, pp. 132, 98; *Despair 2*,

---

[1] In the original Russian there is no mention of *lapta*:

математик получал на бегу крепкий мячик в ребра... (*ZL*, p. 34)

Scammell suggests the translation: 'the mathematics master getting a sizable snowball in the ribs while on the run'.

pp. 44, 116). The choice of Mary to translate *Mashen'ka* was dictated by similar considerations, as Nabokov explains in his Foreword:

> The Russian title of the present novel, *Mashenka*, a secondary diminutive of *Maria*, defies rational transliteration . . . In casting around for a suitable substitute (*Mariette*?, *May*?) I settled for *Mary*, which seemed to match best the neutral simplicity of the Russian title name.   (p. xi.)

Where, again, names have humorous associations or involve word-play, Nabokov sometimes substitutes names which convey analogous comic effects. Here is an example from *Dar*:

> я почему-то особенно ясно запомнил фигуру этого генерала (Х. В. Барановского — в нем было что-то пасхальное)... (pp. 122–3)

This becomes: 'for some reason I can recall especially clearly the figure of this general (X. B. Lambovski—there was something Paschal about him) (p. 106). (Scammell suggested: 'Kh. V. Baranovski—there was something paschal about him'. In *Podlets* Mityushin names Berg's two seconds as Malinin and Burenin. His friend Gnuschke corrects him: '*Ne sovsem tochno — Burenin i polkovnik Magerovsky.*'[1] In the translation (*An Affair of Honor*), the names are given first as Marx and Engels, and then corrected to Markov and Colonel Arkhangelski.[2] The Russian translation of *Lolita* contains several examples of this sort of change. So too does *The Waltz Invention*. The eleven generals in the Russian version of the play are: Berg, Brig, Breg, Brug, Burg, Gerb, Grab, Grib, Gorb, Grob, Grub. Their English counterparts present, to use Nabokov's own words, 'an analogous series of allusive sense'. They become: Bump, Dump, Gump, Hump, Mump, Rump, Stump, Tump, Ump, Zump.

Nabokov's method of translating literary allusions is also subject to variation. He seems intent upon transferring the maximum amount of literary reference from the original to the translation. Most allusions are retained. Some are left unchanged; others, usually—although not invariably—the more obscure ones, are highlighted and elucidated for the foreign reader. Sometimes he draws the reader's attention to a quotation by placing it in inverted

---

[1] *Voz Ch*, p. 119.
[2] *Nabokov's Quartet*, p. 26.

commas or by appending an explanatory phrase, such as 'as the poet sang'. In *Despair*, for instance (versions 1 and 2), he has: 'Things that pass are treasured later, as the poet sang'.[1] Sometimes, he provides the reader with a small clue to the reference. For example, in *Lolita R* he reveals that Mr. Pim is a character from a well-known tragi-comedy.[2] More commonly, and more helpfully, he gives the source of the allusion and names the author. This is his usual practice in *The Gift* and *Despair*, and in *Lolita R* he elucidates many of the tantalizing references in the English original. Not all the allusions are retained, however. There are cases where Nabokov cuts out an allusion altogether. In *Despair*, for example (versions 1 and 2), he omits a reference to Pimen, the monk from Pushkin's *Boris Godunov*. He has: 'but the very chronicler of the crime stories, Dr. Watson himself' (*Despair 2*, pp. 131–2), instead of:

а сам Пимен всей криминальной летописи, сам доктор Ватсон... (p. 110)

In *Despair 2* he omits a reference to an artist named Kern—a name which recalls the Anna Kern of Pushkin's famous lyric (p. 146). Occasionally Nabokov *adds* references to the literature of his adopted language. In *KQKn* he adds a reference to Shaw's play *Candida* (p. 263), and in *Lolita R* he adds this reference to *Evgeny Onegin*:

Никогда не уедет с Онегиным в Италию княгиня N. (p. 245)

Sometimes Nabokov transposes the literary reference and substitutes an allusion from another literature. In *Despair*, for example (versions 1 and 2), he replaces an allusion to Pushkin's short story *Vystrel* by an allusion to *Othello*. Compare:

В школе мне ставили за русское сочинение неизменный кол, оттого что я по-своему пересказывал действия наших классических героев: так, в моей передаче «Выстрела» Сильвио наповал без лишних слов убивал любителя черешен и с ним — фабулу, которую я впрочем знал отлично. (p. 142)

---

[1] *Despair 2*, p. 188. See *Otchayanie*, p. 43: *Chto proidet, to budet milo*. This is the last line of Pushkin's short poem: *Esli zhizn' tebya obmanet*, 1825.)

[2] Compare *Lolita E*, p. 202. The allusion is, in fact, to A. A. Milne's play *Mr. Pim Passes By*.

At school I used, invariably, to get the lowest mark for Russian composition, because I had a way of my own with Russian and foreign classics; thus, for example, when rendering 'in my own words' the plot of *Othello* (which was, mind you, perfectly familiar to me) I made the Moor skeptical and Desdemona unfaithful. (*Despair* 2, p. 56)

In *Lolita R* a corrupted quotation from *Macbeth* is replaced by a quotation from *Evgeny Onegin*. Compare:

'I have not much at the bank right now but I propose to borrow— you know, as the Bard said, with that cold in his head, to borrow and to borrow and to borrow.' (p. 293)[1]

«у меня сейчас маловато в банке, но ничего, буду жить долгами, как жил его отец по словам поэта». (p. 280)[2]

In *Ultima Thule* there is an interesting example taken from children's lore. The narrator in this story is trying to persuade Falter to relate his psychic experience and to disclose the 'riddle of the universe' which, Falter claims, he has accidentally solved. Falter is most unwilling to reveal his secret and the interview begins to resemble a children's guessing-game with the narrator making his suggestions and Falter pointing out how wide of the mark he is. To one of these suggestions Falter replies: '*Barynya prislala sto rublei*.' This is a line from a jingle used in a Russian guessing-game.[3] Falter is again indicating that the narrator is on the wrong track. In the English translation Nabokov substitutes a reference to that circular English children's rhyme, 'This is the house that Jack built', which provides an equally effective comment on the narrator's lack of progress (*RB*, p. 176).

As these few examples show, there is no apparent evolution in Nabokov's method of translating cultural reference. In all translations of his fiction he is concerned to conserve the identity of the original rather than substitute a different identity, but his practice is just as susceptible to variation in the later translations as in those published before the formulation of his theories of literalism.

There is, however, one noteworthy development in Nabokov's translation technique, not directly connected with his theory. This

---

[1] See *Macbeth*, v. v.   [2] See *Evgeny Onegin*, I. iii. 2.
[3] *VF*, p. 305. Here is the rhyme in full:
Барыня прислала сто рублей. / Что хотите, то купите. / «Да» и «нет» не говорите. / Черного и белого не покупайте. / Головою не мотайте. — / Что вы себе купили?

is an increase in the use of Russian in transliteration in the later English translations. Some of this transliterated Russian, admittedly, is included in contexts where English alone would not provide a satisfactory equivalent, and as such might be said to reflect his growing adherence to the principles of literalism. Often, however, the inclusion of the Russian is not indispensable, but imparts a Russian flavour to the text, serving also to provide linguistic interest for those readers with a knowledge of the language. *The Gift*, for example—a novel centred upon Russian *émigrés* and Russian literature—contains a good deal of transliterated Russian, which highlights the individual quality of the Russian cultural heritage. In other novels Nabokov includes a sprinkling of Russian words to distinguish which language is being spoken. This explains some of the Russian interpolations in *Glory*, a novel set in five different countries, where characters speak three different languages. Sometimes, again, the Russian is given when Nabokov is attempting to capture the individuality of a character's mode of expression. In this example from *SM* he uses transliteration to convey the quality of Tamara's epistolary style:

> '*Bozhe moy*' (*mon Dieu*—rather than 'My God'), where has it gone, all that distant, bright, endearing (*Vsyo eto dalyokoe, svetloe, miloe*—in Russian no subject is needed here, since these are neuter adjectives that play the part of abstract nouns, on a bare stage, in a subdued light). (p. 249)

(In previous versions of this passage (E1, E2), Nabokov gives no Russian, and does not omit the subject noun: 'Where has it gone, all that distant, bright, endearing world?') *Glory* provides some interesting examples of Russian included for its linguistic interest. In the following example, Nabokov renders a tricky piece of word play by placing an English equivalent alongside the Russian:

> Vadim had one inevitable jingle, with a limerick arrangement of Russian rhymes: *Priyátno zret', kogdá bol'shóy medvéd' vedyót pod rúchku málen'kuyu súchku, chtob eyo poét'* (What fun to stare when a great big bear walks home arm in arm with a tiny bitch to lay her there). (p. 70)

(In *Podvig* Nabokov omits the punchline *chtob eyo poet'*) (p. 113). Russian readers could presumably be expected to supply this themselves!)[1] In early translations, such as *Despair 1*, Nabokov

---

[1] The rhyme does in fact have a concluding few lines which are rather more obscene and which Nabokov does not give even in his English version.

does not give his readers this two-fold pleasure of appreciating his word play in both English and Russian. The English equivalent alone is given.

This development suggests not so much a move towards literalism but rather a shift in Nabokov's relation to his reading public. In his recent writing he assumes, and quite justifiably, more knowledge and more interest in Russia and the Russian language. But it also seems that, after gaining recognition as a writer of English, he has consciously begun to reassert his 'foreignness'. He not only includes more Russian in his recent translations; he also inserts more French and even some German. Moreover, this reassertion of 'foreignness' is also reflected in some of his recent English fiction. *Pnin*—a story of a Russian *émigré* resident in America—abounds in linguistic entertainment of this kind. Much of Pnin's English speech is built upon Russian constructions, and sprinkled with Russian and French expressions. He speaks, for example, of having 'habitated in Paris from 1925' (pp. 33–4), and asks his prospective landlady: 'What price are you prepared to demand?' (p. 34.) Many of the Russian names in the novel are not without meaning, and furnish some incidental humour. There is Umov, 'the once famous revolutionary' (p. 22); John and Olga Krotki, 'two frail drudges' (p. 39); and Ivan Nagoy, 'a repulsively hairy young composer' (p. 180). In *Ada*, 1969, most of the characters are fluent in English, Russian, and French and slip readily from one language to another. Multi-lingual puns abound and the literary allusions range through American, English, French, and Russian literature.[1] *Transparent Things*, 1972, also features an international cast, and this gives rise to several examples of amusing mistranslation. There are the English twins 'who called gullies Cool Wars and ridges Ah Rates' (p. 89); Julia, who garbles the Russian for 'I love you' as 'yellow blue tibia' (p. 48); Person's father (another American) who translates *Notre vente triomphale de soldes* as 'Our windfall triumphantly sold' (p. 12). The novel also includes a digression on the Russian and French translation of 'snowdrift' (pp. 45–6), and some effective imitation of French idiom—a typical example being Armande's matter-of-fact pronouncement: 'And now one is going to make love' (p. 54).

---

[1] Discussions of literary allusion in *Ada* are contained in Appel, '*Ada* Described'; Bader, *Crystal Land*, Chapter 7; Lokrantz, *The Underside of the Weave*, pp. 87–94. See also Nabokov's notes to the Penguin edition of *Ada*, 1970.

This is not to say that elements of 'cosmopolitanism' are not found in Nabokov's earlier writing. All of his production bears the stamp of the *émigré*, the man of many countries and many cultures. Not only are the characters and settings of many Russian works non-Russian, but the literary reference is by no means confined to Russian literature. The allusions to *Madame Bovary* in *KDV* have already been pointed out in an earlier chapter. In *Otchayanie* there are quotations from Shakespeare and allusions to Oscar Wilde, Conan Doyle, and James Joyce. And in passages of his first English novel, *The Real Life of Sebastian Knight*, Nabokov already renders the flavour of Russian and French speech, using foreign constructions and transliteration.[1] Nevertheless, it is only in his later production that Nabokov parades this 'transnationalism' so openly and with such flamboyance. In these works he manipulates different languages and different cultures with the same virtuosity as he treats style and form. We have here another illustration of the stylized brilliance which characterizes his writing in his later period.

These observations about Nabokov's translation technique apply to his translations of fiction. His practice, however, in the Auto-biography is different and merits separate consideration. In *Drugie berega* Nabokov adapts his reference more completely. Writing under the impulse of memory he allows himself a much freer hand. He readily transposes allusions and adds many more references to Russians and to Russian literature and Russian political affairs. Writing as an expatriate for expatriates, his sentiments and attitudes take on a rather different colouring. There is more emphasis laid on the brutality and pathos of the Revolution. It is only, for example, in *DB* that he likens the fall of the Russian monarchy to the fall of Athens and Rome (p. 165). He also adopts a slightly harsher attitude to expatriate life in Europe. His account of the hardships of the Cambridge winter lacks the humorous understatement of the English version; and it is in Russian alone that he ventures the following frank comment:

Этот мой резиновый tub я взял с собой в эмиграцию, и он, уже заплатанный, был мне сущим спасением в моих бес-численных европейских пансионах: грязнее французской общей ванной нет на свете ничего, кроме немецкой. (p. 67)

[1] See pp. 117–21, 174–5.

In none of Nabokov's translations of fiction does a change of
language bring with it a comparable change in viewpoint. Here
again the dictates of autobiography differ from the dictates of
fiction.

SOUND INSTRUMENTATION AND WORD-PLAY

In *Eugene Onegin*, Nabokov established quite clearly where the
translator's priorities should lie with regard to the translation of
formal stylistic devices. Whilst the ideal aim of every translator
should be an equivalence of both form and meaning, in cases where
this proves impossible he should content himself with conveying
the meaning and sacrifice the formal effects. In *EO* Nabokov
decided to sacrifice the rhyme scheme, though this did not prevent
him from making ingenious attempts to convey rhythm and
alliteration.

When translating his own work, however, Nabokov is always
prepared to reverse these priorities and quite often values the
retention of the stylistic effect more highly than the retention of
meaning. In his translation of alliteration and onomatopoeia, he
will often modify and change his meaning in order to give an
equivalent auditive effect. Some examples will help substantiate
these observations.

Sometimes Nabokov succeeds in rendering the sense as well as
contriving a play on the same consonants:

1. звук мягкий и матовый   (*Mashen'ka*, p. 25)

   MG: even and soft in tone

   VN: mellow and mat in tone   (*Mary*, p. 14)

2. в сумрачные сибирские годы   (*Dar*, p. 246)

   MS: twilight Siberian years

   VN: sombre Siberian years   (*The Gift*, p. 209)

3. с такой-же солидной серьезностью   (*Dar*, p. 268)

   MS: with equally respectable seriousness

   VN: with equally stolid seriousness   (*The Gift*, p. 228)

4. словно из перегородки она превратилась в провал   (*Dar*,
   p. 282)

   MS: as if it had turned from a partition into a gap

   VN: as if it had turned from a partition into a pit   (*The Gift*, p. 240)

5. a brisk bubbling murder (*Lolita E*, p. 86)

   для быстренького булькающего человекоубийства (*Lolita R*, p. 74)

6. she would moisten the glistening nib with susurrous lips (*CE*, p. 66)

   с сырым присвистом слюнила его блестящее острие (*DB*, p. 93)

7. froggy gloss (*CE*, p. 66)

   лягущечьим лоском (*DB*, p. 93)

More frequently, Nabokov renders the sense and provides alliteration on *different* consonants:

1. Любила она меня без оговорок и без оглядок (*Otchayanie*, p. 128)

   She loved me without reservations, without retrospection (*Despair 2*, p. 39; = E1)

2. этот прием был баловнем биоскопа (*Otchayanie*, p. 140)

   this dodge was the darling of the Kinematograph (*Despair 2*, p. 54; = E1)

3. when that pearly language of hers purled and scintillated (*CE*, p. 74)

   когда эта жемчужная речь журчала и переливалась (*DB*, p. 105)

4. когда дружба была великодушна и влажна (*Dar*, p. 248)

   MS: when friendship was generous and moist

   VN: when friendship was magnanimous and moist (*The Gift*, pp. 210–11)

5. резкостью взглядов и развязностью манер (*Dar*, p. 260)

   MS: with the sharpness of his views and the undue familiarity of his manner

   VN: with the harshness of his views and the brashness of his ways (*The Gift*, p. 222)

6. in my dimness of thought, in my darkness of passion (*Lolita E*, p. 70)

   в тумане мечтаний, в темноте наваждения (*Lolita R*, p. 58)

7. Let me rave and ramble on for a teeny while more   (*Lolita E*, p. 68)

   Позвольте мне, еще чуточку побредить и побродить мыслью (*Lolita R*, p. 56)

8. легкую, ласковую, человечную труху   (*Mashen'ka*, p. 130)

   MG: trivial, beloved human rubbish

   VN: fond, fragile, human rubbish   (*Mary*, p. 87)

9. с пронзительным содроганьем стыда   (*Mashen'ka*, p. 36)

   MG: with a piercing twitch of shame

   VN: with a deep shudder of shame   (*Mary*, p. 21)

10. веселым восклицанием   (*ZL*, p. 34)

    MS: with jolly exclamations

    VN: with jolly ejaculations   (*The Defence*, p. 20)

Another group of examples shows Nabokov adjusting the sense but still preserving the play of consonants. Sometimes the play is on different consonants:

1. эти угрюмые господа   (*Mashen'ka*, p. 120)

   MG: those gloomy gentlemen

   VN: those lugubrious scribes   (*Mary*, p. 79)

2. that compound image—shudder and swan and swell   (*CE*, p. 78)

   а именно тот бедный, поздний, тройственный образ: лодка, лебедь, волна   (*DB*, p. 110)

3. the flames fanned by my fancy and grief   (*Lolita E*, p. 253)

   где греза и горе раздували пламя   (*Lolita R*, p. 240)

4. it remained as prim as a prawn   (*Lolita E*, p. 174)

   она осталась столь же чопорной, как чепец   (*Lolita R*, p. 160)

5. between beast and beauty—between my gagged, bursting beast and the beauty of her dimpled body   (*Lolita E*, p. 60)

   между чудом и чудовищем, между моим рвущимся зверем и красотой этого зыбкого тела   (*Lolita R*, p. 48)

More rarely, Nabokov succeeds in making a play on the same consonant:

1. с... прыщиками на переносице   (*CO*, p. 44)

   E1: and pimples on her nose   (*CO*, p. 12)

   VN: and pathetic little pimples just above that kind of small nose (*LD*, p. 10)

2. долбящий, бубнящий звук слов (*Dar*, p. 219)

   MS: the battering and harping sound of the words

   VN: the drubbing-in, rubbing-in tone of each word (*The Gift*, p. 187)

3. they were as different as mist and mast (*Lolita E*, p. 20)

   они были столь же различны между собой, как мечта и мачта (*Lolita R*, p. 10)

4. an aged swan, a large, uncouth, dodo-like creature (*CE*, p. 77)

   Это был старый, жирный, неуклюжий, похожий на удода, лебедь. (*DB*, p. 109)

This last example deserves especial attention since it provides a very clear illustration of how sound-determined Nabokov's writing is. 'Dodo' and *udod* are two very different birds. A dodo is an extinct, flightless bird, about the size of a swan. *Udod* is a hoopoe, a crested bird of variegated plumage, the size of a large thrush. In translating this simile, which evokes the clumsiness of an aged swan, Nabokov is obviously more interested in the sound of the word than its sense. He preserves the ponderous effect of the two 'd's, but sacrifices the associations of size and age which attach to the dodo.[1] Proffer, in his analysis of *Lolita*, has already commented upon this 'sound-determined' quality of Nabokov's style.[2] The evidence of this study not only corroborates his conclusions in respect of Nabokov's English writing, it also enlarges upon his conclusions, showing this to be a feature of Nabokov's Russian as well as English prose, and a feature which is prominent not only in his original writing but also in translation.[3]

[1] Of course, the Russian word for dodo, *dront*, does not enjoy the same currency as in English. It does not occur in any set expression, such as, 'dead as a dodo'. The dodo makes another appearance in *Strong Opinions*, in a re-publication of an interview conducted by Appel: 'Robbe-Grillet's claims are preposterous. Those manifestos, those dodoes, die with the dadas' (p. 62). There is no reference to dodos in the original version of the interview, published in 1967.

[2] See *Keys to Lolita*, pp. 82–97. Nabokov has himself on occasion discussed this aspect of his writing. See, for example, his comments on the choice of the names Lolita and Humbert Humbert in an interview conducted by Toffler, *Playboy*, 1964.

[3] Rowe in his discussion of Nabokov's 'sound effects' (*Nabokov's Deceptive World*, pp. 52–8), makes some interesting observations on Nabokov's use of assonance in English, and the reader is referred to his study for illustration of this point. However, in his choice of examples he fails to discriminate between translations made by the author and those made in collaboration with another

As for the translations of word-play, although in some cases Nabokov does resort to explanation (there are several examples of this in *Lolita R*), and sometimes even omits the pun altogether, he prefers to substitute an equivalent. These equivalents are often extremely ingenious and just as effective as the original. Here are a few typical examples from *Despair* and *Lolita*:

1. сам доктор Ватсон, — чтобы Ватсон был бы, так сказать, виноватсон... (*Otchayanie*, p. 110)

   Dr. Watson himself—Watson, who, so to speak, knew what was Whatson. (*Despair 2*, pp. 131–2; = E1)

2. Что делает советский ветер в слове ветеринар? Откуда томат в автомате? Как из зубра сделать арбуз? (*Otchayanie*, p. 142)

   What is this jest in majesty? This ass in passion? How do God and Devil combine to form a live dog? (*Despair 2*, p. 56; = E1)

3. where girls are taught . . . 'not to spell very well, but to smell very well'. (*Lolita E*, p. 173)

   «учат правилам не столько грамматическим, сколько аро-матическим». (*Lolita R*, p. 159)

Here Nabokov succeeds in conveying the approximate sense of the original, as well as an equivalence of rhyme.

4. In the house, Lolita had put on her favourite 'Little Carmen' record which I used to call 'Dwarf Conductors', making her snort with mock derision at my mock wit. (*Lolita E*, p. 46)

   В доме Лолита поставила свою любимую пластинку «Ма-лютка Кармен», которую я всегда называл «Карманная Кармен», от чего она фыркала, притворно глумясь над моим притворным остроумием. (*Lolita R*, p. 35)

The examination of Nabokov's translation of word-play and sound instrumentation corroborates the conclusions drawn from his translation of cultural reference. The theories of literal translation which he has evolved meet with little reflection in his practice as a translator of his own work. There is no evidence that in later translations Nabokov is nearer to adopting the ruthless, self-abnegatory attitude with which he tackles *Evgeny Onegin*.

translator. He takes several of his examples from *The Gift* and *The Defence*, and in almost every case he is, in fact, quoting Scammell and not Nabokov. Nabokov certainly gave these passages his approval, but they are not his own.

When dealing with translations of his own work he is often prepared to sacrifice literal interpretation for patterns of sound and form. Herein lies the main value of an examination of Nabokov's translation technique—the indications it gives of Nabokov's method of composition and the development of his style. This aspect will be examined further in the following chapter.

9

STYLE

*The best part of a writer's biography is not the record
of his adventures but the story of his style.*[1]

IT would be hard to exaggerate the difficulty Nabokov experienced in turning from the writing of Russian in order to embark upon a literary career in English. He had, as he tells us in the Autobiography, known English well since early childhood. He learnt to read and write in English before Russian, and English and French classics were among his favourite books as a child. Even before he left Russia for Cambridge he had read widely in Western European literature. Nevertheless, Russian was his native language and, what is more important, it was in Russian that he served his literary apprenticeship and forged his individual style. Being a conscious stylist, a writer who regards the craft of his style as a fundamental feature of his writing, Nabokov felt the loss of his Russian tool very keenly. He expresses this sense of loss most clearly in his Foreword to *Drugie berega*, where he contrasts his position with that of Joseph Conrad, another English writer by adoption:

> Совершенно владея с младенчества и английским и французским, я перешел бы для нужд сочинительства с русского на иностранный язык без труда, будь я, скажем, Джозеф Конрад, который, до того, как начал писать по-английски, никакого следа в родной (польской) литературе не оставил, а на избранном языке (английском) искусно пользовался готовыми формулами. Когда, в 1940 году, я решил перейти на английский язык, беда моя заключалась в том, что перед тем, в течение пятнадцати с лишком лет, я писал по-русски и за эти годы наложил собственный отпечаток на свое орудие, на своего посредника. (p. 7)

Nabokov was faced with the challenge of creating a new instrument, a new style, as supple and well-tempered as his Russian:

[1] *Mary*, p. xiii.

Долголетняя привычка выражаться по-своему не позволяла
довольствоваться на новоизбранном языке трафаретами...
(р. 7)

Nabokov took up that challenge, but he has always maintained that
his English style is an imperfect substitute, 'a wistful standby' for
his Russian. His fullest statement on this is contained, interesting-
ly enough, in his Afterword to *Lolita*, the novel which first brought
him world-wide acclaim:

> My private tragedy, which cannot, and indeed should not, be
> anybody's concern, is that I had to abandon my natural idiom,
> my untrammelled, rich and infinitely docile Russian tongue for a
> second-rate brand of English, devoid of any of those apparatuses—
> the baffling mirror, the black velvet backdrop, the implied associa-
> tions and traditions—which the native illusionist, frac-tails flying,
> can magically use to transcend the heritage in his own way.
> (p. 307)

When Nabokov came to translate *Lolita* into Russian some ten
years later, he recognized with disappointment that he had lost his
former mastery of Russian style. In the Afterword to that translation he comments with some poignancy that the strings of his
instrument had 'rusted' through disuse:

> Меня же только мутит ныне от дребезжания моих ржавых
> русских струн.   (р. 296)

This self-criticism seems justified. *Lolita R* is an ingenious and
talented translation, but much of the language is indeed awkward,
unnatural, and strongly influenced by English idiom and English
constructions. Both Soviet and *émigré* Russian readers have commented on the oddness of the language, and a few examples of this
'un-Russian' Russian are given below:

1. Из моего окна... я мог видеть ее идущую через улицу и с
    довольным видом опускающую в ящик письмо...   (р. 78)

    From my window . . . I could see her crossing the street and con-
    tentedly mailing her letter . . .   (p. 89)

2. «Ло! Лола! Лолита!» — слышу себя восклицающим с порога
    в солнечную даль...   (р. 217)

    'Lo! Lola! Lolita!' I hear myself crying from a doorway into the
    sun . . .   (p. 231).

3. Я был горд собой: я выкрал мед оргазма, не совратив мало-
    летней. (p. 50)

    I felt proud of myself. I had stolen the honey of a spasm without
    impairing the morals of a minor. (p. 62)

4. две молодых женщины с понихвостными прическами
    (pp. 267–8)

    two pony-tailed young women (p. 281)

5. Помнил только начальную литеру и конечное число…
    (p. 207)

    What remained of it in my mind were the initial letter and the
    closing figure . . . (p. 221)

Some readers have drawn attention to actual grammatical mistakes,
and one Soviet writer who has had access to an independent
samizdat translation of *Lolita* judges this greatly superior to
Nabokov's own version. Readers who are in a position to compare
Nabokov's Russian version with his English generally find the
Russian linguistically inferior. But there are others who have
praise for his inventiveness and find his use of language refreshing
in its novelty.[1] Clearly many of the anglicisms are quite intentional,
as some of these examples show, and are used to embellish Humbert Humbert's wayward style. It might even be thought that
Nabokov here is giving us a perverse, tongue-in-cheek demonstration of his theory of 'literal translation'. But not all the translation can be dismissed as an elaborate joke. Here—for once—it
would appear that we can take Nabokov at his word and consider
this a quite genuine attempt—a quite genuine disappointment.

This disappointment, however, has not led him to revise his
judgement on his English. In an interview with Herbert Gold in
1967, he said:

> My English, this second instrument I have always had, is however
> a stiffish, artificial thing, which may be all right for describing
> a sunset or an insect, but which cannot conceal poverty of syntax
> and paucity of domestic diction when I need the shortest road
> between warehouse and shop. An old Rolls Royce is not always
> preferable to a plain jeep.

[1] Ellendea Proffer has also investigated Russian reactions to *Lolita R*. Her
conclusions are even more uniformly negative: 'Even Nabokov's most ardent
fans dislike the Russian translation of *Lolita*.' ('Nabokov's Russian Readers',
p. 258.)

Opinions vary on the relative merits of Nabokov's English and Russian. Personally, I would tend to agree with Nabokov that his Russian is superior—if only because it is less uneven and, on the whole, less mannered than his English. However, whatever general view is held of Nabokov's English, it is undeniable that his command of the language has improved over the years and that with time he has evolved a polished and strikingly original prose style.

Comparison of earlier and later English versions of the same work clearly shows an improvement in Nabokov's command of English. The vocabulary of an early work is often restricted and ill chosen; and much of the syntax bears marked influence of Russian constructions. In a later version Nabokov eliminates many examples of aberrant usage and employs a more varied and apt vocabulary. A good illustration of this improvement is provided by the two English translations of *Otchayanie*, the first made in 1937, the second in 1966. The second version is not only a more accurate translation, it also reads more naturally in English.

Nabokov appears to have had some difficulty with English prepositions in the early translation. In E1, some of the prepositions sound rather 'un-English'. For example:

1. R: глядел вдаль, на облый румянец газоема среди ветренной синевы майского дня. (p. 112)

   E1: stared at the red rotundity of that gasometer *on* the blue background of a breezy May day. (p. 14)[1]

   E2: *against* the blue background (p. 18)

2. R: захватил портфель с подозрительным вздутием... (p. 132)

   E1: then he snatched up a leather portfolio (with a suspicious lump *behind* its cheek)... (p. 47)

   E2: then he snatched up a briefcase (with a suspicious lump *in* its cheek)... (p. 44)

3. R: чтобы изредка, — может быть раз в году (p. 83)

   E1: very rarely, *once in a year* perhaps (p. 120)

   E2: very rarely, *once a year* perhaps (p. 97)

He also appears to have experienced some difficulty with the use and sequence of tenses. In E2, Nabokov makes a considerable

---

[1] My italics here and in the following examples.

number of alterations to the verb forms. Here is an example of his correcting a use of the conditional:

R: все, что собираюсь сделать для тебя, сделаю по доброй воле. (p. 74)

E1: if I *intended* helping you, I do so of my own free will.   (p. 105)

E2: if I *intend* helping you, I do so of my own free will.   (p. 87)

Here Nabokov emends the translation of a Russian gerund:

R: Поодаль, около терновых кустов, лежал навзничь, раскинув ноги, с картузом на лице, человек.   (p. 111)

E1: At some distance from me under a thorn bush, flat on his back and with a cap on his face, *a man was sprawling*.   (p. 12)

E2: At some distance from me . . . *there sprawled a man*.   (p. 17)

This second solution is perhaps not altogether a happy one, but at least it removes any suggestion of movement from the description of the sleeping Felix.

E2 also makes several alterations in word order. Many adverbs are shifted to a more natural position. For example:

1. R: Только дару проникать в измышления жизни, врожденной склонности к непрерывному творчеству я обязан тем... (p. 108)

   E1: The gift of penetrating life's devices *alone*, an innate disposition towards the constant exercise of the creative faculty could have enabled me . . .   (p. 7)

   E2: The gift of penetrating life's devices, an innate disposition toward the constant exercise of the creative faculty could *alone* have enabled me . . .   (p. 13)

2. R: но мне редко приходится отводить душу.   (p. 81)

   E1: I have *seldom* occasion to take my soul for an outing.   (p. 117)

   E2: I *seldom* have occasion to take my soul for an outing.   (p. 95)

3. R: а между тем любитель-актер, игравший князя, уже выходил... (p. 86)

   E1: and, as I spoke, the amateur acting his lordship was coming *already* . . .   (pp. 123–4)

   E2: and, as I spoke, the gentleman in the part of the prince was *already* coming . . .   (p. 100)

4. R: А может быть (продолжал я думать, соскакивая с мысли на мысль) он изменился и больше не похож на меня, и я понапрасну сюда приехал.   (p. 158)

E1: but maybe (I went on, skipping from thought to thought) he had changed and now was like me *no more*, and I had come in vain. (p. 92)

E2: but maybe (I went on, skipping from thought to thought) his features had altered and now were *no longer* like mine, and I had come in vain.   (pp. 76–7)

In this last example, the word order of E1 introduces an unnecessarily 'poetic' flavour into what is, in Russian, a stylistically neutral context. In E2 Nabokov reverts to a neutral, non-emotive word-order.

Adjustments are also made in the translation of sentences where the verb precedes the subject. There are several examples in E1 where Nabokov preserves this Russian word order, but reinforces the verb with the adverb 'there'. (Thus: 'there gushed', 'there jumped', 'there came', etc.) The effect is sometimes clumsy or stilted. In E2 Nabokov prefers to put the subject first, judging this to be a more natural and stylistically neutral word order in English. For example:

1. R: В павильоне вроде часовни бил ключ целебной воды... (p. 46)

E1: In a pavilion, reminding one of a chapel, *there gushed* a spring of curative water . . .   (p. 244)

E2: In a pavilion, reminding one of a chapel, a spring of curative water *gushed* . . .   (p. 191)

See also:

2. R: из проймы его ужасного вытянутого трико то и дело выскакивал нательный крест мужицкого образца.   (p. 137)

E1: from the opening in his repulsively flabby bathing suit *there kept jumping out* the cross, of moujik pattern, that he wore next to his skin.   (pp. 54–5)

E2: from the opening in his repulsively flabby bathing suit the silver cross, of moujik pattern, that he wore next to his skin, *kept jumping out* when he jumped in.   (p. 49)

3. R: Навстречу мне с развальцем шли синие почтальоны... (p. 106)

E1: Towards me *there came*, at a leisurely walk, several blue postmen . . . (p. 155)

E2: It was distribution time, and *they came* toward me, at a leisurely
walk, a dozen blue postmen . . . (p. 125)

4. R: В неподвижной воде отражалась гобеленовая пышность
бурой и рыжей листвы... (p. 153)

E1: Below, on the still surface of the water, *there was reflected* the
rich tapestry of brown and rusty-red foliage . . . (p. 86)

E2: Below, on the still surface of the water, *we admired* the exact
replica (ignoring the model, of course) of the park's autumn
tapestry of many-hued foliage . . . (p. 72)

There are many alterations made to vocabulary in E2. First of
all, there are some corrections of words which had been misused
in the earlier version. For example, in E1 'ignore' is used in the
French sense of 'not to know': 'I ignore to this day the exact
manner in which his soul was wrecked.' In E2 this becomes: 'I
never learned the exact manner in which his soul was wrecked'
(p. 148). In E1, again, 'goaded' is used to translate *pronzalo* in the
following context: 'Not the fact of their finding his stick and so
discovering our common name . . . oh, no, not *that* goaded me'
(p. 276). In E2, this is changed to 'galled': 'oh, no, not *that* galled
me' (p. 213). Other alterations, and there are a great many of
these, are of words which reveal strong traces of their Russian
origin, or which sound unusual or 'off-key'. For example:

1. R: яркость воображения (p. 44)

E1: *brightness* of imagination (p. 241)

E2: *vivid* imagination (p. 189)

2. R: Тишина была исключительно хорошего качества. (p. 49)

E1: A silence of *exclusively* fine quality. (p. 249)

E2: A silence of *exceptionally* fine quality. (p. 194)

3. R: хотя уезжал я довольно часто и не говорил куда. (p. 24)

E1: although I used to go away fairly often and never said *whither*.
(p. 206)

E2: although I used to go away fairly often and never said *where*.
(p. 163)

4. R: хорошо запрятаны (p. 125)

E1: *soundly* hidden (p. 36)

E2: *securely* hidden (p. 34)

5. Another echo of a French expression:

> E1: I am trying to make you *seize* the difference between us . . .
> (p. 115; cf. *saisir la différence*)

> E2: I am trying to make you *grasp* the difference between us . . .
> (p. 94)

Another group of changes indicate Nabokov's developed skill in selecting the *mot juste*, the precise or concrete equivalent. Compare, for example, the following variants:

1. E1: Hair comes pressing out from every pore. (p. 33)
   E2: Hair comes sprouting out of every pore. (p. 31)

2. Describing a journey by car:
   E1: Once or twice I struck badly cobbled bits . . . (p. 215)
   E2: Once or twice I struck a badly cobbled stretch . . . (p. 171)

3. Describing how to get to Eichenburg on foot:
   E1: then straight to the east through the wood. (p. 74)
   E2: then bear east through the wood. (p. 64)

There are several examples in E2 where Nabokov seeks an alternative for the translation 'thing' or 'things'. Compare:

1. R: словно все, что произошло, было недобрым делом. (p. 121)
   E1: as if the whole thing had been an evil deed. (p. 26)
   E2: as if the whole experience had been an evil deed. (p. 28)

2. Here Hermann is talking about his literary production:

   > R: воспользовавшись моей бессрочной отлучкой, выдашь мое
   > за свое... (p. 77)

   > E1: you may use my termless removal to give out my thing for your
   > own . . . (p. 110)

   > E2: you may use my termless removal to give out my stuff for your
   > own . . . (p. 91)

3. Here the context is again literary:

   > R: Сочиненьица той зимы я давно уничтожил... (p. 98)

   > E1: The coy little things composed that winter, have been de-
   > stroyed . . . (p. 143)

   > E2: The coy trifles composed that winter have been destroyed . . .
   > (p. 116)

This comparison of the two versions of *Despair* furnishes many indications of Nabokov's increasing grasp of English. The concern which he shows here to emend and improve the quality of his English expression characterizes the whole of his English production, not only in translation but also in works written originally in English. Many chapters of the two later versions of the Autobiography contain emendations of syntax and vocabulary. So too do successive editions of several English short stories: *A Forgotten Poet*, *The Assistant Producer*, and *Symbols and Signs*, for example, all undergo textual changes when they are republished in collections—in *Nine Stories* and in *Nabokov's Dozen*. This continuing concern to improve upon his expression in English can conceivably be attributed, in some measure at least, to his 'foreignness', to the fact that he is writing in a language which is not his own. As has been already pointed out, it is only his English writing which he reworks in this way. He does not retouch work written in his native language, Russian.

This does not mean that examples of aberrant English do not continue to occur in Nabokov's later writing. They do. Clearly, however, not all the 'oddness' of vocabulary and phraseology in his later writing is inadvertent. Nabokov deliberately retains certain russicisms and selects unusual vocabulary in order to impart an originality and individuality to his style. In his later English production it is not possible to draw any clear distinction between what is 'foreign' or 'non-standard' and what is original and calculated to enrich the scope of the English language.

Another general development in Nabokov's use of English which will be touched on briefly here is the increase in americanisms. It is understandable that Nabokov's originally European brand of English should acquire a colouring of American idiom and expression during his twenty years in the United States; and a comparison of *The Real Life of Sebastian Knight* with *Lolita* gives the measure of this development. However, Nabokov's translations and revisions show how conscious and deliberate was his adaptation to American idiom. The americanization of his style is not exactly a gradual process. From the start, Nabokov *assumes* an American voice. As early as 1938, while still resident in Europe, he introduced several americanisms into *LD*—a translation destined for an American publisher. For instance, 'mad on the movies' replaces Winifred Roy's 'was crazy about the cinema';[1] 'cute stories' replaces 'amusing stories';[2] and 'opposite sidewalk' is on one occasion substituted for 'the opposite side.'[3]

Later, when preparing his second version of *Despair*, Nabokov adapts a good deal of the vocabulary of the early London-published translation. He also injects a flavouring of American into the translations prepared by the two Englishmen, Scammell and Glenny. Scammell was actually resident in the States when he began translating for Nabokov and his versions of *The Gift* and *The Defence* already contain a number of americanisms. Glenny's version of *Mary* is, however, consistently English in spelling and idiom and Nabokov's final version introduces a good many more alterations. Here is a small but representative selection of examples from *Mary* and from *Despair*.

Despair:

E1:	lorry (p. 12)	E2:	truck (p. 17)
	the pictures (p. 140)		the movies (p. 114)
	pavement (p. 203)		sidewalk (p. 161)
	post-boxes (p. 154)		mailboxes (p. 125)
	tube station (p. 154)		underground station (p. 125)
	pants (p. 203)		drawers (p. 161)
	dinner jacket (p. 194)		tuxedo (p. 154)
	towards (p. 155)		toward (p. 125)

Mary:

MG:	paraffin	VN:	kerosene (p. 45)
	pavement		sidewalk (p. 88)
	holiday-makers		vacationists (p. 46)
	frightening		spooky (p. 75)
	at the back of beyond		in the sticks (p. 89)

Nabokov, however, is not always entirely consistent in his choice of vocabulary. English and American variants sometimes occur in one and the same version. For example, in the 1938 edition of *LD* he has 'pavement' in the same chapter as 'sidewalk';[4] and in *Despair*[2]

---

[1] See *LD*, p. 17. *CO*, p. 22.

[2] See *LD*, p. 82. *CO*, p. 121.

[3] *CO*, p. 37. 'Sidewalk' is replaced by 'pavement' in the later London editions of 1961 and 1969. See *LD*, p. 28.

[4] As indicated above in n. 3, the 1961 and 1969 London editions have 'pavement' in both instances. See *LD*, pp. 16, 28.

he has 'tuxedo' in one chapter but in another he retains the English 'dinner jacket' (pp. 154, 35). A more serious criticism is that in some of his writing the American vocabulary and up-to-date idiom sits uneasily on top of his essentially literary English prose style. There is in places a noticeable unevenness of style, where old and new elements are not sufficiently blent. But while flaws and lapses can be detected in Nabokov's use of americanisms, there is no disputing his conscious and scrupulous intention to assume the idiom of his adopted country and become 'an American writer'. All his later works, original writings as well as translations, are stamped with this American style.

These general features of the improvement and development of Nabokov's English usage emerge quite plainly from an analysis of his reworkings and revisions. It is a more difficult and complex matter to assess the *individual* features of his English style. There can be no 'straight' comparison of Nabokov's style in English and Russian. In the first place, the structure of any given language necessarily conditions and moulds a writer's expression in that language. The distinctive features of Nabokov's English style will be determined, in some measure, by general differences between the Russian and the English languages. Secondly, we cannot ignore the time-factor. The style of the writer, like the growth of the man, is not static; it is a developing thing, a moving target. The main body of Nabokov's English production post-dates his Russian, and features of his English style will naturally reflect the growing maturity of the man and the writer. Any discussion of the 'individuality' of Nabokov's English must take these two factors into account.

There do exist, however, two later samples of Nabokov's Russian prose—*Drugie berega* (1954) and *Lolita R* (1967) which, it might be hoped, could shed some light on this question of his stylistic individuality. A comparison of Nabokov's earlier and later Russian prose would perhaps throw into relief those features of style which are common to all his mature writing, both in English and in Russian, and thus make it possible to isolate those features which are exclusive to his English. Unfortunately, this line of inquiry is not fruitful. Both *DB* and *Lolita R* are special cases, not suitable for this sort of comparative analysis. *DB* is a memoir. It is about Nabokov's Russian past. Quite understandably, therefore,

the style has close affinities with his early Russian production. (It
was seen in Chapter 7 how out of line *DB* was with the development of the English versions of the Autobiography.) As for the
Russian *Lolita*, the style here bears such strong traces of English
constructions that it cannot safely be treated as an autonomous
piece of Russian. For this reason the two versions have had to be
discounted in the analysis of the development of Nabokov's prose
style.

   One distinctive feature of Nabokov's English is a preference for
precise terms and recherché vocabulary. This preference grows
with continuing practice in the language. When revising an earlier
English version, he frequently replaces a simple English word
with a more unfamiliar or specialized equivalent. There are many
examples of this in the successive editions of the Autobiography
and the development is borne out in all Nabokov's later work,
including his translations. His revisions of the versions submitted
by Scammell and Glenny show just how conscious a feature this is
of his later style. There he frequently substitutes the rare word for
the familiar, the elaborate for the simple. Taking a general view of
this development it would almost seem that Nabokov, in order
to establish an individual style and stamp it with difference and
distinction, was deliberately choosing to step out of the ordinary
in his use of words and quite deliberately preferring the extra-
ordinary. To attempt to clarify this general observation and
identify the nature of 'extraordinariness' in the words he chooses
would lead to analysis under such headings as Latinate words,
technical terms, and purpose-built and invented word forms. In
the following list, examples have been selected from translations
of the novels and grouped under these three headings. Obviously,
though, these compartments are not watertight: some scientific
terms are Latin in origin, and conversely many Latinate words are
used by Nabokov to give an erudite or technical flavour to his
prose. Special attention is focused on examples where Nabokov
alters a version proposed by one of his translators. These are given
first. Examples have also been included from the translations made
in collaboration with Dmitri Nabokov. These sound typically
'Nabokovian' but they cannot be vouched for as Nabokov's own.
They are accordingly given in parentheses. Where words are
known to occur and recur in other English works and translations
a reference is given.

LATINATE WORDS

'vernal'

Mary. Here it is used twice to translate *vesennii* in preference to MG's suggestions: 'springlike' and 'springtime'.

> his gray vernal shadow   (p. 31)
>
> vernal, dusty   (p. 100)

Recurs in: *Glory, The Gift, Spring in Fialta, The Eye, Ada, Lips to Lips, The Circle.*

'auroral'

Mary. It is used in preference to MG's 'of the dawn'.

> the eye accustomed to evening shadows but unfamiliar with auroral ones   (p. 112)

Recurs in: *The Eye* (two examples), *Ada, PF, Pnin, Solus Rex.*

'vesperal'

Mary

> R: небо к вечеру подернулось обморочной бледнотой. (p. 56)
>
> MG: the evening was veiled with a swooning pallor.
>
> VN: the pale sky had dimmed in a vesperal swoon.   (p. 34)

Recurs in : *The Gift.*

'porcine'

The Gift

> R: розовое, как свинья пузо   (p. 377)
>
> MS: a pink pig-like paunch
>
> VN: pink porcine paunches   (p. 318)

Recurs in: *Ada, Ultima Thule.*

'helical'

The Gift

> R: С изогнутой лестницы   (p. 183)
>
> MS: Down the curved staircase
>
> VN: Down the helical stairs   (p. 157)

Another example: p. 21. Recurs in: *The Defence* ('heliced'), *Glory, PF.*

'habitus'

The Gift

R: мысленный быт молодого петербургского литератора-дилетанта (p. 115)

MS: the intellectual life

VN: the intellectual habitus of a young dilettante member of the St. Petersburg literary set (p. 101)

Another example: p. 332. Recurs in: *IB*.

'ingress'

The Gift

R: и затем, весь войдя (p. 209)

MS: then, coming right in

VN: then, ingressing entirely (p. 178)

'crepitate'

Mary

R: Щетина на вытянутой коже... равномерно похрусты-вала (p. 46)

MG: the bristles on his taut skin gave a steady crackle

VN: the bristles on his taut skin steadily crepitated (p. 28)

Recurs in: *Glory*, *The Gift*, *PF*, *Pnin*, *Lips to Lips*, *Solus Rex*.

'reticulate'

The Gift

R: Клетчатое прикосновение ее соленых губ сквозь вуаль. (p. 173)

MS: The trellised touch of her salty lips through the veil.

VN: The reticulate touch of her salty lips through the veil. (p. 149)

Recurs in: *SM* ('the touch of reticulated tenderness').

('vespertine')

Invitation to a Beheading

R: под черным вечерним дубом (p. 128)

E: beneath the black vespertine oak (p. 114)

('crepuscular')

Glory

R: и сумрачное колыхание сирени (p. 130)

E: and the crepuscular undulation of lilacs (p. 143)

Recurs in: *The Potato Elf*.

('lacustrine')

Glory

R: в озерные, камышевые, сосновые окрестности города
(p. 132)

lacustrine, reedy, piny outskirts of the city   (p. 146)

('equine')

Glory

R: добрых седых лошадиных губ   (p. 115)

the gentle equine lips   (p. 128)

('sylvan')

Invitation to a Beheading

R: или лесным разбойником   (p. 134)

or a sylvan robber   (p. 120)

('inutile')

KQKn

R: в упоительную область воображения   (p. 70)

the ravishing realm of inutile imagination   (p. 70)

Recurs in: *The Potato Elf*; and in *Ada* ('utile').

('astral')

The Potato Elf

R: погруженным в астрологические мечты   (*Voz Ch*, p. 170)

E: when immersed in astral fancies   (*RB*, p. 226)

The Bertensson/Kosinska translation has: 'when he was thinking about his magic.'

('ovate')

The Leonardo

R: Вот овальный тополек в своей апрельской пунктирной
зелени   (*VF*, p. 57)

E: Here comes the ovate little poplar, all punctated with April
greenery   (*RB*, p. 11)

('ovine')

Lips to Lips

R: красивыми бараньими глазами   (*VF*, p. 268)

E: beautiful ovine eyes   (*RB*, p. 62)

('vulturine')
  Solus Rex
      R: взгляд голых стервятничьих глаз   (p. 23)
      E: the gaze of his lashless vulturine eyes   (*RB*, p. 205)

('senescent')
  Solus Rex
      R: обручился со стареющей девушкой   (p. 29)
      E: he had become engaged to a senescent virgin   (*RB*, p. 211)

('sinistral')
  Ultima Thule
      R: крепким налево накрененным почерком   (*VF*, p. 279)
      E: strong, sinistral handwriting   (*RB*, p. 154)

('riparian')
  The Circle
      R: Его постоянным товарищем по речной части   (*VF*,
          p. 43)
      E: His constant companion in riparian pastimes   (*RB*, p. 259)

('palpated')
  The Leonardo
      R: Ненавистно все то, что нельзя тронуть, взвесить, сосчи-
          тать.   (*VF*, p. 65)
      E: Hateful is everything that cannot be palpated, measured,
          counted.   (*RB*, p. 18)
  Recurs in: *Torpid Smoke, Pnin.*

('nictate')
  Invitation to a Beheading
      R: и моргая длинными, бледными, как бы даже седыми,
          ресницами   (p. 56)
      E: and her long, pale, almost white lashes nictating   (p. 40)
  Recurs in: *PF* ('nictitation'); *The Leonardo.*

('susurrous')
  Glory
      R: Быстро шелестел открытый таксомотор   (p. 112)
      E: The taxi sped with a susurrous sound   (p. 185)
  Recurs in: *SM.*

('mamillae')

Solus Rex

     R: сосцы добродетели   (p. 28)

     E: the mamillae of merit   (*RB*, p. 209)

('malleation')

Solus Rex

     R: цепь, требовавшую прежде всего постепенности ковки
       (p. 30)

     E: a chain that demanded above all some gradual form of mallea-
       tion   (*RB*, p. 212)

('mollitude')[1]

Solus Rex

     R: кабинетной негой   (p. 29)

     E: the mollitude of his book-lined study   (*RB*, p. 210)

Recurs in: *EO*.

TECHNICAL WORDS

'clavicle'

Mary

     R: он расстегивал ей кофточку, целовал ее в горячую ключицу
       (p. 104)

     MG: he unbuttoned her jacket, kissed her burning collar-bone

     VN: he unbuttoned her blouse, kissed her hot clavicle   (pp. 67–8)

Recurs in: *The Gift*, *The Eye*, *Ada*.

'glabella'

The Gift

     R: переносица   (p. 250)

     MS: the bridge of the nose

     VN: the glabella   (p. 213)

Recurs in: *The Defence*, *The Eye*.

---

[1] This was one of the words which Edmund Wilson cited as an example of
Nabokov's 'addiction to rare and unfamiliar words' in his review of *EO*, 1965.
Nabokov countered this criticism in his 'Reply to My Critics', 1966.

'viscera'

The Gift

    R: показывает образованному миру все свои внутренности
       (p. 277)

    MS: showing the educated world the whole of his inside

    VN: showing the educated world all his viscera   (p. 235)

'auricular'

The Gift

    R: величиной с согнутый мизинец   (p. 349)

    MS: the size of a bent little finger

    VN: the size of a bent auricular finger   (p. 296)

Recurs in: *The Defence, IB, KQKn, PF.* (Note: In French, *l'auriculaire* is a common alternative for *le petit doigt.*)

'pabulum'

The Gift

    R: люди, духовно передовые, понимали, что одним «искус-
       ством», одной «лирой» сыт не будешь.   (p. 340)

    MS: spiritually progressive people understood that mere 'art'
       and the 'lyre' was not enough.

    VN: spiritually progressive people understood that mere 'art' and
       the 'lyre' were not a sufficient pabulum.   (p. 289)

'hemicycle'

The Gift

    R: Между эстрадой и передним полукругом аудитории
       (p. 289)

    MS: Between the platform and foremost semicircle of the audi-
       torium

    VN: Between the platform and foremost hemicycle of the audi-
       torium   (p. 246)

'maculation'

The Gift

    R: с кровавым крапом у корней   (p. 134)

    MS: the specks of blood at their roots

    VN: the blood-red maculation at their roots   (p. 116)

Recurs in: *IB* ('macules of light').

'*Epicnaptera* moth'

   The Gift

      R: шелкопряд   (p. 108)

      MS: silkworm

      VN: *Epicnaptera* moth   (p. 96)

'peba'

   The Gift

      R: кожа у него была, как броня у некоторых насекомоядных. (p. 214)

      MS: his skin was like the armour on an anteater.

      VN: his skin was like the armour on a peba.   (p. 183)

'lampyrid'

   Mary

      R: бледно-зеленого светляка   (p. 112)

      MG: a pale green glowworm

      VN: one of the pale green lampyrids   (p. 73)

   (Nabokov also has 'glowworm' on the same page.)

'aments'

   Mary

      R: скользких от ольховых сережек   (p. 86)

      MG: slippery with alder catkins

      VN: slippery with alder aments   (p. 56)

('achenes'/'papillae')

   KQKn

      with such nice, plump, lumpy, glossy red strawberries positively crying to be bitten into, all their achenes proclaiming their affinity with one's own tongue's papillae . . . (p. 2)

   (This is added in the English version.)

('chorea')

   KQKn

      he managed to convey the impression of acute chorea . . . (p. 194)

   (This is added in the English version.)

('exfoliating')

KQKn

> They were now in front of the house where another good anecdote was in the process of what botanically minded folklorists call 'exfoliating'. (p. 220)

(This is added in the English version.)

('stridulation')

Ultima Thule

> R: где вырабатывали свой ночной цинк кузнечики (*VF*, p. 283)

> E: while crickets zinked the night with their stridulation (*RB*, p. 157)

Recurs in: *A Russian Beauty*.

('axilla')

The Potato Elf

> R: присосался губами к бритой мышке, к горячей, чуть колючей впадине. (*Voz Ch*, p. 169)

> E: glued his lips to the hot pricklish hollow of her shaven axilla. (*RB*, p. 225)

The Bertensson/Kosinska translation has: 'fastened his lips to to her shaven, hot, slightly prickly armpit.'

3. INVENTED WORDS AND UNUSUAL WORD FORMATIONS

'racemosa'

This is a noun formed from adjective 'racemose', and is first used in *EO* to translate *cheremukha* (VI. vii. 9).

Recurs in: *Mary, SM, The Circle*.

('sculptitory')

Ultima Thule

> R: силой своей ваятельской воли (*VF*, p. 280)

> E: by the power of his sculptitory will (*RB*, p. 155)

In the first appearance of *Ultima Thule* in *The New Yorker* Nabokov uses the variant 'sculptatory'.

('capitaled')

Torpid Smoke

R: завивался вверх, как легкий столб, шум автомобиля, венчаясь гудком на перекрестке... (*VF*, p. 76)

E: the noise of a car would curl up like a wispy column to be capitaled by a honk at the crossing . . . (*RB*, p. 28)

Particularly common word formations are combinations with the prefix 'fore-' and the diminutive suffixes '-let' and '-icle'. Not all the examples are neologisms but many are rare.

('fore-')

Glory

R: не совпадало с мечтой о нем   (p. 118)

E: not matching exactly its foredream   (p. 131)

The Gift

R: и предугадать все подробности   (p. 16)

E: and fore-fancy all the details   (p. 17)

KQKn

R: ибо его руки она особенно любила   (p. 102)

E: for she particularly loved his forelimbs   (p. 104)

Glory

R: так щедро отвечал на предчувствия   (p. 178)

E: so generously fulfilled his forefeeling   (p. 33)

The Potato Elf

R: Человек не может провидеть, какой именно день достанется ему... (*Voz Ch*, p. 175)

E: A person cannot foreknow which day exactly will fall to his lot . . . (*RB*, p. 231)

The Bertensson/Kosinska translation has: 'No one can foresee which day will be his . . .'.

Analogous formations are found in Nabokov's original English works. For example:

Pnin: forehear, forelimbs
Lolita: foreglimpsed, forehanging
PF: forevision, foretime, forefeels
Despair 2 (Foreword): foreread
Ada: foreglimpse
Transparent Things: foresmell

'-icle'

The Gift

R: стишки, посвященные войне   (p. 146)

MS: verses dedicated to the war

VN: versicles dedicated to the war   (p. 126)

Recurs in: *Lips to Lips*.

The Gift

R: живое ядрышко   (p. 135)

MS: each a living nucleus

VN: each a live orbicle   (p. 117)

('-let')

KQKn

R: Подул ветерок, сорвал бумажку...   (p. 244)

E: A sudden breeze took possession of the paper baglet...   (p. 258)

Glory

R: цепляясь за кустики жестких цветов   (p. 127)

E: clutching at shrublets of rough flowers   (p. 85)

Invitation to a Beheading

R: заводные, двухместные «часики»   (p. 81)

E: spring-powered, two-seat 'clocklets'   (p. 66)

Ultima Thule

R: данная истинка   (*VF*, p. 300)

E: a given truthlet, to coin a diminutive   (*RB*, p. 172)

('-kins')

Ultima Thule

R: и таких... зовут трупсиками.   (*VF*, p. 276)

E: and that such children . . . were known as cadaverkins.   (*RB*, p. 151)

Other translations contain 'streamlet', 'chainlet', 'rootlet', 'heart-let', 'tearlet', 'treelet'. This form of diminutive also proliferates in Nabokov's later original works. *Lolita* has 'faunlet', coined as a male equivalent of 'nymphet'. This diminutive recurs in *PF* which in addition has 'circlet', 'roundlet', 'wavelet', and 'cloudlet'. *Pnin* has 'townlet', 'bunchlet', and '*émigré* rhymesterettes'. *Transparent Things* has 'flaglets' and 'flamelet'. *Ada* contains even more exotic formations: apart from 'droplet' and 'vaselet', there is 'nipplet', 'flowlets', 'wartlet', 'floweret', 'poodlet', 'beardlet', and 'whorelet'!

Certain features of this vocabulary deserve especial comment. Although only a small selection of examples has been given here, in fact a large proportion of the added specialist terms have to do with plants and insects and reflect Nabokov's interest in the natural sciences, entomology and lepidoptery in particular. Nabokov's interest in these fields dates right back to early childhood and his Russian works contain a considerable number of scientific terms. (*Dar* has a great many.) English, however, possesses greater resources of technical vocabulary than Russian, and in his later writing Nabokov draws upon and exploits these resources. To a certain extent, therefore, Nabokov's development in this area of vocabulary can be said to be partly conditioned by language.

Many other words appear to have been chosen simply because Nabokov likes the sound of them. Words such as 'crepitate', 'susurrous', and 'nictate' have an obvious onomatopoeic value. Others are combined into patterns of alliteration and assonance: 'beautiful ovine eyes', for example, or 'the mamillae of merit'. And the word 'racemosa', as Nabokov explains in his commentary to *EO*, was coined to evoke something of the beauty of this tree in bloom:

> The Russian word [*cheremukha*], with its fluffy and dreamy syllables, admirably suits this beautiful tree, distinguished by its long racemes of flowers, giving the whole of it, when in bloom, a gentle pendulous appearance. . . . I now formally introduce the simple and euphonious 'racemosa' used as a noun and rhyming with 'mimosa'.[1]

We have here further illustration of the point made in Chapter 8 (pp. 176–9) about the sound-determined quality of much of Nabokov's writing.

What also emerges clearly from these examples is that some of the unusualness of Nabokov's English vocabulary can be traced to the influence of Russian. To this Russian influence might be ascribed the free use of the prefix 'fore-', by analogy with the common Russian prefix *pred-*, and also the predilection for diminutive suffixes. Whilst it must be acknowledged that Nabokov's

---

[1] Vol. 3, pp. 11–12.

Russian already contains some novel diminutives—*istinka* and *trupsiki*, for example—his use of the form in English is unquestionably more inventive and more unusual. It is arguable, too, that Nabokov's fondness for such Latinate adjectives as 'vernal', 'vesperal', 'equine', etc. derives from the influence of Russian, where adjectives can readily be formed from the corresponding nouns. For example, *vesna/vesennii* (spring), *vecher/vechernyi* (evening), *loshad'/loshadinyi* (horse), *ozero/ozernyi* (lake), *rassvet/ rassvetnyi* (dawn). It is equally clear that Nabokov's preference for these forms does not derive from an imperfect knowledge of English and registers of English style. *Vesennii* and *vechernyi* are not everywhere translated by the poetic 'vernal' and 'vesperal'. Nabokov also employs the neutral English equivalents 'spring-like', 'spring', and 'evening'. Similarly, Russian diminutives are not invariably translated by the suffixes '-let' and '-icle'. In the majority of cases, Nabokov is quite prepared to use a qualifying adjective such as 'little' or 'diminutive'. Nor are these Russian-inspired forms encountered only in the translations. They also recur in his original English works. Nabokov, in his later writing, is consciously drawing upon the resources of his native language in order to add colour and variety to his English style. It is not only in the use of prefixes and suffixes that the Russian influence on Nabokov's English style is apparent. Rowe, in *Nabokov's Deceptive World*, has pointed out the continuing influence of Russian in Nabokov's word order, in his choice of colour adjectives and in the attention he pays to the roots and component parts of words.[1] And, more generally, Nabokov's 'foreignness' can be traced in his fresh and unorthodox approach to the language. His viewpoint is different, his perception not dulled by familiarity. Thus he can contrive unusual word combinations, patterns of sound and meaning, which would not readily occur to a native speaker.

It cannot, however, be expected that a list of examples can give an adequate, or even a balanced representation of the unusualness of Nabokov's English vocabulary. Quotations, stripped of their contexts, lose their resonance. They show the incidence of a given feature, but they do not enable us to judge whether it has been

---

[1] pp. 26–42. Rowe's observations seem entirely valid. A criticism could, however, be made of his choice of examples. Here again, as in his discussion of assonance, he fails to allow for the part played by Nabokov's collaborators. The examples from *The Gift* and *The Defence* which he quotes on p. 28 and pp. 29–30, are all in Scammell's manuscript. They are not Nabokov's own.

well chosen. Any evaluation of Nabokov's vocabulary needs to be based on an examination of the words in their settings. Where Nabokov does employ a rare or unusual word it is often with telling stylistic effect. The intended effect may be poetic, as in the example from *Mary* where the hero, Ganin, is evoking the distant memory of Sevastopol: 'This was how Sevastopol remained in his memory—*vernal*, dusty, in the grip of a kind of lifeless, dreamy disquiet' (p. 100; my italics). Or it may be ironic, as in the example from *Lips to Lips*, where Nabokov is mimicking the hackneyed romanticism of his hero's novelistic style: 'Ilya Borisovich naively delighted in the gleam of its rich knob, and did not foresee, alas, what claims that valuable article would make, how painfully it would demand mention, when Dolinin, his hands feeling the curves of a supple young body, would be carrying Irina across a *vernal* rill' (*RB*, p. 48). Or, as in *Ultima Thule* and *Solus Rex*, Nabokov may deliberately be cultivating an eccentric style, fitted to the tortured, lunatic atmosphere of his narrative. At other times unusual words serve to distance the events of the narrative: a technical word, judiciously placed, can puncture the 'realism' of a description. The positioning of 'axilla' in *The Potato Elf* is an effective instance of this sort of distancing. A dwarf is pathetically attempting to relieve his pent-up sexual frustrations on two circus acrobats:

> Finally, when frolicsome Arabella drew him to her and fell backward upon the couch, Fred lost his head and began to wriggle against her, snorting and clasping her neck. In attempting to push him away, she raised her arm and, slipping under it, he lunged and glued his lips to the hot pricklish hollow of her shaven *axilla*. (*RB*, p. 225)

A rarefied vocabulary, however, requires rare handling. In the wrong contexts these words can jar and sound idiosyncratic, at times precious. Wherein, for example, lies the emotive impact of 'clavicle', which intrudes upon more than one highly-charged scene? Here is Ganin at his rendezvous with Mary:

> And amid the hubbub of the autumn night, he unbuttoned her blouse, kissed her hot *clavicle*; she remained silent—only her eyes glistened faintly, and the skin of her bared breast slowly turned cold from the touch of his lips and the humid night wind. (*Mary*, pp. 67–8)

Here is the final scene between Zina and Fyodor in *The Gift*:

> The mist of some sorrow had enveloped Zina—her cheeks, her
> narrowed eyes, her throat pit, her fragile *clavicle*—and this was
> somehow enhanced by the pale smoke from her cigarette. The
> scuffing of passers-by seemed to stir up the thickening darkness.
> (p. 342)

Here is Smurov fantasizing about his beloved Vanya in *The
Eye*:

> yes, everything about her was excruciating and somehow irre-
> mediable, and only in my dreams, drenched with tears, did I at
> last embrace her and feel under my lips her neck and the hollow
> near the *clavicle*. (p. 73)

These examples have, for this reader at least, a certain quaint
charm. Perhaps, here again, Nabokov simply likes the sound of
the word. But elsewhere his touch is rather heavier and the effect
mannered and pretentious. It is the more to be regretted that this
'cleverness with words' has become a more prominent feature in
his writing. In *Transparent Things*, in the person of the writer R., he
throws out a barely veiled challenge to potential critics of his own
practice. R. has once been taken to task by a 'clownish critic' for
the phrase 'umbral companion' (p. 98). R.'s novel, *Tralatitions*,
provides his proof-reader, Hugh Person, with some thorny
problems:

> Sometimes he wondered what the phrase really meant—what
> exactly did 'rimiform' suggest and how did a 'balanic plum' look,
> or should he cap the 'b' and insert a 'k' after 'l'? The dictionary
> he used at home was less informative than the huge battered one
> in the office and he was now stumped by such beautiful things as
> 'all the gold of a kew tree' and 'a dappled nebris'. He queried the
> middle word in the name of an incidental character 'Adam von
> Librikov', because the German particle seemed to clash with the
> rest; or was the entire combination a sly scramble? (p. 75)

In an interview first published in *Strong Opinions* Nabokov again
turns defence into attack: 'My books, all my books, are addressed
not to 'dunderheads'; not to the cretins who believe that I like
long Latinate words' (p. 196).

While Nabokov's command of English undoubtedly improves,
it does not for all that become more conventional. He continues
to draw upon his knowledge of Russian and consciously strives

after unusual, striking effects. Sometimes the intention is playful and the brilliance merely superficial, but where the intention is serious the stylistic effect can sometimes be arresting and deeply satisfying. As Granville Hicks said in an article in 1967:

> He takes pleasure—a malicious pleasure, it sometimes seems—in using rare words and rare forms of words. . . . But it must also be remembered that he often uses the uncommon word because it is for him the right word. I should not leave the impression that as a stylist Nabokov is merely a gamester; on the contrary . . . he is serious in intention and possessed of a marvelous command of the resources of the English language.

The examination of Nabokov's developing English style can be carried beyond mere choice of words and their harmonies to larger units and the rhythmical grouping of words. Nabokov is attentive to the rhythm and harmony of his prose. Rhythmic, even metrical prose is a marked feature of his Russian writing, and he carries this feature over into his English production. The experimental pastiches of Blok and Bely, for example, which are contained in *Dar* may be matched against the prose poems which begin both *Bend Sinister* and *Lolita*.

A distinctive rhythmical feature of Nabokov's English style which has been chosen for comment here is his preference for balanced pairs of words and phrases. Certainly, examples of this type of balanced construction are to be found in all Nabokov's production, both English and Russian, but the results of this investigation show this to be a less common and less prominent feature of his Russian style. The pairing may be of identical, similar, or of contrasting elements and is often highlighted by alliteration, word-play, or even rhyme. It is a feature, like the recherché vocabulary, which becomes more pronounced in his later English writing. It is noticeable in the later translations, but more particularly in works written originally in English. Proffer, in his study of *Lolita*, has set out a number of groups of these 'doublets', as he calls them, and the reader is referred to this study for examples from this novel.[1] The following selection of examples is taken from Nabokov's other English novels and from the English translations. Examples from the translations prepared by Dmitri Nabokov are again put in parentheses.

[1] *Keys to Lolita*, pp. 90–5.

ANTITHETICAL PAIRS

LD

R: заходила вразвалку   (p. 44)

E1: her walk turned into a waddle

LD: her careless walk changed to a careful waddle   (p. 11)

Pnin

and the little bright house was securely locked up in the large dark night.   (p. 173)

PF

with a heavy heart and a puzzled mind   (p. 90)

with the sounds of new life in the trees cruelly mimicking the cracklings of old death in my brain   (p. 96)

Ada

the place's tall bookcases and short cabinets, its dark pictures and pale busts   (p. 41)

The early afternoon sun found new places to brighten and old places to toast.   (p. 81)

looking down, with old wistfulness and an infant's curiosity (p. 81)

SEMANTIC PARALLELISM AND REPETITION

(KQKn)

R: Марта… нисколько не была похожа на вчерашнюю даму, которая позевывала, как тигрица.   (pp. 29–30)

Martha bore no resemblance at all to the lady in the train who had glowed like a picture and yawned like a tigress.   (p. 27)

two different radios on two different levels   (p. 53)

(This is added in the English version.)

PF

last smokes and last grins   (p. 83)

Ada

the coming of a first pause in late August, a first silence in early September.   (p. 139)

the head of the arrow, the point of the pain.   (p. 192)

PAIRING INVOLVING ALLITERATION AND ASSONANCE

(*KQKn*)

> R: именно по... природному знанию пряностей и зелий, полезного и вредного... (p. 158)

because of . . . an instinctive knowledge of spices and herbs, of the healthful and the harmful. (pp. 161–2)

> R: Лужи состояли уже не просто из пресной воды, а из какой-то синей, искрящейся жидкости. (p. 167)

Puddles consisted not of liquid mud but limpid pigments . . . (p. 171)

Pnin

It had body but it lacked bouquet. (p. 146)

PF

the hint of a haze (p. 92)

I could distinguish the expression of passionate interest, rapture and reverence . . . (p. 89; see also p. 88)

Here are the great mansions of madness, the impeccably planned dormitories—bedlams of jungle music . . . (p. 92)

in my tender and terrible boyhood (p. 88)

Ada

drizzly and warm, gauzy and green (p. 4)

with limpid limbs and a leaden head (p. 27)

pernicious fads and popular fantasies (p. 73)

at possible failings and fadings, at the fatigue of its fugue (p. 139)

Transparent Things

imitation aragonite, carved and colored in the Grumbel jail by a homosexual convict (p. 13)

with a nobiliary particle between castle and crag (p. 24)

amidst the clanging and knocking wilderness of clay and cranes (p. 37)

the clink of crockery. (p. 48)

Once, however, he was sure he had caught her, floating and flashing, red-anoraked, bare-headed, agonizingly graceful . . . (p. 53)

PAIRING INVOLVING WORD-PLAY AND RHYME

(*KQKn*)

R: Тикали часы.   (p. 126)

E: The clock tocked rather than ticked, the tock clicked and clocked.   (p. 128)

PF

with a hapless, and capless, policeman riding two seats behind him   (p. 99)

Ada

a book addressed to young laymen and lemans—and not to grave men or gravemen.   (p. 17)

the collected works of unrecollected authors   (p. 41)

This list is not intended to be exhaustive. There are more examples in every one of the works cited. Examples occur most frequently in Nabokov's original English works and especially in *Ada*. The growth of this feature in Nabokov's English writing undoubtedly reflects inherent differences between English and Russian syntax and word formation. English, with its abundance of short and monosyllabic words offers more opportunity for these cryptic and pithy combinations of sound and sense. But there is also another factor—Nabokov's own maturation as a writer. These carefully balanced phrases, like the recherché vocabulary, demonstrate the controlled and self-conscious brilliance which distinguishes all of his mature writing, both in style (the added alliteration and word-play) and in the handling of plot and characterization. Ultimately, therefore, it must be recognized that Nabokov's creative development is inextricably bound up with his adoption of the English language and continuing experiment in that new medium.

The final comment is perhaps best left with Nabokov himself. In a paragraph in his Afterword to the Russian *Lolita* he summarizes what he sees as some of the essential differences between Russian and English and gives some suggestions as to what each language is more suited to describe. But in so doing he illuminates the very point which has been central to this argument regarding his own personal development as an author. When he contrasts the 'greenness' of Russian with the 'ripeness' of English he is expressing his own view on general differences between the two languages, but it is tempting and, indeed, more rewarding, to read into this an allegorical description of his own literary evolution, from youth to maturity:

Телодвижения, ужимки, ландшафты, томление деревьев, запахи, дожди, тающие и переливчатые оттенки природы, все нежно-человеческое (как ни странно!), а также все мужицкое, грубое, сочно-похабное, выходит по-русски не хуже, если не лучше, чем по-английски; но столь свойственные английскому тонкие недоговоренности, поэзия мысли, мгновенная перекличка между отвлеченнейшими понятиями, роение односложных эпитетов, все это, а также все относящееся к технике, модам, спорту, естественным наукам и противоестественным страстям — становится по-русски топорным, многословным и часто отвратительным в смысле стиля и ритма. Эта невязка отражает основную разницу в историческом плане между зеленым русским литературным языком и зрелым, как лопающаяся по швам смоква, языком английским: между гениальным, но еще недостаточно образованным, а иногда довольно безвкусным юношей, и маститым гением, соединяющим в себе запасы пестрого знания с полной свободой духа. Свобода духа! Все дыхание человечества в этом сочетании слов.[1]

[1] pp. 296–7.

CONCLUSION

I'm the shuttlecock above the Atlantic, and how bright
and blue it is there in my private sky, far from the
pigeonholes and the clay pigeons.[1]

NABOKOV has on several occasions expressed his distaste for
the *gestation de l'œuvre* type of criticism. For him only
the final printed version has any validity. Rough drafts,
galleys, manuscripts are of no value and should be destroyed:

> for he belonged to that rare type of writer who knows that nothing
> ought to remain except the perfect achievement: the printed book;
> that its actual existence is inconsistent with that of its spectre,
> the uncouth manuscript flaunting its imperfections like a revenge-
> ful ghost carrying its own head under its arm; and that for this
> reason the litter of the workshop, no matter its sentimental or
> commercial value, must never subsist.

This is a description of Sebastian Knight, a writer who shares
many of the literary beliefs of his creator.[2] But paradoxical though
it may seem Nabokov is himself an incorrigible reviser. He is
continually refashioning the same material in different contexts,
in different works, and in different versions of the same work. In
his translations Nabokov frequently makes substantial changes,
changes which give some clear indications of his method of composition and his evolution as a writer. In the novels which undergo
major revisions—*Despair 2*, *Laughter in the Dark*, *King, Queen,
Knave*, and *The Eye*—the mechanism of the plot is tightened and
made more dramatic. Character and situation are treated with more
colour and more humour. There is more vivid detail, and more
blatant and ribald treatment of sex. The style is also embellished
with striking alliterative and rhythmic effects. But the colour and
verve which Nabokov adds in these translations is accompanied by
a greater display of authorial irony and detachment. The artifice
of literary creation is openly exposed; the characterization is more
stylized, the language more brilliant and more obtrusive.

---

[1] Interview with Nabokov conducted by Nicholas Garnham, 1968.
[2] *The Real Life of Sebastian Knight*, p. 34.

It has been suggested earlier that this blend of stylization and enlivenment which characterizes Nabokov's revisions perhaps results from the restrictive conditions attending a rewrite. The author can emend, touch up, and elaborate his earlier work, but, at several years' remove, he cannot recapture the original creative impulse. The work is already done, finished, and the author remains outside it. There may well be some truth in this. However, the changes which Nabokov makes cannot be regarded simply as afterthoughts 'tacked on' to an earlier work. They are always in keeping with the original design. What is more, they are consistent with his conception of art and with the general development of his creative writing.

Nabokov has always reacted strongly against conventional notions of 'realism', or the belief that a novel should contain ideas and have a message. For him art has always been its own justification and created its own reality. 'Although I do not care for the slogan "art for art's sake" . . . there can be no question that what makes a work of fiction safe from larvae and rust is not its social importance but its art, only its art.' Nabokov made this statement in interview in 1964.[1] Earlier, in his Afterword to *Lolita*, he had declared: 'For me a work of fiction exists only in so far as it affords me what I shall bluntly call aesthetic bliss.'[2]

Nabokov has a rare talent for conveying a feel of reality, of creating a memorable character and evoking the atmosphere of a place and an epoch. But Nabokov's 'aesthetic bliss' is not just derived from portraiture, the depiction of *mœurs* or the telling of a good story. His pleasure, his greater pleasure, is rather in the combination of these elements into a pattern which may mimic the form of external reality but which has meaning and justification finally only in its own terms—the patterning of art. The story of Nabokov's development as a writer is the story of a developing preoccupation with pattern and artifice.

There are aspects of this development in which Nabokov's Russian and English writings exhibit a certain parallelism. One of these aspects is his use of fantasy. The imaginary land is a recurrent theme in his work, but it assumes greatest prominence at points when his skill in depicting surrounding reality is most apparent. This happened in his Russian period. In *Dar*, his last

---

[1] Interview conducted by Alvin Toffler, *Playboy*, 1964.
[2] *Lolita*, p. 305.

Russian novel, Nabokov gave his most complete and vivid picture of Russian *émigré* life in Europe; the setting and the characters are masterfully drawn, and combined with an absorbing investigation into the nature of art and the workings of artistic creation. But after *Dar* Nabokov turned increasingly to fantasy: in his play, *Izobretenie Val'sa*, and then in his two last Russian stories, *Ultima Thule* and *Solus Rex*. Nabokov's writing in English follows an analogous curve of development. The imaginary land is still a recurrent theme, but it again assumes greater prominence after Nabokov has demonstrated his skill in depicting his new surroundings. After the brilliant evocation of American life in *Lolita* and *Pnin* Nabokov once more turns away from realistic settings. There follows *Pale Fire* which juxtaposes an American and an imaginary setting; then *Ada*, where the setting is entirely imaginary; and in 1972, *Transparent Things*, set in a highly stylized version of Switzerland where every place-name is fictitious.

If it is possible, as in this instance, to see some parallelism in the development of Nabokov's Russian and English productions, nevertheless, a study of his revisions shows that preoccupation with artifice is both a continuing and an increasingly marked feature of his writing. This is apparent in his reworking of his autobiography, and it can be seen, too, in his translations where he imposes pattern and design upon earlier Russian works. Perceptive and admiring critics have always rightly laid stress on the importance of artifice in his writing. Khodasevich, for example, said as early as 1930 in a review of *Zashchita Luzhina* that it contained that 'noble artificiality, which is the necessary accompaniment of all art':

> В ней есть и та благородная искусственность, которая неизбежно и необходимо сопутствует всякому искусству. Профаны и дилетанты ее пугаются — мастера без нее не работают.

In Nabokov's continued and developing cultivation of artifice there is much that a contemporary Khodasevich would find to admire. There are indeed many ways in which an earlier work is improved by the changes which he makes. It is difficult, however, to give unreserved approval to all Nabokov's later additions. Deployment of artifice is not to be equated with exhibition of artifice, and there is in Nabokov's later writing and in his revisions of earlier works what can only be termed an exhibitionist tendency. It is hard to describe in other terms the increasing emphasis on those aspects of his writing which have attracted the attention and in some cases the censure of critics, be it his verbal dexterity or his predilection for unsavoury subjects. Nabokov's projection of his popular literary image is often parodic, and often humorous; but this is self-conscious, not conscious art. And it does not reflect that 'curiosity, tenderness, kindness, ecstasy', which is Nabokov's own definition of art,[1] and which is the effect of the best of his writing.

The question remains to what extent the change of language has influenced Nabokov's development. It could be suggested, perhaps, that the increased detachment and stylization of his later writing derives in part at least from his position as an outsider, a foreigner writing in an alien language. Perhaps, even, his liberal and free treatment of sex is not unconnected with the freedom from social and linguistic inhibitions which is enjoyed by any stranger in foreign parts, speaking a foreign tongue. Perhaps. But these are shadowy suppositions, hypotheses altogether too vague. Only on the level of style is it possible to see clearly how the change of language has influenced Nabokov's development. The brilliance of Nabokov's later English style owes not a little to his viewpoint as a foreigner. He sees the English language through different eyes. He sees patterns of sound and potential meanings in words which the native speaker, his perception dulled through familiarity, would simply pass over. He deviates more readily from set modes of expression and conventional registers of style, inventing new and arresting word combinations, employing high-flown, recherché vocabulary alongside the most mundane colloquialisms. The results are not always successful—some of Nabokov's English writing is uneven, some is mannered and contrived—but at its best this 'foreignness', this fresh, off-centre vision, can make for that 'strangeness', that *ostranenie* which, as a fictitious Nabokov has acknowledged in interview,[2] is central to all true artistic perception.

---

[1] Afterword to *Lolita*, p. 305.

[2] 'Viktor Shklovskij, formerly a fine critic, author of *The Knight's Move*, once coined the term "ostranenie" or "making strange". American Slavists are quick to use it. But is it to refer to Tolstoy's naive Natasha alone? It might just as well apply to the metaphysical conceit. . . . What doesn't make strange, estrange, strangify in a book if the author is a genuine artist?' See Lubin's parody of an interview with Nabokov, in 'Kickshaws and Motley', pp. 202–3.

It is interesting, finally, to project the scope of the argument beyond the narrow confines of the translations and make a few general observations about Nabokov's standing in relation to the mainstream of Russian and English/American literature. Here it is relevant to recall the criticism levelled against him by some *émigré* critics that his Russian writing was in some respects 'foreign', 'un-Russian'. This charge of un-Russianness was brought on three main counts. Firstly, Nabokov was criticized for choosing to describe non-Russian settings and characters. Secondly, it was argued that his formal and compositional brilliance was foreign to the Russian literary tradition. The third, and the most fundamental criticism of all, was that his works lacked the 'love of humanity' which had been the moving force of most great writing.[1] There was a good measure of conservatism, a modicum of sentimentality, and even a touch of envy underlying these criticisms, which is understandable enough given the difficult, pressured conditions of an expatriate literature. If a writer's choice of settings, for example, were to be regarded as a criterion of his affiliation to a particular literary tradition, then the number of 'foreign' writers would indeed be legion. In making this charge the *émigrés* were simply expressing their regret that Nabokov was not putting his talents directly to the service of the expatriate cause, that he was not helping to build up a specifically expatriate literature and consolidate the expatriate identity. But to recognize the limitations of these criticisms is not to deny them all substance. With hindsight, and in the light of Nabokov's subsequent development, his detachment from the expatriate scene does have some significance. We have already noted his fondness for imaginary settings. This leads him in *Solus Rex* to experiment for the first time with an imaginary language—an experiment which he was to continue in two English novels, *Bend Sinister* and *Pale Fire*. There is a parallel here with another bilingual writer, Stefan George, who invented two languages of his own and wrote poetry in both of them. Leonard Forster, who discusses this case in his study of bilingualism points out that George devised his 'lingua romana' at a time when he felt unsure in which language he ought to write. It is perhaps not without significance that Nabokov's experiments were begun at an equivalent moment in his career, when his linguistic

---

[1] A selection of *émigré* critical opinion is given in Appendix E: 'Nabokov in Russian Criticism.'

affiliation was still undecided. And another of Forster's comments has relevance to Nabokov's situation: 'A man who goes to these lengths to exercise himself in an untried medium may be expected to do the same in existing languages too.'[1]

It should be added that the opinion of Nabokov's foreignness was not unanimously held by his *émigré* critics. There were other critics who were equally keen to recognize his links with the Russian literary tradition. Some of them rightly discerned his affinities with Gogol and saw him as an inheritor of that irrational, comic, and linguistically inventive tradition which passed through Dostoevsky to Andrey Bely, and in Soviet Russia to, among others, Nabokov's contemporary, Yury Olesha. But this view is also somewhat one-sided. Nabokov has never identified himself exclusively with any one national literary tradition. In an interview which he gave in 1934, he discussed this question of influence and declared that it was in Russia that he had felt greatest affinity with Western culture; in the West, on the other hand, he found himself more conscious of the 'fascination' of Gogol and of Chekhov:

> Говорят о влиянии на меня немецких писателей, которых я и не знаю. Я ведь вообще плохо читаю по-немецки. Можно говорить скорее о влиянии французском: я люблю Флобера и Пруста. Любопытно, что близость к западной культуре я почувствовал в России. Здесь же, на Западе, я ничему сознательно не научился. Зато особенно остро почувствовались обаяние Гоголя и — ближе к нам — Чехова.[2]

Nabokov cannot be neatly fitted into any national pigeon-hole, and this *was* recognized by one or two of his contemporaries, notably Weidlé and Nikolay Andreyev. They were prepared to take a wider view, and see Nabokov's connections both with the Russian and the Western European tradition. This study has shown that Nabokov's Russian writing does indeed show marked traces of French and English as well as of Russian literary

---

[1] *The Poet's Tongues*, pp. 56–9.

[2] Interview conducted by Sedykh, in *Poslednie novosti*, 1934. Subsequently, in the Forewords to several of his translations, Nabokov showed himself less indulgent to these 'comparison-seekers': see, for example the Foreword to *IB*: 'Incidentally, I could never understand why every book of mine invariably sends reviewers scurrying in search of more or less celebrated names for the purpose of passionate comparison' (pp. 5–6). He acknowledges only one influence on the writing of *IB*—that of the 'altogether delightful Pierre Delalande, whom I invented'.

influence. Thus it is difficult to escape the general conclusion
that whilst his Russian was by no means divorced from Russian
influence it was none the less being fed by Western European
traditions and was to a certain degree 'out of line' with Russian
writing of his time.

It is this stance of non-alignment which Nabokov has preserved
as a writer of English. Certainly he has made every effort to forge
an individual prose style; he adapts his settings and he explores
and plunders the resources of the English literary tradition. If
Dar is Nabokov's homage to Russian literature, *Lolita* is his
homage to the English language and English literature.[1] But
throughout he has never severed his links with Russian, nor
indeed with French. On the contrary, with time he has made
increasing parade of his status as a 'trans-national' writer. In
Transparent Things the characters are Russian, French, and
American, and all three languages are represented. But *Ada*
remains his most flamboyantly cosmopolitan work. There he
conjures up a fantasy world which combines features of Russia,
Western Europe, and North America and which presents the
reader with an imaginative potpourri of settings, languages, and
cultures. Only when Nabokov is considered in relation to these
multiple attachments can the unity of the man and the writer be
perceived across and through the changes in language, and only
then is it possible to put in its proper perspective the question of
whether Nabokov is a Russian, or an American, or even a European writer.

[1] See Nabokov's Foreword to *The Gift*: 'Its heroine is not Zina but Russian
Literature' (p. 8). See the Afterword to *Lolita*: '. . . an American critic suggested
that *Lolita* was the record of my love affair with the romantic novel. The
substitution "English language" for "romantic novel" would make this elegant
formula more correct' (p. 307).

APPENDIX A

TRANSLATIONS OF NABOKOV'S WORKS
INTO ENGLISH AND RUSSIAN

THIS appendix includes all translations published up to the end of 1975. They are listed in chronological order for easy reference. Dates are given of the works' first appearance in print where this is known. Full details of publication are given in the Bibliography. Translations made independently of the author have not been included.

Translation into English

	Translation	Original	
Novels			
1936	*Camera Obscura*	*Camera Obscura*	1932–3
1937	*Despair 1*	*Otchayanie*	1934
1938	*Laughter in the Dark*	*Camera Obscura*	1932–3
1959	*Invitation to a Beheading*	*Priglashenie na kazn'*	1935–6
1963	*The Gift*	*Dar*	1937–8
1964	*The Defence*	*Zashchita Luzhina*	1929–30
1965	*The Eye*	*Soglyadatai*	1930
1966	*Despair 2*	*Otchayanie*	1934
1968	*King, Queen, Knave*	*Korol', dama, valet*	1928
1970	*Mary*	*Mashen'ka*	1926
1971	*Glory*	*Podvig*	1931–2
Plays			
1966	*The Waltz Invention*	*Izobretenie Val'sa*	1938
Short Stories			
1941	*Cloud, Castle, Lake*	*Oblako, ozero, bashnya*	1937
1941	*The Aurelian*	*Pil'gram*	1930
1947	*Spring in Fialta*	*Vesna v Fial'te*	1936
1963	*The Visit to the Museum*	*Poseshchenie muzeya*	1939
1963	*Terra Incognita*	*Terra Incognita*	1931
1964	*Lik*	*Lik*	1939
1966	*An Affair of Honor*	*Podlets*	192?
1971	*Lips to Lips*	*Usta k ustam*	1956
		(The date of composition is given by Field as December 1931.)	

1971	A Dashing Fellow	Khvat	193?
1972	The Circle	Rasskaz	1934
		(later entitled *Krug*)	
1973	Perfection	Sovershenstvo	1932
1973	A Russian Beauty	Krasavitsa	1934
1973	The Leonardo	Korolek	1933
1973	Torpid Smoke	Tyazhelyi dym	1935
1973	Breaking the News	Opoveshchenie	1934
1973	Ultima Thule	Ultima Thule	1942
1973	Solus Rex	Solus Rex	1940
1973	The Potato Elf	Kartofel'nyi El'f	1924
1973	Bachmann	Bakhman	1924
1974	A Nursery Tale	Skazka	1926
1975	Tyrants Destroyed	Istreblenie tiranov	1938
1975	Music	Muzyka	1932
1975	Recruiting	Nabor	1935
1975	Terror	Uzhas	1927
1975	The Admiralty Spire	Admiralteiskaya igla	1933
1975	A Matter of Chance	Sluchainost'	1924
1975	In Memory of L. I. Shigaev	Pamyati L. I. Shigaeva	193?
1975	Vasily Shishkov	Vasily Shishkov	1939
1975	Christmas	Rozhdestvo	1925

Autobiography

1966	Speak, Memory	Drugie berega	1954

Translation into Russian

Novels

1967	Lolita	Lolita	1955

Autobiography

1954	Drugie berega	Conclusive Evidence	1951

APPENDIX B

ADDED AND REWRITTEN PASSAGES IN
KING, QUEEN, KNAVE

Added Passages

Only passages over twelve lines in length are listed here. Lesser interpolations have not been included.

Chapter 3: A conversation between Martha and Franz:

'Where is Mr. Tom today?' . . . The workmen were moving as in a dream. (pp. 51–2)

Chapter 3: The description of Franz's job:

He accepted with alacrity the tedium of his job . . . had embarrassing manners. (p. 80)

Chapter 5: The description of Franz and Martha making love:

Then, his desire exposed . . . His vocabulary was even more primitive. (pp. 96–7)

Chapter 7: The conversation between Martha and Dreyer after the Christmas party:

'Either of the two . . .' Hopelessly bad stenographers, both of them. (p. 147)

Chapter 9: The description of Martha and Franz rehearsing a murder plan:

And while Dreyer was actually sitting in that armchair . . . that she and Franz were so diligently planning. (p. 181)

Chapter 11: The description of the cinema advertising *King, Queen, Knave*:

He walked slowly, looking right and left . . . or something along those lines. (pp. 215–16)

Chapter 11: Martha's preparations for her departure to Gravitz:

She wrote to her sister Hilda . . . and the old soldier shrugged his consent. (pp. 224–5)

Chapter 12: The description of the hotel guests:

Hardly anybody hired any of the poor boats . . . slipped off the seat and vanished. (pp. 232–3)

Chapter 12: The description of Schwartz and Weiss playing chess:

The two young fellows . . . 'Old idiot', muttered Black, whose position was desperate. (p. 241)

Rewritten Passages

These are the most substantially reworked passages of the novel:

Chapter 3: Martha's biography:

> Her mother had died when Martha was three . . . not very interesting recollections. (pp. 65–6)

Chapter 9: The tennis game:

> On the terra-cotta red courts . . . Martha could bear it no longer. (pp. 186–9)

Chapter 11: A visit to the inventor:

> The sculptor who looked like a scientist . . . 'we want her to roll them, and that is difficult.' (pp. 218–19)

Chapter 11: Dreyer's biography:

> Secretly he realised that he was a businessman by accident . . . his gentle bumbling father. (pp. 223–4)

Chapter 13: Another visit to the inventor; Dreyer's return to Gravitz; his conversation with the doctor:

> At home, the gardener informed him of Tom's death . . . 'Your uncle is here.' (pp. 260–5)

Chapter 13: Franz's activities on the day of Martha's death:

> Before leaving with her for the hospital . . . And the fools say second sight does not exist. (pp. 267–71)

APPENDIX C

VERSIONS OF THE AUTOBIOGRAPHY

THIS appendix lists the successive versions of each chapter of the Autobiography. Full details are given of the first appearance of these chapters in periodicals.[1]

Chapter 1:   E1:   *The Perfect Past, The New Yorker*, 15 April 1950
              E2:   *CE*
              R: *DB*
              E3:   *SM*

Chapter 2:   E1:   *Portrait of My Mother, The New Yorker*, 9 April 1949
              E2:   *CE*
              R: *DB*
              E3:   *SM*

Chapter 3:   E1:   *Portrait of My Uncle, The New Yorker*, 3 January 1948
              E2:   *CE*
              R: *DB*
              E3:   *SM*

Chapter 4:   E1:   *My English Education, The New Yorker*, 27 March 1948
              E2:   *CE*
              R: *DB*
              E3:   *SM*

Chapter 5:[2]   F: *Mademoiselle O, Mesures* (Paris), No. 2, 1936
              E1:   *Mademoiselle O, The Atlantic Monthly* (Boston), January 1943
              E2:   *Mademoiselle O, Nine Stories*
                   CE
                   Mademoiselle O, Nabokov's Dozen
              R: *DB*
              E3:   *SM*

---

[1] The separate chapters were composed and published in random sequence.
[2] Chapter 5 and Chapter 7 were included in collections of short stories—in *Nine Stories* and *Nabokov's Dozen*. These versions are identical with *CE*.

Chapter 6: E1: *Butterflies, The New Yorker*, 12 June 1948
             E2: *CE*
             R: *DB*
             E3: *SM*

Chapter 7:[1] E1: *Colette, The New Yorker*, 31 July 1948
             E2: *CE*
                  First Love, Nabokov's Dozen
             R: *DB*
             E3: *SM*

Chapter 8: E1: *Lantern Slides, The New Yorker*, 11 February 1950
             E2: *CE*
             R: *DB*
             E3: *SM*

Chapter 9: E1: *My Russian Education, The New Yorker*, 18 September 1948
             E2: *CE*
             R: *DB*
             E3: *SM*

Chapter 10: E1: *Curtain-Raiser, The New Yorker*, 1 January 1949
            E2: *CE*
            R: *DB*
            E3: *SM*

Chapter 11:[2] E1: *First Poem, Partisan Review* (New York), September 1949
            E2: *CE*
            E3: *SM*

Chapter 12: E1: *Tamara, The New Yorker*, 10 December 1949
            E2: *CE*
            R: *DB* (Chapter 11)
            E3: *SM*

Chapter 13: E1: *Lodgings in Trinity Lane, Harper's Magazine* (New York), January 1951
            E2: *CE*
            R: *DB* (Chapter 12)
            E3: *SM*

[1] See note 2 on previous page.
[2] There is no Russian version of Chapter 11 (*First Poem*).

Chapter 14: E1: *Exile, Partisan Review* (New York), January/
February 1951
E2: *CE*
R: *DB* (Chapter 13)
E3: *SM*

Chapter 15: E1: *Gardens and Parks, The New Yorker,* 17 June 1950
E2: *CE*
R: *DB* (Chapter 14)
E3: *SM*

APPENDIX D

NABOKOV'S USE OF AUTOBIOGRAPHICAL MATERIAL IN FICTION

Novels and Stories containing Autobiographical Material

1926   *Mashen'ka* (Tamara theme)
1930   *Zashchita Luzhina* (childhood; French governess)
1931   *Obida* (childhood, including lantern slides shown by a Russian tutor)
1931–2 *Podvig* (childhood; life at Cambridge)
1932   *Lebeda* (childhood, including an account of the father's involvement in a duel)
1933   *Admiralteiskaya igla* (Tamara theme)
1934   *Rasskaz*[1] (the village schoolmaster)
1937–8 *Dar* (childhood; first poems)
1941   *The Real Life of Sebastian Knight* (childhood, including visit to French governess in Switzerland)

Some Parallel Passages

Podvig

Picture of a forest in the bedroom: Chapter 2, pp. 152–3   Compare: *My English Education*, p. 26; *DB*, p. 75; *SM*, pp. 85–6.

Train model: Chapter 2, p. 154   Compare: *Colette*, p. 17; *DB*, p. 130; *SM*, p. 141.

Train journeys to Biarritz: Chapter 6, pp. 166–8   Compare: *Colette*, pp. 17–18; *DB*, pp. 131–5; *SM*, pp. 141–146. Compare also: *The Perfect Past*, p. 34; *DB*, pp. 14–15; *SM*, p. 24.

The beach at Biarritz: Chapter 6, pp. 168–9   Compare: *Colette*, pp. 18–19; *DB*, pp. 136–7; *SM*, pp. 146–8.

Childhood visits to Berlin: Chapter 6, p. 169; Chapter 32, pp. 120–2   Compare: *Curtain-Raiser*, p. 20; *DB*, pp. 186–9; *SM*, pp. 204–8.

[1] First published under this title. Collected, under the title *Krug*, in *Vesnu v Fial'te i drugie rasskazy*.

Rooms in Cambridge: Chapter 14, pp. 100-1

Compare: *Lodgings in Trinity Lane*, pp. 85-6; 88-9; *DB*, pp. 221-2, 227; *SM*, pp. 259-260, 266-7.

Mashen'ka

Physical description of Mashen'ka: pp. 71, 88

Compare: *Tamara*, p. 35; *DB*, pp. 198-9; *SM*, pp. 230-1.

Her dress, in the country: pp. 74-5

Compare: *Tamara*, p. 35; *DB*, p. 198; *SM*, p. 230.

Her dress, in St. Petersburg: p. 107

Compare: *DB*, p. 202; *SM*, p. 234.

The pavilion: pp. 86-7

Compare: *First Poem*, p. 885; *SM*, pp. 215-16.

Stained glass: pp. 86-7

Compare: *First Poem*, p. 885; *SM*, pp. 215, 216. Compare also: *MO*, p. 159; *DB*, pp. 96-97; *SM*, pp. 106-7.

Interior of the country house: p. 90

Compare: *MO*, p. 154; *DB*, p. 89; *SM*, p. 100.

Uncle's house and estate: pp. 90-1, 103-4

Compare: *Portrait of My Uncle*, p. 25; *DB*, pp. 59-60, 199-200; *SM*, pp. 64, 72, 232-3.

Bicycle ride to rendezvous: pp. 103-4

Compare: *Tamara*, p. 35; *DB*, pp. 200-1; *SM*, p. 233.

Nocturnal rendezvous: pp. 103-4

Compare: *Tamara*, p. 35; *DB*, pp. 200-1; *SM*, pp. 233-4.

Meetings in St. Petersburg: pp. 106-8

Compare: *Tamara*, pp. 35-6; *DB*, pp. 202-5; *SM*, pp. 234-7.

Meeting on the train: pp. 112-14

Compare: *Tamara*, p. 37; *DB*, p. 209; *SM*, pp. 240-1.

Mashen'ka's letters: pp. 132-9

Compare: *Tamara*, p. 39; *DB*, p. 216; *SM*, pp. 249-50.

Description of the Crimea: pp. 133-4

Compare: *Tamara*, p. 35; *DB*, p. 213; *SM*, pp. 244-5.

The passages from *Mashen'ka* and *Speak, Memory* describing the Crimea are reproduced here for comparison:

Ганин вспомнил, как получил это письмо, как пошел в этот далекий январский вечер по крутой каменистой тропе, мимо татарских частоколов, увенчанных там и сям конскими черепами, и как сидел над ручьем, тонкими струями омывающим белые гладкие камни, и глядел сквозь тончайшие, бесчисленные, удивительно-отчетливые сучки голой яблони на розовато-млеющее небо, где блестел, как прозрачный обрезок ногтя, юный месяц, и рядом с ним, у нижнего рога, дрожала светлая капля — первая звезда.

Он написал ей в ту-же ночь, — об этой звезде, о кипарисах в садах, об осле, ревущем утром за домом, в татарском дворе. Он писал ласково, мечтательно, припомнил мокрые сережки на скользком мостике беседки, где они встретились. (*Mashen'ka*, pp. 133–4)

The whole place seemed completely foreign; the smells were not Russian, the sounds were not Russian, the donkey braying every evening just as the muezzin started to chant from the village minaret (a slim blue tower silhouetted against a peach-colored sky) was positively Baghdadian. And there was I standing on a chalky bridle path near a chalky stream bed where separate, serpentlike bands of water thinly glided over oval stones—there was I, holding a letter from Tamara. I looked at the abrupt Yayla Mountains, covered up to their rocky brows with the karakul of the dark Tauric pine; at the maquis-like stretch of evergreen vegetation between mountain and sea; at the translucent pink sky, where a self-conscious crescent shone, with a single humid star near it; and the whole artificial scene struck me as something in a prettily illustrated, albeit sadly abridged, edition of *The Arabian Nights*. Suddenly I felt all the pangs of exile. There had been the case of Pushkin, of course—Pushkin who had wandered in banishment here, among those naturalized cypresses and laurels—but though some prompting might have come from his elegies, I do not think my exaltation was a pose. Thenceforth for several years, until the writing of a novel relieved me of that fertile emotion, the loss of my country was equated for me with the loss of my love. (*SM*, pp. 244–5)

Duplicate Passages

Compare the following passages from *Mademoiselle O* and *Zashchita Luzhina*:

Он вспоминал, как в петербургском доме ее астматическая тучность предпочитала лестнице старомодный, водой движимый лифт, который швейцар пускал в ход при помощи рычага на стене вестибюля. «В путь-дорогу», — неизменно говорил швейцар, закрывая за ней дверные половинки, и тяжкий, отдувающийся, вздрагивающий лифт медленно полз вверх по толстому бархатному шнуру, и мимо лифта, по облупленной стене, видной сквозь стекло, медленно спускались темные географические пятна, те пятна сырости и старости, среди которых, как и среди небесных облаков, господствует мода на очертания Черного моря и Австралии. Иногда маленький Лужин поднимался вместе с ней, но чаще оставался внизу и слушал, как в вышине, за стеной, трудно взбирается лифт, — и он всегда надеялся, маленький Лужин, что лифт на полпути застрянет. Частенько так и случалось. Шум прекращался, из неизвестного междустенного пространства доносился вопль о помощи; швейцар внизу двигал, гакая, рычагом, и открывал дверь в черноту и, глядя вверх, деловито спрашивал: «Поехали?» Наконец что-то содрогалось, приходило в движение, и через некоторый срок спускался лифт — уже пустой. Пустой. Бог весть, что случилось с ней, — быть может, доехала она уже до небес и там осталась, со своей астмой, лакричными конфетами и пенснэ на черном шнурке. (*ZL*, p. 175)

Dans la maison de Pétersbourg, elle préférait à l'escalier de marbre le petit ascenseur démodé à propulsion hydraulique que le concierge mettait en branle au moyen d'une manivelle fixée au mur du vestibule. «En route, marche!» disait-il infailliblement en fermant les deux moitiés de la porte sur Mademoiselle, qui s'écroulait lentement sur la banquette. Et le lourd ascenseur, soufflant et craquant, montait avec une lenteur incroyable le long du gros câble recouvert de velours, tandis qu'avec lenteur sur le mur écaillé que l'on apercevait par la vitre, descendaient de sombres taches qui faisaient songer à un atlas géographique: taches d'humidité et de vétusté, où l'on reconnaissait ces contours de mer Noire ou d'Australie que les nuages et les taches prennent à tout propos. Pour moi, qui étais resté en bas, j'écoutais grimper péniblement la machine et j'avais toujours l'espoir mauvais qu'elle s'arrêterait à mi-chemin. Cela arrivait parfois. Le bruit cessait. On n'entendait que la chute d'un peu de plâtre qui s'effritait quelque part. Puis, d'un espace mystérieux entre les murailles arrivait le «gdié, gdié», si connu, le cri de Mademoiselle en détresse. Alors le Suisse en bas poussait avec effort la manivelle, puis ouvrait la porte dans le noir et regardait en haut pour voir si cela marchait. Enfin, l'ascenseur s'ébranlait, et quelque temps après on retrouvait Mademoiselle en larmes dans sa chambre, — prétendant que le concierge le faisait exprès, qu'elle ne pesait pas tant que ça, voyons. «Ah, les affres que j'ai pu souffrir là-haut, suspendue toute seule dans le vide!»   (*MO*, pp. 163–4)

This appendix is not intended to be exhaustive. Only novels and stories containing a substantial amount of textual correspondence with the Autobiography have been included. Mere thematic echoes have not been noted, though exception has been made for one interesting recurrence of the Tamara theme in *Admiralteiskaya igla*. Small details, the objects which turn up in different contexts, have also not been included. These details are often no more than 'lost property', to borrow the title of Sebastian Knight's most autobiographical work. Whilst it might amuse Nabokov to send his readers off on a paperchase throughout his production,[1] one may be permitted to doubt the virtues of such an undertaking. At best, the replacement of a detail in

---

[1] See Nabokov's Foreword to *KQKn* (p. vii), where he points out the reappearance of a cigarette case in *SM*.

a new context can illuminate Nabokov's continuing preoccupation with the rearrangement of his material. At worst, these recurrences are repetitive and tedious to follow up.

It will be noted that all the works listed appeared before *Conclusive Evidence*, and all of them except for *The Real Life of Sebastian Knight* were written in Russian. In his later production Nabokov's personal experience appears in a less recognizable form. Though still a major source for much of his creative writing, there it is digested, sometimes even parodied. Only one example has been found of a wholesale borrowing from an earlier work. This is the description of the French governess in the lift, which was included first in *Zashchita Luzhina* in 1930, and reused in the French version of *Mademoiselle O* in 1936. In all other cases Nabokov adapts and reworks his material. He does not just translate. While there is, therefore, evidence to suggest that Nabokov used his Russian production as a source of material in the writing of his English autobiography, it cannot be imputed that he abused that source and simply reissued earlier work in a different language.

APPENDIX E

NABOKOV IN RUSSIAN CRITICISM

THIS appendix gives a selection of *émigré* opinions on the literary influences on Nabokov's writing, and on his 'un-Russianness'. These opinions were not always entirely consistent. Critics who levelled the charge of foreignness against Nabokov elsewhere showed themselves keen to see his relation to the mainstream of Russian literature. If, on the one hand, he was compared to Kafka, Proust, Céline, and Giraudoux, on the other his name was linked with those of Chekhov, Bunin, Saltykov-Shchedrin, Leonid Andreev, and—with a good deal more relevance—Bely and Gogol. What cannot be adequately represented here is the amount of praise which Nabokov's work elicited from his Russian reviewers, three of his discerning admirers being Khodasevich, Struve, and Nikolay Andreyev. Reviews which have already been quoted in the text are not duplicated here. Full details of publication are given in the Bibliography.

General Discussions of Literary Influences on Nabokov's Writing and of Nabokov's Place in Russian Literature

BERBEROVA: 'Nabokov i ego *Lolita*', 1959.

KARLINSKY: 'Vladimir Nabokov's novel *Dar* as a Work of Literary Criticism', 1963.

—— 'Nabokov and Chekhov', 1970.

STRUVE: 'Current Russian Literature: Vladimir Sirin', 1934.

—— *Russkaya literatura v izgnanii*, 1956.

—— 'Notes on Nabokov as a Russian Writer', 1967.

Discussion of the Influence of Individual Writers on Nabokov

ADAMOVICH: Though Adamovich admired Nabokov's writing he did not, on his own admission, *like* it: «мне лично его писания были не по душе».

In several reviews he compared Nabokov to Gogol, whom he saw as another writer who was incapable of infusing life into his characters. He more than once expressed fears that Nabokov might come to an equally tragic creative *impasse*. See:

—— Review of *SZ*, No. 55, 1934 (containing a part of *Otchayanie*). Here Adamovich also sees similarities with Sologub, another 'Gogolian' writer.

—— Review of *SZ*, No. 56, 1934 (containing a part of *Otchayanie*).

—— 'Perechityvaya *Otchayanie*', 1936.

—— Review of *Russkie zapiski*, No. 2, 1937 (containing *Oblako, ozero, bashnya*).

See also:

ADAMOVICH : Review of *Russkie zapiski*, Aug.–Sept., 1938 (containing *Istreblenie tiranov*). Here Adamovich sees a thematic resemblance to Dostoevsky's *Zapiski iz podpol'ya* and Olesha's *Zavist'*. A summary of these views is contained in the chapter on Nabokov in Adamovich's book, *Odinochestvo i svoboda*, 1955.

BERBEROVA: 'Nabokov i ego *Lolita*', 1959. Nabokov is seen here as a direct descendant of Gogol, Dostoevsky, and Bely.

BITSILLI: 'Vozrozhdenie allegorii', 1936. A comparison is made with Saltykov-Shchedrin and Gogol. Certain affinities are seen with Céline's *Voyage au bout de la nuit*, but the possibility of direct influence is ruled out. Adamovich disputed the comparison with Saltykov-Shchedrin in his review of *SZ*, No. 61, 1936 (containing *Vesna v Fial'te*).

CHERVINSKAYA: 'Po povodu *Sobytiya* V. Sirina', 1938. The comparison with Gogol is considered:

Гоголь не раз вспоминается при чтении Сирина. Но на самой глубине сходство исчезает. Гоголь смеется, но нигде не усмехается. О Сирине иногда кажется, что он издевается над всем и когда-нибудь в этом признается.

DIKS: Review of *SZ*, No. 30, 1927 (containing *Uzhas*). German influences are cited here, in particular the tradition of Kleist:

В «фактуре» чувствуется сильное влияние немецкой школы — точнее, того ее течения, которое в короткой новелле опирается на традиции Клейста.

KANTOR : 'Bremya pamyati', 1934. Kantor discusses the theme of memory in Nabokov's writing, and finds the treatment more limited than in Proust.

KHODASEVICH: Review of *Sobytie*, 1938. A comparison is made with Gogol's *Revizor*.

MOCHUL'SKY: 'Roman V. Sirina', 1926. A review of *Mashen'ka*. Mochul'sky sees a Chekhovian colouring in the characterization of

Alfyorov and Ganin. He also finds the 'idyllic' Russian scenes reminiscent of Bunin and Turgenev. He concludes:

> Здесь особенно чувствуется большая литературная культура автора, мешающая ему найти свой собственный стиль.

STRUVE: Review of *Mashen'ka*, 1926. Struve concedes the influence of Turgenev, and finds close similarities with Bunin:

> Для тех, кто любит сравнивать и прослеживать влияния, скажем, что на романе Сирина если не считать Тургенева, больше всего сказалось влияние Бунина. Бунин вправе гордиться им, как своим учеником.

—— 'Tvorchestvo Sirina', 1930. Struve acknowledges some similarities with Chekhov, Tolstoy, Bunin, Bely, Gogol, and also with Hoffmann and Proust. He denies any similarities with Leonid Andreev.

—— 'Les "romans-escamotage" de Vladimir Sirine', 1931. Nabokov is compared with Giraudoux.

TSETLIN: Review of *Korol', dama, valet*, 1928. An analogy is drawn with Bunin's *Petlistye ushi*. Similarities are also seen with the methods of the German expressionists and also with the writing of Leonid Andreev.

—— Review of *Vozvrashchenie Chorba: rasskazy i stikhi*, 1930. Nabokov is again compared with Leonid Andreev.

Discussions of Nabokov's 'un-Russianness' and overriding concern with form and style

ADAMOVICH: Review of *SZ*, No. 41, 1930 (containing a part of *ZL*).

> «Защита Лужина» написана чрезвычайно искусно и, так сказать, по последней литературной моде. Первая часть романа особенно ясно отражала французские влияния...

—— Review of *SZ*, No. 46, 1931 (containing a part of *Podvig*).

> Это проза холодная и опустошенная, но, по своему, привлекательная. О жизни в ней и воспоминания нет, слабого следа от нее здесь не осталось. Человек и душа его здесь и «не ночевали»... Замечу, в заключение, что, если Сирину суждено «остаться» в нашей литературе и запомниться ей — о чем сейчас можно еще только гадать и догадываться — то это будет, вероятно, наименее русский из всех русских писателей.

—— Review of *SZ*, No. 48, 1932 (containing a part of *Podvig*).

> Когда-то Лев Шестов сказал о Чехове, что его писания — это «творчество из ничего». О Сирине можно было бы повторить эти слова, придав им смысл и оттенок, которые к Чехову относиться не могут, — оттенок несравненно большей «опустошенности», большей механичности и странной, при этом, беспечности.

—— Review of *SZ*, No. 58, 1935 (containing a part of *Priglashenie na kazn'*).

...нет (и, кажется, никогда в русской литературе не было) писателя, для которого вопросы композиции, построения, фабулы, действия, развития, вся вообще область «архитектоники», имели бы большее значение.

Adamovich goes on to admit that he was, and still is, disconcerted by Sirin's 'un-Russianness', and acknowledges that this has probably prevented him hitherto from giving Sirin's work its due share of praise.

—— Review of *SZ*, No. 59, 1935 (containing a part of *Priglashenie na kazn'*).

Только вот в чем беда: это мир его, — его и больше ничей! Невозможно туда, в это пугающе-волшебное царство, полностью проникнуть, и невозможно в нем дышать!

—— 'Perechityvaya *Otchayanie*', 1936. Adamovich here discusses the coldness of Nabokov's writings, and cites the example of the story *Opoveshchenie* which he had heard Nabokov read at a literary soirée. It is a sad story, full of pathos, and beautifully told, *but*:

Одно странно: всем любуешься, но никого не жалеешь. В голову даже не приходит мысль о сочувствии... Люди, о которых рассказал Сирин, очерчены с необычайной меткостью, но, как у Гоголя, им чего-то недостает, чего-то неуловимого и важнейшего: последнего дуновения, или, может быть, проще: души.

...Он на очень страшном пути, а помочь себе может только сам, если хочет этого... Отчаянием все-таки жить нельзя, и даже в изощреннейшей литературе нет от него убежища.

—— Review of *Russkie zapiski*, No. 4, 1938 (containing *Sobytie*).

Сирин — бесспорно виднейший из писателей «по-революционного» поколения....

Только странный это писатель, холодный, запальчиво-безразличный, и в ответ лишь безразличное любование возбуждающий.

ANDREYEV: 'Sirin', 1930.

Вот — писатель, который изумительным и обещающим силуэтом поднялся в наши изгнаннические годы, сочетав в себе культурное наследие прошлого с духом молодых поколений, русскую литературную традицию со смелым новаторством, русскую устремленность к психологизму с западной занимательностью сюжета и совершенством формы.

KANTOR: 'Bremya pamyati', 1934.

Поскольку Сирин остается во власти чисточувственного восприятия мира, искусство его обречено оставаться ограниченным и внешним.

KHODASEVICH: 'O Sirine', 1937.

При тщательном рассмотрении Сирин оказывается по преимуществу художником формы, писательского приема, и не только в том общеизвестном и общепризнанном смысле, что формальная сторона его писаний отличается исключительным разнообразием, сложностью, блеском и новизной. Все это потому и признано, и известно, что бросается в глаза всякому. Но в глаза-то бросается потому, что Сирин не только не маскирует, не прячет своих приемов, как чаще всего поступают все и в чем Достоевский, например, достиг поразительного совершенства, — но напротив: Сирин сам их выставляет наружу, как фокусник, который, поразив зрителя, тут же показывает лабораторию своих чудес. Тут, мне кажется, ключ ко всему Сирину.

KHOKHLOV: Review of *Vozvrashchenie Chorba: rasskazy i stikhi*, 1930. Khokhlov here is speaking of the title story in the collection:

В нем он свободно и просто отходит от почтенной традиции некоторой части русской литературы: писать так, чтобы не видно было автора, чтобы было «как настоящее».

...Сирин — писатель профессионал, для которого мир дороже в своих отвержениях, чем в самом себе. Сирин влюблен в тему, а не в действительность...

OSOKIN: Review of *Priglashenie na kazn'*, 1939.

...чуть не впервые от романа Сирина можно провести отчетливые линии к русской литературе (до сих пор Сирин нам казался писателем исключительно западным) — к «Носу» Гоголя и к «Моим запискам» Леонида Андреева.

...Последние годы Сирин стал на очень опасный путь — внешней акробатики и внутренней схематизации и упрощения.

OSORGIN: Review of *Podvig*, 1932.

Про В. Сирина говорят, что он по темам и по форме не совсем русский писатель; но я не знаю, почему русский писатель обязан быть русаком и не перекладывать страницы рукописи использованной копировальной бумагой. Традиция русской литературы — не слишком дорожить традициями.

—— Review of *Camera Obscura*, 1934.

Его последний роман, «Камера обскура», опять очень хороший и талантливый, утверждает взгляд на Сирина, как на писателя эмиграции, не только почти совершенно оторванного от живых российских вопросов и интересов, но и стоящего вне прямых влияний русской классической литературы. Его сюжеты интернациональны, герои — иностранцы, язык чужд присущих русскому писателю исканий и ограничен готовым установившимся словарем, стиль — европейской обработки, легко переложимый на любой иностранный язык. Холодный блеск — не в русском духе и у нас не ценится, — но было бы, конечно, нелепым ставить это Сирину в упрек: наоборот — новое достижение, известный вклад, о ценности которого стоит и подумать и поспорить.

STRUVE: 'Tvorchestvo Sirina', 1930.

Неоднократно указывалось на «нерусскость» Сирина. Мне это указание представляется неверным в общей форме. Но у Сирина есть «нерусские» черты, вернее, черты не свойственные русской литературе, взятой в целом. У него отсутствует, в частности, столь характерная для русской литературы «любовь к человеку» (по мнению — спорному — Н. А. Бердяева, из больших русских писателей, у Гоголя не было этой черты). Почти все персонажи Сирина — «отрицательные». Он питает художническое пристрастие к изображению уродов, моральных и физических, но в его изображении напрасно было бы искать, как у Достоевского, любви и жалости к этим уродам. Сирин в своем подходе всегда художнически бесстрастен и безжалостен... Однако в «Защите Лужина» Сирин — может быть, вопреки своей воле — выходит как будто из этого круга «нелюбви к человеку»: в судьбе душевно и духовно беззащитного урода и морального недоноска Лужина есть что-то подлинно и патетически человеческое.

VARSHAVSKY: Review of *Podvig*, 1933.

Все чрезвычайно сочно и красочно, и как-то жирно. Но за этим разлившимся в даль и в ширь половодьем — пустота, не бездна, а плоская пустота, пустота как мель, страшная именно отсутствием глубины.

WEIDLÉ: Weidlé touched on the question of Nabokov's 'un-Russianness' in several review articles, and related the characteristic features of his writing to current trends in contemporary literature. See:

—— Review of *SZ*, No. 42, 1930 (containing part of *ZL*).

—— 'Russkaya literatura v emigratsii: novaya proza', 1930.

—— Review of *SZ*, No. 44, 1930 (containing *Soglyadatai*).

—— 'Dvadtsat' let evropeiskoi literatury', 1939. Here Nabokov is named alongside Virginia Woolf, Giraudoux, Kafka, Dos Passos, and others, as a writer who has sought new forms.

ZAITSEV, B. 'Dnevnik pisatelya', 1930.

У Пескова есть Бог и есть дьявол. У Сирина Бога бесспорно нет, а пожалуй, и дьявола тоже.

BIBLIOGRAPHY

T H I S bibliography contains only those works to which reference has been made in the text. The most complete bibliography of Nabokov's works is by Andrew Field: *Nabokov: a Bibliography* (New York, 1973). This supersedes his earlier bibliography in *Nabokov: his Life in Art* (New York and London, 1967). Prior to this two bibliographies had been published: one in *L'Arc* (Aix-en-Provence), No. 24, 1964, and another, more complete and more reliable, by Dieter E. Zimmer, *Vladimir Nabokov: Bibliographie des Gesamtwerks*, revised edition (Hamburg, 1964).

WORKS BY VLADIMIR NABOKOV

Works are entered under their original titles, and are listed in chronological order.

Novels

Mashen'ka (Berlin, 1926)

> *Mary*, English translation by Michael Glenny in collaboration with the author (New York, 1970, and London, 1971).

Korol', dama, valet (Berlin, 1928). Reprinted: New York, 1968.

> *King, Queen, Knave*, English translation by Dmitri Nabokov in collaboration with the author (New York and London, 1968).

Soglyadatai, SZ, No. 44, 1930. Included in *Soglyadatai*, a collection of thirteen stories (Paris, 1938).

> *The Eye*, English translation by Dmitri Nabokov in collaboration with the author (New York, 1965, and London, 1966).

Zashchita Luzhina, serialized in 3 parts in *SZ*, Nos. 40–2, 1929–30. Book edition: Berlin, 1930. Reprinted: Paris, 1967.

> *The Defence*, English translation by Michael Scammell in collaboration with the author (New York and London, 1964).

Podvig, serialized in 4 parts in *SZ*, Nos. 45–8, 1931–2. Book edition: Paris and Berlin, 1932.

> *Glory*, English translation by Dmitri Nabokov in collaboration with the author (New York, 1971, and London, 1972).

Camera Obscura, serialized in 4 parts in *SZ*, Nos. 49–52, 1932–3. Book edition: Paris and Berlin, 1932.

> *Camera Obscura*, English translation by Winifred Roy (London, 1936). *Laughter in the Dark*, revised English translation by the author (New York, 1938). Revised editions: London, 1961, 1969.

Otchayanie, serialized in 3 parts in *SZ*, Nos. 54–6, 1934. Book edition: Berlin, 1936.

> *Despair*, English translation by the author (London, 1937). Revised edition: New York and London, 1966.

Priglashenie na kazn', serialized in 3 parts in *SZ*, Nos. 58–60, 1935–6. Book edition: Paris and Berlin, 1938.

> *Invitation to a Beheading*, English translation by Dmitri Nabokov in collaboration with the author (New York, 1959, and London, 1960).

Dar, serialized in 5 parts in *SZ*, Nos. 63–7, 1937–8, without the fourth chapter. Complete edition: New York, 1952.

> *The Gift*, English translation by Dmitri Nabokov and Michael Scammell in collaboration with the author (New York and London, 1963).

The Real Life of Sebastian Knight (Norfolk, Conn., and London, 1941).

Bend Sinister (New York, 1947, and London, 1960).

Lolita (Paris, 1955, New York, 1958, and London, 1959).

> *Lolita*, Russian translation by the author (New York, 1967).

Pnin (New York and London, 1957).

Pale Fire (New York and London, 1962).

Ada or Ardor: a Family Chronicle (New York and London, 1969).

Transparent Things (New York, 1972, and London, 1973).

Look at the Harlequins! (New York, 1974, and London, 1975).

Collections of Short Stories

Vozvrashchenie Chorba: rasskazy i stikhi, collection of fifteen stories and twenty-four poems (Berlin, 1930).

Soglyadatai, collection of thirteen stories (Paris, 1938).

Nine Stories (Norfolk, Conn., 1947).

Vesna v Fial'te i drugie rasskazy, collection of fourteen stories (New York, 1956).

Nabokov's Dozen, collection of thirteen stories (New York, 1958, and London, 1959).

Nabokov's Quartet, collection of four stories (New York, 1966, and London, 1967).

A Russian Beauty and Other Stories, collection of thirteen stories (New York and London, 1973).

Tyrants Destroyed and Other Stories, collection of thirteen stories (New York and London, 1975).

Short Stories: Separate Appearances

Kartofel'nyi El'f, *Russkoe ekho* (Berlin), 8, 15, 22, 29 June 1924. Reprinted in *Rul'* (Berlin), 15, 17, 18, 19 December 1929. Collected in *Vozvrashchenie Chorba: rasskazy i stikhi*.

The Potato-Elf, English translation by Serge Bertensson and Irene Kosinska, *Esquire* (New York), December 1939. Included in *The Single Voice*, ed. Jerome Charyn (New York, 1969).

The Potato Elf, English translation by Dmitri Nabokov in collaboration with the author, *A Russian Beauty and Other Stories*.

Sluchainost', *Segodnya* (Riga), 22 June 1924.

A Matter of Chance, English translation by Dmitri Nabokov in collaboration with the author, *Tyrants Destroyed and Other Stories*.

Bakhman, *Rul'* (Berlin), 2, 4 November 1924. Collected in *Vozvrashchenie Chorba: rasskazy i stikhi*.

Bachmann, English translation by Dmitri Nabokov in collaboration with the author, *Vogue* (New York), December 1973. Collected in *Tyrants Destroyed and Other Stories*.

Rozhdestvo, *Rul'* (Berlin), 6, 8 January 1925. Collected in *Vozvrashchenie Chorba: rasskazy i stikhi*.

Christmas, English translation by Dmitri Nabokov in collaboration with the author, *The New Yorker*, 29 December 1975.

Vozvrashchenie Chorba, *Rul'* (Berlin), 12, 13 November 1925. Collected in *Vozvrashchenie Chorba: rasskazy i stikhi*.

The Return of Tchorb, English translation by Gleb Struve, *This Quarter* (Paris), IV, No. 4, June 1932.

Skazka, *Rul'* (Berlin), 27, 29 June 1926. Collected in *Vozvrashchenie Chorba: rasskazy i stikhi*.

A Nursery Tale, English translation by Dmitri Nabokov in collaboration with the author, *Playboy* (Chicago), January 1974. Collected in *Tyrants Destroyed and Other Stories*.

Uzhas, *SZ*, No. 30, 1927. Collected in *Vozvrashchenie Chorba: rasskazy i stikhi*.

Terror, English translation by Dmitri Nabokov in collaboration with the author, *Tyrants Destroyed and Other Stories*.

Passazhir, *Rul'* (Berlin), 6 March 1927. Collected in *Vozvrashchenie Chorba: rasskazy i stikhi*.

The Passenger, English translation by Gleb Struve, *Lovat Dickson's Magazine* (London), II, No. 6, 1934. Included in *A Century of Russian Prose and Verse: from Pushkin to Nabokov*, ed. Struve (New York, 1967).

Pil'gram, *SZ*, No. 43, 1930. Collected in *Soglyadatai*.

The Aurelian, English translation by Peter Pertzov in collaboration with the author, *The Atlantic Monthly* (Boston, Mass.), November 1941. Collected in *Nine Stories* and *Nabokov's Dozen*.

Obida, *PN*, 12 July 1931. Collected in *Soglyadatai*.

Terra Incognita, PN, 22 November 1931. Collected in *Soglyadatai.*

Terra Incognita, English translation by Dmitri Nabokov in collaboration with the author, *The New Yorker,* 18 May 1963. Collected in *A Russian Beauty and Other Stories.*

Lebeda, PN, 31 January 1932. Collected in *Soglyadatai.*

Muzyka, PN, 27 March 1932. Collected in *Soglyadatai.*

Musique, French translation by the author, *Les Nouvelles littéraires* (Paris), 14 May 1959.

Music, English translation by Dmitri Nabokov in collaboration with the author, *Tyrants Destroyed and Other Stories.*

Sovershenstvo, PN, 3 July 1932. Collected in *Soglyadatai.*

Perfection, English translation by Dmitri Nabokov in collaboration with the author, *The New Yorker,* 19 May 1973. Collected in *Tyrants Destroyed and Other Stories.*

Admiralteiskaya igla, PN, 4 June 1933. Collected in *Vesna v Fial'te i drugie rasskazy.*

The Admiralty Spire, English translation by Dmitri Nabokov in collaboration with the author, *Playboy* (Chicago), February 1975. Collected in *Tyrants Destroyed and Other Stories.*

Korolek, PN, 23, 24 July 1933. Collected in *Vesna v Fial'te i drugie rasskazy.*

The Leonardo, English translation by Dmitri Nabokov in collaboration with the author, *A Russian Beauty and Other Stories.*

Rasskaz, PN, 11, 12 March 1934. Collected in *Vesna v Fial'te i drugie rasskazy,* under the title *Krug.*

The Circle, English translation by Dmitri Nabokov in collaboration with the author, *The New Yorker,* 29 January 1972. Collected in *A Russian Beauty and Other Stories.*

Opoveshchenie, PN, 8 April 1934. Collected in *Soglyadatai.*

Breaking the News, English translation by Dmitri Nabokov in collaboration with the author, *A Russian Beauty and Other Stories.*

Krasavitsa, PN, 18 August 1934. Collected in *Soglyadatai.*

A Russian Beauty, English translation by Simon Karlinsky in collaboration with the author, *Harper's Bazaar and Queen* (London), October 1973. Collected in *A Russian Beauty and Other Stories.*

Tyazhelyi dym, PN, 3 March 1935. Collected in *Vesna v Fial'te i drugie rasskazy.*

Torpid Smoke, English translation by Dmitri Nabokov in collaboration with the author, *Tri-Quarterly* (Evanston, Ill.), No. 27, Spring 1973. Collected in *A Russian Beauty and Other Stories.*

Nabor, PN, 18 August 1935. Collected in *Vesna v Fial'te i drugie rasskazy.*

Recruiting, English translation by Dmitri Nabokov in collaboration with the author, *Tyrants Destroyed and Other Stories.*

Vesna v Fial'te, SZ, No. 61, 1936. Collected in *Vesna v Fial'te i drugie rasskazy.*

Spring in Fialta, English translation by Peter Pertzov in collaboration with the author, *Harper's Bazaar* (New York), May 1947. Collected in *Nine Stories* and *Nabokov's Dozen.*

Oblako, ozero, bashnya, Russkie zapiski (Paris), No. 2, 1937. Collected in *Vesna v Fial'te i drugie rasskazy.*

Cloud, Castle, Lake, English translation by Peter Pertzov in collaboration with the author, *The Atlantic Monthly* (Boston, Mass.), June 1941. Collected in *Nine Stories* and *Nabokov's Dozen.*

Istreblenie tiranov, Russkie zapiski (Paris), August–September 1938. Collected in *Vesna v Fial'te i drugie rasskazy.*

Tyrants Destroyed, English translation by Dmitri Nabokov in collaboration with the author, *Tyrants Destroyed and Other Stories.*

Lik, Russkie zapiski (Paris), No. 14, February 1939. Collected in *Vesna v Fial'te i drugie rasskazy.*

Lik, English translation by Dmitri Nabokov in collaboration with the author, *The New Yorker*, 10 October 1964. Collected in *Nabokov's Quartet* and *Tyrants Destroyed and Other Stories.*

Poseshchenie muzeya, SZ, No. 68, 1939. Collected in *Vesna v Fial'te i drugie rasskazy.*

The Visit to the Museum, English translation by Dmitri Nabokov in collaboration with the author, *Esquire* (New York), March 1963. Collected in *Nabokov's Quartet* and *A Russian Beauty and Other Stories.*

Vasily Shishkov, PN, 12 September 1939. Collected in *Vesna v Fial'te i drugie rasskazy.*

Vasily Shishkov, English translation by Dmitri Nabokov in collaboration with the author, *Tyrants Destroyed and Other Stories.*

Solus Rex, SZ, No. 70, 1940.

Solus Rex, English translation by Dmitri Nabokov in collaboration with the author, *A Russian Beauty and Other Stories.*

Ultima Thule, Novyi zhurnal (New York), No. 1, 1942. Collected in *Vesna v Fial'te i drugie rasskazy.*

Ultima Thule, English translation by Dmitri Nabokov in collaboration with the author, *The New Yorker*, 7 April 1973. Collected in *A Russian Beauty and Other Stories.*

The Assistant Producer, The Atlantic Monthly (Boston, Mass.), May 1943. Collected in *Nine Stories* and *Nabokov's Dozen.*

A Forgotten Poet, The Atlantic Monthly (Boston, Mass.), October 1944. Collected in *Nine Stories* and *Nabokov's Dozen.*

Symbols and Signs, The New Yorker, 15 May 1948. Collected under the title *Signs and Symbols* in *Nabokov's Dozen.*

Usta k ustam, first published in *Vesna v Fial'te i drugie rasskazy,* 1956.

 Lips to Lips, English translation by Dmitri Nabokov in collaboration with the author, *Esquire* (New York), September 1971. Collected in *A Russian Beauty and Other Stories.*

Undated Short Stories

Exact dates of publications have not yet been traced for the following:

Podlets, Rul' (Berlin), 192?. Collected in *Vozvrashchenie Chorba: rasskazy i stikhi.*

 An Affair of Honor, English translation by Dmitri Nabokov in collaboration with the author, *The New Yorker,* 3 September 1966. Collected in *Nabokov's Quartet* and *A Russian Beauty and Other Stories.*

Khvat, Segodnya (Riga), 193?. Collected in *Soglyadatai.*

 A Dashing Fellow, English translation by Dmitri Nabokov in collaboration with the author, *Playboy* (Chicago), December 1971. Collected in *A Russian Beauty and Other Stories.*

Pamyati L. I. Shigaeva, 193?. Collected in *Vesna v Fial'te i drugie rasskazy.*

 In Memory of L. I. Shigaev, English translation by Dmitri Nabokov in collaboration with the author, *Tyrants Destroyed and Other Stories.*

Drama

Sobytie, Russkie zapiski (Paris), No. 4, 1938.

Izobretenie Val'sa, Russkie zapiski (Paris), No. 11, November 1938.

 The Waltz Invention, English translation by Dmitri Nabokov in collaboration with the author (New York, 1966).

Collections of Poetry

Stikhotvoreniya, a collection of sixty-eight poems (St. Petersburg, 1916).

Vozvrashchenie Chorba: rasskazy i stikhi, a collection of fifteen stories and twenty-four poems (Berlin, 1930).

Stikhotvoreniya: 1929-1951, a collection of fifteen poems (Paris, 1952). All included, with English translations, in *Poems and Problems.*

Poems, a collection of fourteen poems (New York, 1959, and London, 1961). All included in *Poems and Problems.*

Poems and Problems, including thirty-nine Russian poems with English translations and fourteen English poems (New York, 1970, and London, 1972).

Poems: Separate Appearances

Universitetskaya poema, SZ, No. 33, 1927.

Poety, signed Vasily Shishkov (pseud.), *SZ*, No. 69, 1939. Collected in *Stikhotvoreniya: 1929–1951*. Reprinted with an English translation, *The Poets*, in *Tri-Quarterly* (Evanston, Ill.), No. 17, Winter 1970, and with a different English translation in *Poems and Problems*.

Obrashchenie, signed Vasily Shishkov (pseud.), *SZ*, No. 70, 1940. Collected (without a title) in *Stikhotvoreniya: 1929–1951*, and (under the title *K Rossii*) in *Poems and Problems* with an English translation.

'On Translating "Eugene Onegin"', *The New Yorker*, 8 January 1955. Collected in *Poems* and (with a different last line) in *Poems and Problems*.

Memoirs

For details of the publication of separate chapters of the Autobiography see Appendix C.

Conclusive Evidence: a Memoir (New York, 1951). Published in England under the title *Speak, Memory: a Memoir* (London, 1951).

Drugie berega (New York, 1954).

Speak, Memory: an Autobiography Revisited (New York, 1966, and London, 1967).

Translations

Nikolka Persik, translation of *Colas Breugnon*, a novel by Romain Rolland (Berlin, 1922).

Anya v strane chudes, translation of Lewis Carroll's *Alice in Wonderland* (Berlin, 1923).

Maiskaya noch', translation of Alfred de Musset's poem *La Nuit de mai*, in *Rul'* (Berlin), 20 November 1927.

Dekabr'skaya noch', translation of Alfred de Musset's poem *La Nuit de décembre*, in *Rul'* (Berlin), 7 October 1928.

P'yanyi korabl', translation of Rimbaud's poem *Le Bateau ivre*, in *Rul'* (Berlin), 16 December 1928.

Dans le désert du monde . . ., translation of Pushkin's poem *Tri klyucha*, in *NRF*, XLVIII, No. 282, 1937, p. 373.

Ne me les chante pas, ma belle, translation of Pushkin's poem *Ne poi, krasavitsa, pri mne*, in *NRF*, XLVIII, No. 282, 1937, p. 374.

Je ne puis m'endormir . . ., translation of Pushkin's poem *Mne ne spitsya, net ognya*, in *NRF*, XLVIII, No. 282, 1937, p. 375.

Pourquoi le vent troublant la plaine . . ., translation of *Zachem krutitsya vetr v ovrage*, one of Pushkin's *Ezersky* stanzas, *NRF*, XLVIII, No. 282, 1937, p. 375.

Three Russian Poets: Selections from Pushkin, Lermontov and Tyutchev (Norfolk, Conn., 1944). All included in *Pushkin, Lermontov, Tyutchev: Poems* (London, 1947), with some added translations from Pushkin and Lermontov.

'Pushkin: rhymed paraphrases of three stanzas from *Eugene Onegin*', *The Russian Review* (New York), IV, No. 2, 1945.

Nikolai Gogol, including translations of extracts from *Mertvye dushi, Revizor, Shinel'*, and some letters (Norfolk, Conn., 1944). Corrected edition, 1961.

A Hero of our Time, translation of Lermontov's *Geroi nashego vremeni*, by Dmitri Nabokov with the collaboration of Vladimir Nabokov (New York, 1958).

In noon's heat, in a dale of Dagestan, translation of Lermontov's poem *Son*, in *A Hero of our Time*, p. v. An earlier different translation of this poem is contained in *Three Russian Poets*, entitled *The Triple Dream*.

The Song of Igor's Campaign: an Epic of the Twelfth Century, translation of *Slovo o polku Igoreve* (New York, 1960, and London, 1961).

Eugene Onegin, translation of Pushkin's *Evgeny Onegin*, 4 vols. (New York and London, 1964).

'Tis time, my dear, 'tis time . . ., translation of Pushkin's lyric *Pora, moi drug, pora . . .*, in *Despair*, revised edition, p. 10.

Articles and Works of Criticism

'Chto vsyakii dolzhen znat' ?', *Novaya gazeta* (Paris), No. 5, May 1931, p. 3.

'Pouchkine ou le vrai et le vraisemblable', *NRF*, XLVIII, No. 282, 1937, pp. 362–78.

Nikolai Gogol (Norfolk, Conn., 1944). Corrected edition, 1961.

Povesti: N. V. Gogol': Predislovie (New York, 1952).

'Problems of Translation: *Onegin* in English', *Partisan Review* (New York), No. 22, 1955, pp. 496–512.

'Zametki perevodchika', *Novyi zhurnal* (New York), No. 49, 1957, pp. 130–44.

'Zametki perevodchika II', *Opyty* (New York), No. 8, 1957, pp. 36–49.

'The Servile Path', *On Translation*, ed. Reuben Brower (Cambridge, Mass., 1959).

'On Translating Pushkin: Pounding the Clavichord', *The New York Review of Books*, 30 April 1964, pp. 14–16. Reprinted in *Strong Opinions*.

Postscript to W. Arndt's article 'Goading the Pony', *The New York Review of Books*, 30 April 1964, p. 16.

'Reply to My Critics', *Encounter* (London), February 1966. Reprinted, with some modifications, in *Strong Opinions*, pp. 241–67.

Strong Opinions, a collection of interviews, letters to editors, and articles (New York, 1973, and London, 1974).

Interviews

'U V. V. Sirina.' Interview conducted by Andrey Sedykh in *PN*, 3 November 1932, p. 2.

'Vladimir Nabokov on His Life and Work.' Interview conducted by Peter Duval-Smith in *The Listener* (London), 22 November 1962. Included in *Strong Opinions*, pp. 9–19.

'Playboy Interview: Vladimir Nabokov.' Interview conducted by Alvin Toffler in *Playboy* (Chicago), January 1964. Included in *Strong Opinions*, pp. 20–45.

'An Interview with Vladimir Nabokov.' Interview conducted by Alfred Appel Jr. in *Nabokov: the Man and his Work*, ed. L. S. Dembo (Madison, 1967), pp. 19–44. Included in *Strong Opinions*, pp. 62–92.

'The Art of Fiction XL.' Interview conducted by Herbert Gold in *The Paris Review* (Paris), No. 41, 1967, pp. 92–111. Included in *Strong Opinions*, pp. 93–107.

'The Strong Opinions of Vladimir Nabokov.' Interview conducted by Nicholas Garnham in *The Listener* (London), 10 October 1968, pp. 463–4. Included in *Strong Opinions*, pp. 115–19.

'Prospero's Progress', a biographical article by Martha Duffy and Ron Sheppard based on an interview with Nabokov, *Time* (New York), 23 May 1969. The text of this interview is included in *Strong Opinions*, pp. 120–30.

'Vladimir Nabokov Talks about Nabokov.' Interview conducted by Allene Talmey in *Vogue* (New York), December 1969. Included in *Strong Opinions*, pp. 153–8.

Unpublished interview, 1972. Included in *Strong Opinions*, pp. 194–6.

CRITICISM OF NABOKOV AND OTHER WORKS CONSULTED

ADAMOVICH, Georgy, Review of *SZ*, No. 40 (containing a part of *ZL*), *PN*, 31 October 1929, p. 2.

—— Review of *SZ*, No. 41 (containing a part of *ZL*), *PN*, 13 February 1930, p. 3.

—— Review of *SZ*, No. 42 (containing a part of *ZL*), *PN*, 15 May 1930, p. 3.

—— Review of *SZ*, No. 46 (containing a part of *Podvig*), *PN*, 4 June 1931, p. 2.

—— Review of *SZ*, No. 48 (containing a part of *Podvig*), *PN*, 11 February 1932, p. 2.

—— 'O knige Lorensa', *PN*, 7 April 1932, p. 3.

—— 'O "pafose Moskvy"', *PN*, 26 May 1932, p. 2.

—— 'Sirin', *PN*, 4 January 1934, p. 3.

—— Review of *SZ*, No. 55 (containing a part of *Otchayanie*), *PN*, 24 May 1934.

—— Review of *SZ*, No. 56 (containing a part of *Otchayanie*), *PN*, 8 November 1934, p. 3.

—— Review of *SZ*, No. 58 (containing a part of *Priglashenie na kazn'*), *PN*, 4 July 1935, p. 2.

—— Review of *SZ*, No. 59 (containing a part of *Priglashenie na kazn'*), *PN*, 28 November 1935, p. 3.

—— 'Perechityvaya *Otchayanie*', *PN*, 5 March 1936, p. 3.

—— Review of *SZ*, No. 61 (containing *Vesna v Fial'te*), *PN*, 30 July 1936, p. 3.

—— Review of *Russkie zapiski*, No. 2 (containing *Oblako, ozero, bashnya*), *PN*, 16 December 1937, p. 3.

—— Review of *Russkie zapiski*, No. 4 (containing *Sobytie*), *PN*, 21 April 1938, p. 3.

—— Review of *Russkie zapiski*, August–September 1938 (containing *Istreblenie tiranov*), *PN*, 15 September 1938.

—— Review of *SZ*, No. 69 (containing *Poety*), *PN*, 17 August 1939, p. 3.

—— 'Literaturnye zametki', *PN*, 22 September 1939, p. 3.

—— *Odinochestvo i svoboda* (New York, 1955).

Affaire Lolita, L', including articles by F. W. Dupee, Vladimir Nabokov, Maurice Girodias, and Daniel Bécourt (Paris, 1957).

ANDERSON, Quentin, 'Nabokov in Time', *The New Republic* (New York), 4 June 1966.

ANDREYEV, Nikolay E., 'Sirin', *Nov'* (Tallin), October 1930. English translation in *The Complection of Russian Literature*, ed. Andrew Field (London, 1971).

—— 'Ob osobennostyakh i osnovnykh etapakh razvitiya russkoi literatury za rubezhom', in *Russkaya literatura v emigratsii*, ed. N. Poltoratsky (Pittsburg, 1972).

APPEL, Alfred, Jr., '*Lolita*: the Springboard of Parody', *Nabokov*, ed. Dembo, pp. 106–43.

—— ed., *Vladimir Nabokov: the Annotated Lolita* (New York, 1970).

—— '*Ada* Described', *Nabokov*, ed. Appel and Newman, pp. 160–86.

APPEL, Alfred, Jr. and NEWMAN, Charles, ed., *Nabokov: Criticism, Reminiscences, Translations and Tributes* (London, 1971). First published in *Tri-Quarterly* (Evanston, Ill.), No. 17, 1970. This edition contains a supplement, 'Anniversary Notes', in which Nabokov comments on articles in the collection.

ARNDT, Walter, 'A Reply to Vladimir Nabokov: Goading the Pony', *The New York Review of Books*, 30 April 1964, p. 16.

AUTY, Robert, 'Prešeren's German Poems', *Oxford Slavonic Papers*, new series, vol. 6, 1973, pp. 1–11.

BADER, Julia, *Crystal Land: Artifice in Nabokov's English Novels* (Berkeley, 1972).

BERBEROVA, Nina, 'Nabokov i ego *Lolita*', *Novyi zhurnal* (New York), No. 57, 1959, pp. 92–115.

BITSILLI, P. M., 'Vozrozhdenie allegorii', *SZ*, No. 61, 1936, pp. 191–204. English translation, 'The Revival of Allegory', in *Nabokov*, ed. Appel and Newman, pp. 102–18.

—— Review of *Priglashenie na kazn'* and *Soglyadatai*, *SZ*, No. 68, 1939, pp. 474–7.

BROWER, Reuben A., ed., *On Translation* (Cambridge, Mass., 1959).

CATFORD, J. C., *A Linguistic Theory of Translation* (London, 1965).

CHERVINSKAYA, L., 'Po povodu *Sobytiya* V. Sirina', *Krug* (Paris), No. 3, 1938, pp. 168–70.

COHN, Ruby, 'Samuel Beckett Self-Translator', *PMLA*, No. 76, 1961.

DEMBO, L. S., ed., *Nabokov: the Man and his Work* (Madison, 1967).

DEMUROVA, N., 'Golos i skripka: k perevodu ekstsentricheskikh skazok L'yuisa Kerrolla', *Masterstvo perevoda* (Moscow, 1970), pp. 150–85.

DIKS (pseud. of B. A. Leman), Review of *SZ*, No. 30 (containing *Uzhas*), *Zveno* (Paris), No. 211, 13 February 1927, p. 8.

DUPEE, F. W., 'A Preface to *Lolita*', *Anchor Review* (New York), No. 2, 1957.

FIELD, Andrew, *Nabokov: his Life in Art* (London, 1967).

FLETCHER, John, *The Novels of Samuel Beckett* (London, 1964).

FORSTER, Leonard, *The Poet's Tongues: Multilingualism in Literature* (Dunedin, 1970).

HICKS, Granville, 'A Man of Many Words', *Saturday Review* (New York), 28 January 1967, pp. 31–2.

HUGHES, Robert P., 'Notes on the Translation of *Invitation to a Beheading*', *Nabokov*, ed. Appel and Newman, pp. 284–92.

IVANOV, Georgy, Review of *SZ*, No. 33 (containing *Universitetskaya poema*), *PN*, 15 December 1927, p. 3.

—— Review of *Mashen'ka*, *Korol', dama, valet*, *Zashchita Luzhina*, *Vozvrashchenie Chorba*, in *Chisla* (Paris), No. 1, 1930, pp. 233–6.

JANVIER, Ludovic, *Pour Samuel Beckett* (Paris, 1966).

KANTOR, M., 'Bremya pamyati', *Vstrechi* (Paris), No. 3, March 1934, pp. 125–8.

KARLINSKY, Simon, 'Vladimir Nabokov's Novel *Dar* as a Work of Literary Criticism: a Structural Analysis', *SEEJ*, new series, VII, No. 3, 1963, pp. 284–90. French translation in *L'Arc* (Aix-en-Provence), 1964, pp. 48–54.

—— 'Nabokov and Chekhov: the Lesser Russian Tradition', *Nabokov*, ed. Appel and Newman, pp. 7–16.

—— 'Anya in Wonderland: Nabokov's Russified Lewis Carroll', *Nabokov*, ed. Appel and Newman, pp. 310–15.

KHODASEVICH, V. F., Review of *Zashchita Luzhina*, *Vozrozhdenie* (Paris), 11 October 1930, p. 2.

—— 'O Sirine', *Vozrozhdenie* (Paris), 13 February 1937, p. 9. Reprinted in *Literaturnye stat'i i vospominaniya* (New York, 1954). English translation (abridged), 'On Sirin', in *Nabokov*, ed. Appel and Newman, pp. 96–101.

—— Review of *Sobytie*, *SZ*, No. 66, 1938, pp. 424–7.

KHOKHLOV, German, Review of *Vozvrashchenie Chorba: rasskazy i stikhi*, *Volya Rossii* (Prague), No. 2, February 1930, pp. 190–1.

LOKRANTZ, Jessie Thomas, *The Underside of the Weave: Some Stylistic Devices used by Vladimir Nabokov* (Uppsala, 1973).

LUBIN, Peter, 'Kickshaws and Motley', *Nabokov*, ed. Appel and Newman, pp. 187–208.

MOCHUL'SKY, K., 'Roman V. Sirina', *Zveno* (Paris), No. 168, 18 April 1926, pp. 2–3.

NOVIK, Al. (pseud. of German Khokhlov), Review of *Zashchita Luzhina*, *SZ*, No. 45, 1931, pp. 514–17.

OSOKIN, Sergey, Review of *Priglashenie na kazn'*, *Russkie zapiski* (Paris), No. 13, 1939, pp. 198–9.

OSORGIN, Mikhail, Review of *Korol', dama, valet*, *PN*, 4 October 1928, p. 3.

—— Review of *Podvig*, *PN*, 27 October 1932, p. 3.

—— Review of *Camera Obscura*, *SZ*, No. 54, 1934, pp. 458–60.

PROFFER, Carl R., 'From *Otchaianie* to *Despair*', *Slavic Review* (New York), XXVII, No. 2, 1968, pp. 258–67.

—— *Keys to Lolita* (Bloomington, Ind., 1968).

—— 'A New Deck for Nabokov's Knaves', *Nabokov*, ed. Appel and Newman, pp. 293–309.

PROFFER, Ellendea, 'Nabokov's Russian Readers', *Nabokov*, ed. Appel and Newman, pp. 253–60.

ROWE, William Woodin, *Nabokov's Deceptive World* (New York, 1971).

STRUVE, Gleb, Review of *Mashen'ka*, *Vozrozhdenie* (Paris), 1 April 1926, p. 3.

—— Review of *Universitetskaya poema*, *Rossiya* (Paris), 10 December 1927, p. 4.

—— 'Tvorchestvo Sirina', *Rossiya i slavyanstvo* (Paris), 17 May 1930, p. 3.

—— 'Les "romans-escamotage" de Vladimir Sirine', *Le Mois* (Paris), No. 4, April 1931, pp. 145–52.

—— 'Current Russian Literature: Vladimir Sirin', *SEER*, XII, No. 35, January 1934, pp. 436–44.

—— *Russkaya literatura v izgnanii* (New York, 1956).

—— 'Notes on Nabokov as a Russian Writer', *Nabokov*, ed. Dembo, pp. 45–56.

TERAPIANO, Yury, Review of *Camera Obscura*, *Chisla* (Paris), No. 10, 1934, pp. 287–8.

TSETLIN, M. O., Review of *Korol', dama, valet*, *SZ*, No. 37, 1928, pp. 536–8.

—— Review of *Vozvrashchenie Chorba: rasskazy i stikhi*, *SZ*, No. 42, 1930, pp. 530–1.

VARSHAVSKY, V., Review of *Lady Chatterley's Lover*, *Chisla* (Paris), No. 6, 1932, pp. 259–62.

—— Review of *Podvig*, *Chisla* (Paris), No. 7–8, 1933, pp. 266–7.

'Vecher V. V. Sirina', (unsigned notice), *PN*, 17 November 1932, p. 3.

WEAVER, Warren, *Alice in Many Tongues: the Translations of Alice in Wonderland* (Madison, 1964).

WEIDLÉ, Wladimir, Review of *SZ*, No. 42 (containing a part of *ZL*), *Vozrozhdenie* (Paris), 12 May 1930, p. 3.

—— 'Russkaya literatura v emigratsii: novaya proza', *Vozrozhdenie* (Paris), 19 June 1930, pp. 3–4.

—— Review of *SZ*, No. 44 (containing *Soglyadatai*), *Vozrozhdenie* (Paris), 30 October 1930, p. 2.

—— 'Dvadtsat' let evropeiskoi literatury', *PN*, 10 February 1939, p. 3.

WILSON, Edmund, 'The Strange Case of Pushkin and Nabokov', *The New York Review of Books*, 15 July 1965, pp. 3–6.

ZAITSEV, Boris, 'Dnevnik pisatelya', *Vozrozhdenie* (Paris), 16 March 1930, p. 3.

MANUSCRIPTS

GLENNY, Michael, English translation of *Mashen'ka*, submitted to Nabokov.

SCAMMELL, Michael, English translation of *Dar* (Chapters 2–5), submitted to Nabokov.

—— English translation of *Zashchita Luzhina*, submitted to Nabokov.

INDEX

Page references for Nabokov's works are given under the original titles. Fictional characters and characters from Nabokov's autobiography are not included.

Ada or Ardor: a Family Chronicle, 6, 12, 25 n., 58, 103, 112, 113, 115, 116, 133, 144, 146 n., 164–5, 174, 194, 196, 198, 202, 203–4, 209, 210, 211, 215, 219
Adamovich, G. V., 3, 24–5, 79, 81, 117, 132, 232–3, 234–5
Admiralteiskaya igla (*The Admiralty Spire*), 221, 227, 230
Admiralty Spire, The, see *Admiralteiskaya igla*
Affair of Honor, An, see *Podlets*
Anderson, Q., 132
Andreev, L. N., 232, 234, 236
Andreyev, N. E., 2, 218, 232, 235
Anya v strane chudes (translation of *Alice in Wonderland*), 19–21, 168
Appel, A., Jr., 57 n., 115 n., 146 n., 174 n.; interview with Nabokov, 2, 5, 16 n., 132, 137, 156 n., 179 n.
Arndt, W., 18
Assistant Producer, The, 136, 190
Aurelian, The, see *Pil'gram*
Autobiography, the, 10–11, **139–66**, 182, 190, 192–3, 224–6, 227–31. See also *Conclusive Evidence, Drugie berega, Speak, Memory*
Auty, R., 2 n.

Bachmann, see *Bakhman*
Bader, Julia, 4, 25 n., 174 n.
Bakhman, 221
Balzac, H. de: *Eugénie Grandet*, 92
Beckett, S., 2, 3 n.
Bely, A. (pseud. of B. N. Bugaev), 208, 218, 232, 233, 234
Bend Sinister, 6, 26, 208, 217
Berberova, Nina, 1, 232, 233
Berdyaev, N. A., 237
Bertensson, S., 5, 196, 201, 202
Bitsilli, P. M., 85 n., 233
Blok, A. A., 160–1, 208
Borges, J. L., 58
Breaking the News, see *Opoveshchenie*

Bunin, I. A., 1, 232, 234
Busch, W., 109
Butterflies, 225. See also Autobiography, the
Byron, Lord, 15; *Don Juan*, 58

Camera Obscura (*Laughter in the Dark*), 5, 7, 9, 21, **23–58**, 59, 60, 62, 68, 80, 81–2, 89, 91, 108, 110, 112–14, 116, 119 n., 131, 133, 136, 138, 169, 178, 190–1, 209, 213, 220
Carroll, L. (pseud. of C. L. Dodgson): *Alice in Wonderland*, see *Anya v strane chudes*
Catford, J. C., 168 n.
Céline, L. F. (pseud. of L. F. Destouches), 232, 233
Cervantes, M. de: *Don Quixote*, 58
Chekhov, A. P., 154, 218, 232, 233, 234
Chernyshevsky, N. G., 81
Chervinskaya, Lidiya, 233
Christmas, see *Rozhdestvo*
'Chto vsyakii dolzhen znat'', 116
Circle, The, see *Rasskaz*
Cloud, Castle, Lake, see *Oblako, ozero, bashnya*
Cohn, Ruby, 3 n.
Coleridge, S. T., 15
Colette, 225, 227. See also Autobiography, the
Conclusive Evidence: a Memoir, 6, 11, 177, 178, 179, 221. See also Autobiography, the
Conrad, J., 2, 182
Curtain-Raiser, 225, 227. See also Autobiography, the

Dar (*The Gift*), 6, 7–8, 9, 10, 25, 81, 119, 120, 133, 140, 170, 171, 173, 176, 177, 179, 180 n., 191, 194, 195, 198, 199, 200, 202, 203, 204, 205 n., 207, 208, 214–15, 219, 220, 227
Dashing Fellow, A, see *Khvat*

Defence, The, see *Zashchita Luzhina*
Demurova, N., 21 n.
Despair, see *Otchayanie*
Diks (pseud. of B. A. Leman), 233
Donizetti, G.: *Lucia di Lammermoor,* 92
Dos Passos, J. R., 237
Dostoevsky, F. M., 76, 218, 233, 236, 237; *The Idiot,* 46 n.
Doyle, Sir A. Conan, 175; Dr. Watson, 171, 180
Drugie berega, 10, 11, 175–6, 177, 178, 179, 182–3, 192–3, 221. *See also* Autobiography, the
Duffy, Martha: interview with Nabokov, 16 n.
Dupee, F. W., 115 n.
Duval-Smith, P.: interview with Nabokov, 132–3

Eugene Onegin (translation of *Evgeny Onegin*), 14–18, 22, 168, 176, 180, 198, 201, 204
Exile, 226. *See also* Autobiography, the
Eye, The, see *Soglyadatai*

Fel'zen, Yu. (pseud. of N. B. Freudenstein), 1
Field, A., 34 n., 41 n., 49, 51, 82 n., 134 n., 138 n., 157 n., 220
First Poem, 145, 163, 225, 228. *See also* Autobiography, the
Flaubert, G., 218; *Madame Bovary,* 91–2, 175
Fletcher, J. W., 3 n.
Forgotten Poet, A, 190
Forster, L. W., 2 n., 217–18
Freud, S., 116

Gardens and Parks, 226. *See also* Autobiography, the
Garnham, N. R.: interview with Nabokov, 213
Gazdanov, G., 1
George, S. A., 217
Gift, The, see *Dar*
Giraudoux, J., 232, 234, 237
Glenny, M. V., 7 n., 8, 120, 124–31, 162 n., 169, 191, 193, 194, 195, 198, 200
Glory, see *Podvig*
Gogol, N. V., 218, 232, 233, 234, 235, 236, 237; *Dead Souls,* 92. *See also*

Gogol', N. V.: povesti; Nikolay Gogol
Gogol', N. V.: povesti: introduction by Vladimir Nabokov, 10
Gold, H.: interview with Nabokov, 132 n., 166 n., 184

Hero of our Time, A (translation of *Geroi nashego vremeni*), 13, 14, 18, 19, 21, 22
Hicks, G., 208
Hitchcock, A. J., 113
Hoffmann, E. T. A., 234
Hughes, R. P., 4 n., 120 n.

In Memory of L. I. Shigaev, see *Pamyati L. I. Shigaeva*
'In noon's heat, in a dale of Dagestan' (translation of *Son*), 18
interviews with Nabokov, *see* under name of interviewer. See also *Strong Opinions*
Invitation to a Beheading, see *Priglashenie na kazn'*
Istreblenie tiranov (*Tyrants Destroyed*), 221
Ivanov, G. V., 3, 116 n.
Izobretenie Val'sa (*The Waltz Invention*), 6, 7, 9, 133, 136, 170, 215, 220

Janvier, L., 3 n.
Joyce, J. A., 175

Kafka, F., 232, 237
Kamera obskura, see *Camera Obscura*
Kantor, M. L., 233, 235
Karlinsky, S., 7, 21 n., 232
Kartofel'nyi El'f (*The Potato Elf*), 5, 134, 135, 195, 196, 201, 202, 206, 221
Keats, J., 15
Kerensky, A. F., 147
Khodasevich, V. F., 4, 215, 232, 233, 236
Khokhlov, G. D. (pseud. Al. Novik), 132, 236
Khvat (*A Dashing Fellow*), 79, 80, 221
King, Queen, Knave, see *Korol', dama, valet*
Kleist, H. von, 233
Koni, A. F., 154

Korff, Anna-Christina von, 147
Korol', dama, valet (King, Queen, Knave), 2–3, 6, 7, 8, 9, 23–8, 51, 66 n., 80–1, 90–114, 119, 120, 131, 133, 144, 146 n., 167, 168–9, 171, 175, 196, 199, 200, 201, 202, 203, 209, 210, 211, 213, 220, 222–3, 230 n.
Korolek (The Leonardo), 196, 197, 221
Kosinska, Irene, 5, 196, 201, 202
Krasavitsa (A Russian Beauty), 7, 201, 221
Krug, see Rasskaz

Lantern Slides, 225. See also Autobiography, the
Laughter in the Dark, see Camera Obscura
Lawrence, D. H.: Lady Chatterley's Lover, 79–80
Lebeda, 227
Leonardo, The, see Korolek
Lermontov, M. Yu., 14, 18, 20; Geroi nashego vremeni, see Hero of our Time, A; Son, see 'In noon's heat, in a dale of Dagestan'
Lik, 134, 220
Lips to Lips, see Usta k ustam
Lodgings in Trinity Lane, 225, 228. See also Autobiography, the
Lokrantz, J. T., 138 n., 174 n.
Lolita, 6, 9, 10, 12, 23, 24, 26, 57, 58, 66 n., 81, 91 n., 114–16, 119, 120, 121, 122–3, 124, 131, 132, 133, 146 n., 170, 171, 172, 177, 178, 179, 180, 183–4, 190, 192–3, 202, 203, 208, 211–12, 214, 215, 216, 219, 221
Louis XVI, king of France, 147
Lubin, P., 166, 216

Mademoiselle O, 11, 139, 140, 147–55, 224, 228–30, 231. See also Autobiography, the
Mary, see Mashen'ka
Mashen'ka (Mary), 6, 7 n., 8, 9, 25, 119, 120, 121–2, 124–31, 133, 156–66 passim, 169, 170, 176, 178, 182, 191, 194, 195, 198, 200, 201, 206, 220, 227–9
Matter of Chance, A, see Sluchainost'
Maturin, C. R.: Melmoth the Wanderer, 66 n.

Mérimée, P.: Carmen, 58
Milne, A. A.: Mr. Pim Passes By, 171
Mochul'sky, K. V., 233–4
Music, see Muzyka
Musique, see Muzyka
Musset, A. de, 11
Muzyka (Music), 11–12, 59, 221
My English Education, 145, 224, 227. See also Autobiography, the
My Russian Education, 144–5, 225. See also Autobiography, the

Nabokov, Dmitri V. (son), 5 n., 7, 8, 9, 14, 82, 90, 193, 208
Nabokov's Dozen, 8, 140, 190, 224 n.
Nabor (Recruiting), 221
Narcissus, 69
Nikolay Gogol, 13–14, 21, 27
Nikolka Persik (translation of Colas Breugnon), 11
Nine Stories, 190, 224 n.
Novik, Al., see Khokhlov, G. D.
Nursery Tale, A, see Skazka

Obida, 227
Oblako, ozero, bashnya (Cloud, Castle, Lake), 7, 56, 113, 133, 220
Obrashchenie ('To Russia'), 117
Olesha, Yu. K., 218, 233
'On a Book entitled Lolita', 114–15
'On Translating "Eugene Onegin"', 15, 17
Opoveshchenie (Breaking the News), 221
Osokin, S. (?pseud.), 236
Osorgin, M. (pseud. of M. A. Il'in), 2–3, 236–7
Otchayanie (Despair), 5, 7, 9, 10, 18–19, 21, 23–8, 44 n., 59–82, 87, 89, 91, 110, 112–14, 119, 131, 133, 134, 136, 167, 169–70, 171, 173–4, 175, 177, 180, 185–90, 191–2, 202, 213, 220

Pale Fire, 115–16, 133, 194, 195, 197, 199, 202, 203, 209, 210, 211, 215, 217
Pamyati L. I. Shigaeva (In Memory of L. I. Shigaev), 221
Passazhir (The Passenger), 5
Passenger, The, see Passazhir
Perfect Past, The, 224, 227. See also Autobiography, the

Perfection, see *Sovershenstvo*
Pertzov, P., 7, 8
Peskov, G. (pseud. of Elena Deisha-Sionitskaya), 237
Peter I, tsar of Russia ('the Great'), 154
Pil'gram (*The Aurelian*), 7, 133, 134–5, 220
Plato, 156 n.
Pnin, 6, 25 n., 46 n., 113 n., 126 n., 133, 136–8, 163 n., 174, 194, 195, 197, 202, 203, 209, 210, 215
Podlets (*An Affair of Honor*), 135–6, 170, 220
Podvig (*Glory*), 6, 7, 9, 12, 25, 27 n., 82 n., 119, 120, 121, 122, 124, 133, 169, 173, 194, 195, 196, 197, 202, 203, 220, 227–8
Poems and Problems, 7
'Poets, The', see *Poety*
Poety ('The Poets'), 117
Pope, A., 15
Portrait of My Mother, 224. See also Autobiography, the
Portrait of My Uncle, 224, 228. See also Autobiography, the
Poseshchenie muzeya (*The Visit to the Museum*), 220
Potato Elf, The, see *Kartofel'nyi El'f*
'Pouchkine ou le vrai et le vraisemblable', 11, 13
Prešeren, F., 2 n.
Priglashenie na kazn' (*Invitation to a Beheading*), 7, 9, 23 n., 27 n., 119, 120, 123–4, 131–2, 133, 195, 196, 197, 199, 203, 218 n., 220
'Problems of Translation', 14, 15, 16, 17–18
Proffer, C. R., 4 n., 23–4, 57 n., 65, 72 n., 77, 98 n., 113 n., 179, 208
Proffer, Ellendea, 184 n.
Proust, M., 42, 218, 232, 233, 234
Pushkin, A. S., 11, 13, 18, 20, 161, 171; *Boris Godunov*, 171; *Evgeny Onegin*, 171, 172 (see also *Eugene Onegin*); *Pora, moi drug, pora . . .*, see '''Tis time, my dear, 'tis time . . .'; *Vystrel*, 171

Racine, J., 151; *Athalie*, 150
Rambouillet, Mme de, 150
Rasskaz (*The Circle*), 134, 135, 194, 197, 201, 221, 227

Real Life of Sebastian Knight, The, 1 n., 6, 49 n., 175, 190, 213, 227, 230, 231
Recruiting, see *Nabor*
Remizov, A. M., 1
'Reply to My Critics', 16 n., 19 n., 198 n.
Return of Tchorb, The, see *Vozvrashchenie Chorba*
Rimbaud, A., 11
Robbe-Grillet, A., 179 n.
Rolland, R.: *Colas Breugnon*, see *Nikolka Persik*
Rowe, W. W., 179 n., 205
Roy, Winifred, 5, 27, 29, 49, 56, 60, 191
Rozhdestvo (*Christmas*), 221
Russian Beauty, A, see *Krasavitsa*
Russian Beauty and Other Stories, A, 7

Saltykov-Shchedrin, M. E., 232, 233
Scammell, M., 8, 119 n., 169 n., 170, 180 n., 191, 193, 194, 195, 198, 199, 200, 203, 205 n.
Sedykh, A.: interview with Nabokov, 59, 218
'Servile Path, The', 14 n., 15
Shakespeare, W., 175; *Macbeth*, 172; *Othello*, 171–2
Shaw, G. B.: *Candida*, 92, 171
Shestov, L. (pseud. of L. I. Shvartsman), 234
Shishkov, V. (pseud. of Vladimir Nabokov), 116–18
Shklovsky, V. B., 216 n.
Signs and Symbols, see *Symbols and Signs*
Sirin, V.: pseud. of Vladimir Nabokov
Skazka (*A Nursery Tale*), 221
Slovo o polku Igoreve, see *Song of Igor's Campaign, The*
Sluchainost' (*A Matter of Chance*), 221
Soglyadatai (*The Eye*), 7, 10, 23–8 *passim*, **82–9**, 110, 112–14, 119 n., 131, 133, 194, 198, 207, 213, 220
Soglyadatai (collection of stories), 80, 82
Sologub, F. (pseud. of F. K. Teternikov), 233
Solus Rex, 10 n., 79, 80, 136, 194, 195, 197, 198, 206, 215, 217, 221
Song of Igor's Campaign, The (translation of *Slovo o polku Igoreve*), 18

Sovershenstvo (*Perfection*), 221
Speak, Memory: an Autobiography Revisited, 11, 13, 34 n., 113 n., 117 n., 173, 195, 197, 201, 221, 228–9. See also Autobiography, the
Spring in Fialta, see *Vesna v Fial'te*
Stikhotvoreniya (collection of poems: 1916), 157–8
Stikhotvoreniya: 1929–1951, 10
Strong Opinions, 179 n., 207
Struve, G. P., 2 n., 5, 7, 82 n., 117 n., 132 n., 232, 234, 237
Symbols and Signs, 136, 190

Talmey, A.: interview with Nabokov, 139, 157 n.
Tamara, 155, 157–66 *passim*, 225, 228. See also Autobiography, the
Tati, J. (J. Tatischeff), 49
Terapiano, Yu. K., 24 n., 116
Terra Incognita, 110 n., 220
Terror, see *Uzhas*
Three Russian Poets: Selections from Pushkin, Lermontov and Tyutchev, 18
''Tis time, my dear, 'tis time . . .' (translation of *Pora, moi drug, pora* . . .), 18–19
'To Russia', see *Obrashchenie*
Toffler, A.: interview with Nabokov, 179 n., 214
Tolstoy, L. N., 216 n., 234; *Anna Karenina*, 91 n., 92; *Otets Sergey*, 58
Torpid Smoke, see *Tyazhelyi dym*
Transparent Things, 113 n., 115, 133, 174, 202, 203, 207, 210, 215, 219
Tsetlin, M. O., 80–1, 90 n., 234
Turgenev, I. S., 72, 76, 234
Tyazhelyi dym (*Torpid Smoke*), 113 n., 197, 202, 221
Tyrants Destroyed, see *Istreblenie tiranov*

Tyrants Destroyed and Other Stories, 7
Tyutchev, F. I., 18

Ultima Thule, 10, 135, 172, 194, 197, 201, 203, 206, 215, 221
Universitetskaya poema, 116 n.
Usta k ustam (*Lips to Lips*), 134, 135, 194, 195, 196, 206, 220
Uzhas (*Terror*), 221

Varshavsky, V. S., 80, 237
Vasily Shishkov, 117, 221
Veidle, V. V., *see* Weidlé, W.
Vesna v Fial'te (*Spring in Fialta*), 7, 58, 66 n., 133, 135, 194, 220
Visit to the Museum, The, see *Poseshchenie muzeya*
Vladimir II, grand prince of Kiev (Monomakh), 21
Vozvrashchenie Chorba (*The Return of Tchorb*), 5

Waltz Invention, The, see *Izobretenie Val'sa*
Ward, Hilda, 11, 139
Weaver, W., 21 n.
Weidlé, W., 117 n., 218, 237
Wilde, O., 66 n., 175
William I, king of England ('the Conqueror'), 21
Wilson, E., 198 n.
Woolf, Virginia, 237

Zaitsev, B. K., 237
'Zametki perevodchika', 14 n., 15
'Zametki perevodchika II', 14 n., 18 n.
Zashchita Luzhina (*The Defence*), 3, 6, 8, 9, 10, 12, 25, 27 n., 119, 120, 122, 131, 132, 133, 169, 178, 180 n., 191, 194, 198, 199, 205 n., 215, 220, 227, 229–31
Zhukovsky, V. A., 17 n.